ECONOMICS OF AQUACULTURE DIVERSIFICATION IN INDIAN SUNDARBAN

About the Author

Dr. Jaydev Misra, a Ph.D. in Economics from Visva Bharati, Santiniketan, is currently an Assistant Professor of Economics in Dhruba Chand Halder College under the University of Calcutta. His present assignment includes research in Aquaculture Economics, Health Economics as well as Efficiency Analysis using Non-parametric methodologies. Dr. Misra has served as a fellow or investigator in number of sponsored research project and has published several articles in the national and international journals. Dr. Misra is also a life member of Inland Fisheries Society of India and Agricultural Economics Research Association of India. His previous book is entitled as "Sustaining Pond Aquaculture" published in 2011.

Economics of Aquaculture Diversification in Indian Sundarban

Jaydev Misra

CONCEPT PUBLISHING COMPANY PVT. LTD.
NEW DELHI-110059

ISBN-13: 978-93-86682-50-5

First Published 2018

Published and Printed by

Since 1974

Concept Publishing Company Pvt. Ltd.
A/15-16, Commercial Block, Mohan Garden,
New Delhi-110059 (India)
T : 91 11 25351460, 91 11 25351794
E : publishing@conceptpub.com, *W*: www.conceptpub.com

Cataloging in Publication Data--Courtesy: D.K. Agencies (P) Ltd. <docinfo@dkagencies.com>

Misra, Jaydev, author.
Economics of aquaculture diversification in Indian Sundarban / Jaydev Misra.
pages cm
Includes bibliographical references and index.
ISBN 9789386682505

1. Fisheries—Economic aspects—Sundarbans (Bangladesh and India) 2. Fisheries—Economic aspects—India—West Bengal. 3. Fish culture—Economic aspects—Sundarbans (Bangladesh and India) 4. Fish culture—Economic aspects—India—West Bengal. 5. Fishes—Variation—Sundarbans (Bangladesh and India) 6. Fishes—Variation—India—West Bengal. I. Title.

LCC SH300.W47M57 2018 DDC 338.3727095414 23

Preface

India, particularly, West Bengal is blessed with adequate diversity of Small Indigenous Fish Species (SIFS). It is usually believed that integration of those fish species in the form of commercial culture, along with present carp based production system can increase the overall efficiency of aquaculture production in the country, as well as, can provide food and nutritional security to the poor fish farmers. There is no denying the fact that such diversification of aquaculture has been started to experience in West Bengal within the ambit of commercial management practices. The Government has recently taken steps for intensifying aquaculture diversification and considerable investment has already been committed. Extension services have been geared at the village level. Training programmes for the fish farmers regarding new commercially viable SIFS have been introduced. Despite all these efforts and enormous potentials for intensified aquaculture diversification, the production level and productivity are still not adequate to meet the large gap between potential and actual yields of fish. Sometimes, recipients of improved technology have been found to follow only a part of adoption strategy as they are generally circumscribed by different socio-economic factors. It is, therefore, important to locate the efforts of aquaculture diversification and its effect on efficiency of overall aquaculture production on more secure foundation of data and methodology.

Present book is a case study of Indian Sundarban. In this study, attempts have been made to examine the structural and operational features of tanks and ponds and to identify the factors that enhance the potential for aquaculture diversification as well as the factors impede the development of fisheries in Indian Sundarbans. Technical efficiency of diversified aquaculture practices is also estimated in this study. Efforts are also made to evaluate the role of adoption of improved technologies towards development of diversified fisheries. The study is based on the data collected from selected fish farmers from different villages in few blocks of Sundarban. This book is largely based on the report of Minor Research Project entitled "Economics of Aquaculture Diversification in Indian Sundarban: Nature, Extent and Impact on Efficiency", which was undertaken with the financial support from the University Grants Commission. I express my deep sense of gratitude to the UGC for their support.

I wish to express my thanks in abundance to Dr. Sourabh Kumar Dubey, West Bengal University of Fishery Science and Dr. Priyadarshini Mallick, Assistant Professor, Dhruba Chand Halder College who consistently took the trouble of providing the data and preparing the manuscript appropriate for this exercise. Through my frequent interactions with the Professors like Dr. Debasis Mandal, Indian Institute of Technology, Delhi; Dr. Sib Ranjan Misra, ex-Professor, Visva Bharati; Dipankar Coondoo, Institute of Development Studies, Kolkata; Professor Subhas C. Ray, Professor, University of Connecticut, UK, I have been able to enhance my understanding about the different dimensions of diversified aquaculture in Sundarban. I owe a special debt of gratitude to all of them for shaping my thought about it.

A word of warm appreciation is due to District Magistrate of South 24-Parganas; Agriculture Development Officer and members of the Panchayat Samities of the Study area. My obligation is due to Smt. Sumita Mitra Dev, Director of Fisheries, West Bengal; Dr. Madhumita Mukherjee, Additional Director of Fisheries; Dr. Prasanta Kumar Jana, Joint Director of Fisheries; Dr. Shamik Das, DDF, Planning, Department of Fisheries, West Bengal; Dr. Tapas Paria, Assistant Director of Fisheries, South 24-Parganas, West Bengal; Sri Sumanto De, CEO, South 24-Parganas, West Bengal; Mr. Timir Ganguly, ADF, Kalyani Fish Farm, Government of West Bengal; A.K. Gorai, Fishery Extension Officer, Malda and Sri N. Barik, Assistant Director of Fisheries, Birbhum, West Bengal, who provided us with most of the facts and figures and many of the ideas which are set out below. It is thanks to their expertise and unfailing courtesy. To the numerous fish farmer respondents of our study, we owe a debt which no expression of gratitude can fully redeem. We like to acknowledge his contribution in making the study what it is.

I am also thankful to Prof. A.P. Sharma, Director, CIFRI, Barrackpore for his valuable suggestions. Thanks also owe to Dr. (Mrs.) A. Sinha, Principal Scientist & OIC, CIFRI, Kolkata Centre; Dr. A.S. Ghosh, Dy. Project Director (Fishery), Sundarban Development Board; Mr. S. Ghosh, Junior Project Officer (Fishery), Sundarban Development Board for their unstinted support. A word of heartfelt thanks is due to Dr. A. Mishra, Secretary, Paribesh Unnayan Parishad and Biswajit Mahakur, Secretary, Joygopalpur Gram Vikash Kendra (JGVK) for their active cooperation during survey. I am thankful to the staff members of the Department of Economics, Dhruba Chand Halder College and Dr. Satyabrata Sahoo, Principal, Dhruba Chand Halder College for their support during the course of this investigation and finalization of this report.

Jaydev Misra
Department of Economics
Dhruba Chand Halder College
University of Calcutta
Kolkata (W.B.)

Contents

List of Tables and Figures

LIST OF TABLES

LIST OF FIGURES

1
Introduction

> There can be no peace without food security in the world. You cannot talk peace to a hungry man.
>
> — *Dr. Vijay Gupta,* Winner of Sunhak Peace Prize

1.1 Food Insecurity and Poverty in India

Despite steady economic growth and development in many parts of the world, a significant proportion of the global population continues to suffer from food insecurity and malnutrition. Millennium Development Goals (MDGs) of United Nations recognizes that hunger and food insecurity are the core afflictions of poor people, and specifically sets out to halve the proportion of extremely poor and hungry people in the world. Although the situation has improved till 1990s, the rate of improvement remains far short of that required to attain these targets. Recent data of International Food Policy Research Institute shows that India continues to have serious levels of widespread hunger forcing it to be ranked a lowly 97 among 118 developing countries for which the Global Hunger Index (GHI) was calculated in 2016 (IFPRI, 2017). Countries worse than India include extremely poor African countries such as Niger, Chad, Ethiopia and Sierra Leone besides two of India's neighbours: Afghanistan and Pakistan. Other neighbours like Sri Lanka, Bangladesh, Nepal and China are all ranked above India. Its hunger status, with an index value of 28.5, is classified as 'serious', notwithstanding the reduction in index value compared to the year 2000. The Hunger Index has three dimensions: inadequate food supply measured through

If we look into per capita protein and calorie intake through foods of animal and crop origin, it can be found that the overall protein and calorie intake marginally increased during 1987-1993 to 2005-2010. Importantly, the share of food of animal origin in protein as well as calorie intake of households has improved over time, though marginally. The relative share of foods of animal origin in protein intake has increased from 15.6 per cent in 1987-1993 to 19.0 per cent in 2005-2010. The relative share of foods of animal origin in calorie intake has increased from 7.0 per cent during 1987-1993 to 8.7 per cent during 2005-2010. These results of Table 1.2 can easily be associated with trends in per capita consumption of major food commodities in India as evident in Table 1.3. Diversification of Indian diet leads the consumers to

Table 1.2: Per capita protein and calorie intake from animal food and crop in India

Period	*Protein Intake (grams/day)*			*Calorie Intake (kcal/day)*		
	Animal	*Crop*	*Total*	*Animal*	*Crop*	*Total*
1987-93	8.6	46.6	55.2	156	2090	2246
	(15.6)	(84.4)	(100)	(7.0)	(93.1)	(100)
1994-99	9.5	45.9	55.4	175	2108	2283
	(17.2)	(82.9)	(100)	(7.7)	(92.3)	(100)
2000-04	9.6	45.1	54.7	181	2076	2257
	(17.6)	(82.5)	(100)	(8.0)	(92.0)	(100)
2005-10	10.7	45.5	56.2	201	2110	2311
	(19.0)	(81.0)	(100)	(8.7)	(91.3)	(100)

Note: The figures in the parentheses depicts percentage of respective total.
Source: NCAER, 2014.

Table 1.3: Trends in per capita consumption of major food commodities in India

(kg/year)

Food Commodity	*Rural*			*Urban*		
	1987-88	1999-2000	2009-10	1987-88	1999-2000	2009-10
Rice	83.0	80.0	73.0	64.0	62.0	53.0
Wheat	55.0	54.0	52.0	53.0	54.0	50.0
Pulses	7.9	10.2	7.9	9.4	12.2	9.6
Milk	38.9	46.1	50.1	51.8	62.1	65.2
Eggs	6.3	13.2	21.1	17.4	25.1	32.5
Fish	1.9	2.6	3.3	2.1	2.7	2.9

Source: NCAER, 2014.

move away from cereals type of food grains to high-value food commodities such as milk, egg, meat, and fruits and vegetables (NCAER, 2014 b; Viswanathan and Satyasai, 1996). Other factors contributing to the change in food consumption pattern are the increasing urbanization and globalization. Further, there has been a significant shift in consumption pattern away from rice, wheat and coarse cereals over the past two decades in both rural and urban segments of the country (Table 1.4). The decline in consumption of coarse cereals, however, has been steeper, in the rural areas. The consumption of pulses increased up to the year 1999-2000 and later decreased in both rural and urban India. There was a steady increase in the consumption of edible oils and food products of animal origin (milk, eggs, fish and chicken) over the years from 1987 to 2010.

Table 1.4: Production of major food commodities in India

Food Commodity	*TE 1993-94*	*TE 2003-04*	*TE 2014-15*
Food grains	177.37	200.28	257.94
Cereals	164.66	187.14	239.44
Pulses	12.71	13.14	18.50
Milk	58.07	86.23	138.80
Eggs	1.15	1.98	3.45
Fish	4.35	6.13	9.49

Source: CMIE, Directorate of Economics and Statistics, 2016.

Another point deserves particular mention here. Protein, as an important source of building block of human body has already been recognized by the scientists. But, by concentrating only on protein, one really misses the point that human body also requires many micronutrients and minerals like calcium and zinc, and vitamins. Though protein is essential, it is not a limiting nutrient. Micronutrient deficiency, sometimes termed as "hidden hunger", since it is difficult to see, is a big problem in south and South-east Asian countries like India (Roos *et al.*, 2007). About 250 million children worldwide, for example, are estimated to be at risk of vitamin A deficiency, and an equal or more number of children is at risk of deficiencies of other minerals like iron, zinc and calcium. Deficiency of vitamin A is widespread in India, particularly among women and children. Calcium is an important nutrient for growth in young children, foetal growth and milk production.

Indian agriculture has made remarkable strides during past five decades achieving high levels of production and productivity to address food and nutrition security of its 1.3 billion people which is 17.84 per cent of world population in 2016 (CIA, 2016). The agriculture sector contributes just 15 per cent to India's Gross Domestic Product (GDP), but over 55 per cent of the population still depends on it. More importantly, the some nutritional need of many of the consumers in India is fulfilled through production of nutrient-rich crops. But, unfortunate enough is that agricultural policies in India, while continuing to focus on ways of increasing supply from traditional crop farming, have overlooked the role of diversified production, employment and income generation on farms in achieving food and nutritional security as well as to mitigate problem of hidden hunger (Ahmed *et al.*, 1999). This view is, however, fast changing. Increasingly being recognized is the role of a balanced nutrition, including critical vitamins and minerals in the diet of the poor, which are related to income and purchasing power improvement, rather than just food production and consumption. Hence, the cereals and crop commodity supply perspective of food security has now changed to include products such as fish and livestock (Ahmed *et al.*, 1999; Delgado *et al.*, 1999).

1.3 Can Fisheries be an Option?

In many of developing countries, fish and fisheries play an important role in the diets, livelihoods, and income of many poor population groups who suffer from protein, vitamin and mineral deficiencies. Fish are a rich source of high quality protein, a range of micronutrients, and fatty acids essential for human brain development (Tacon and Metian, 2013). They are also of ten the cheapest and most frequently consumed animal-source food in low income food deficit countries (World Bank, 2006), making an important contribution to diversity in otherwise monotonous diets dominated by prudishstaples (Thilsted, 2013). The significant growth in fish consumption has enhanced people's diets around the world through diversified and nutritious food. In 2013, fish accounted for about 17 per cent of the global population's intake of animal protein and 6.7 per cent of all protein consumed. Moreover, fish provided more than 3.1 billion people with almost 20 per cent of their average per capita intake of animal protein. In addition to being a rich source of easily digested, high quality proteins containing all essential amino acids, fish provides essential fats (e.g. long chain omega-3 fatty acids), vitamins (D, A and B) and minerals (including calcium, iodine, zinc, iron and selenium), particularly if eaten whole. Even small quantities of fish can have a significant positive nutritional impact on plant based diets, and this is the case in many LIFDCs and least-developed countries. Fish is usually high in unsaturated fats and provides health benefits in protection against cardiovascular diseases. It also aids foetal and infant development of the brain and nervous system. With its valuable nutritional properties, it can also play a major role in correcting unbalanced diets and, through substitution, in countering obesity.

In order to meet increasing demand for fish, its production is still increasing. Globally fish and seafood already represent 16.6 per cent of all animal protein intake and this proportion has been increasing (FAO, 2014). Yet, there are substantial geographical variations in global seafood supply and demand, and active international seafood trade importantly contributes to smoothing regional imbalances. In fact, seafood is among the most heavily traded food commodities, with 37–38 per cent of all fish produced being exported in 2010–12 (FAO, 2012). In contrast, rapid expansion of global aquaculture production has continued with no sign of reaching its peak: during the past three decades, global aquaculture production expanded at an average annual rate of over 8 per cent, from 5.2 million tons in 1981 to 66.6 million tons in 2012 (FishStat). China represents the single largest seafood producing and consuming nation, and its influence on the global fish markets and trade has intensified (Zhang *et al.*, 2014). China consumed 35 per cent of global seafood in 2011 (FAO, 2012). Although Asia accounted for 88 per cent of world aquaculture production by volume in 2012, China alone accounted for 62 per cent. China is both an importer and exporter of fish. China became the third-largest fish-importing country by value in 2011 after Japan and the United States; part of the fish imports is raw-material to be re-exported after processing. China now represents 13 per cent of world fish export in value, amounting to $17.0 billion in 2011 and $18.2 billion in 2012 (FAO, 2013). Apart from marine fisheries, world aquaculture production of fish accounted for 44.1 per cent of total production (including for non-food uses) from capture fisheries and aquaculture in 2014, up from 31.1 per cent in 2004. All continents have shown a general trend of an increasing share of aquaculture production in total fish production, although in Oceania this share has declined in the last three years.

Despite of these facts, fishery, as a capable means of food and nutritional security, livelihood enhancement and diversification has been debated since the early 1990s, when doubts started cropping up about the capacity of marine fisheries to contribute sustainably to livelihoods, especially of the poor. These doubts sprang from the fact that most fisheries had begun to show signs of distress. A number of factors could have contributed to this distress: overfishing and destructive fishing; urban, agricultural, and industrial pollution; destruction of critical coastal habitats and nurseries; reduced flows of freshwater. Whatever the causes, both fish catches and productivity have fallen, incomes have declined, the sector's contribution to the national economy has declined or remained static. Fishing operations have suffered mounting losses, the misery of fishers aggravated by rampant indebtedness, high maintenance costs and reduction or withdrawal of various subsidies, direct and indirect. Some responses to the changing conditions—such as policy measures to conserve or manage coastal biodiversity—may also have added to the problems. FAO recently estimated that worldwide 18 per cent of the fish stocks or species groups are overexploited, while 10 per cent have become significantly depleted, or are recovering from depletion (FAO, 2002). For the World Environment Day (5 June, 2004), the United Nations Environment Programme (UNEP) chose the slogan "Wanted! Seas and Oceans, Dead or Alive?". This two-way link, that is, fish depletion leading to poverty and poverty leading to fish depletion became the serious concern for the international agencies.

Against this background, role and importance of small-scale fisheries to the livelihoods of rural populations and as a means to break the nexus of poverty and food insecurity in developing countries has gained momentum. In November 2001, an International Workshop on "Small-scale fisheries, Poverty and the Code of Conduct" was organized in Cotonou, which brought together experts from the South and North to debate and share their experience about small-scale fisheries in West Africa and their relation to poverty (Neiland and Béné, 2004). Academics also started to refocus their attention on the relatively neglected issue of poverty (their cause, their origins) in fisheries and some key papers were published in major international journals, which raised the profile of both the sector itself and the contribution that research in this sector can make to the more general debate about poverty (*e.g.* Allison and Ellis, 2001; Béné, 2003). At the same time, FAO through its Advisory Committee on Fisheries Research (ACFR) and its Committee of Fisheries (COFI) recognized that small scale fisheries had not received the attention that they deserved considering the important contribution that they seem to make to nutrition and food security, sustainable livelihoods and poverty alleviation, especially in developing countries. In its Twenty-sixth session in February 2003 the COFI discussed "strategies for increasing the sustainable contribution of small-scale fisheries to food security and poverty alleviation" (FAO, 2003), and also welcomed the suggestion made by the FAO fisheries department to elaborate, in the context of the Code of Conduct for Responsible Fisheries, a series of "Technical Guidelines for increasing the contribution of small-scale fisheries to food security and poverty alleviation". These guidelines are currently being developed. Finally, in November 2003, an ACFR Working Party on Small-scale Fisheries was convened in Bangkok with the participation of 18 experts to undertake an evaluation of the role and importance of small-scale fisheries, elaborate a research agenda, and review strategies and mechanisms to bridge the gap between research and action (FAO, 2004). All these various initiatives have produced and continue to generate major progress in our understanding of the relationship between poverty and fisheries.

1.4 Small is Beautiful

In developing countries like India, where fish consumption tends to be based on locally available products, role of consumption and production of small indigenous fish species as a means of diversified aquaculture practices has highly been recognized in recent years. In many parts of the south and South-east Asia, including India, a large diversity of small indigenous fish species is found in fresh water systems. These small indigenous freshwater fish species (SIFFS) form a major component of food consumed by families, especially those living closer to freshwater resources. Daniels (2002) indicates that of 750 species of freshwater fish species found in India, a large number of the mare familiar only to the local population. Small indigenous fish species of freshwater origin are not only a source of vital protein to the rural poor, but also of micro-nutrients such as calcium, zinc, iron and fatty acids (Roos *et al.*, 2007; Halwart, 2008). Indigenous knowledge about these species and about their health benefits is high among rural population. For example, such species are often considered an essential part of the diet of pregnant women and lactating mothers. Research has proved that the bio-availability of calcium from these small indigenous freshwater fish species is at par with that derived from milk (Roos *et al.*, 2007). Species-wise investigation reveals that, *mola (Amblypharyngodon mola)*, commonly found in eastern and north-east India, is often included in the diet of pregnant and lactating mothers, for its nutritive value. This is not only the case in India but also in other countries in Asia such as Laos, Cambodia, Vietnam and China (**Halwart & Bartley, 2005**). One of the noted advantages of SIFFS is that people, even the poor, can buy them in quantities they can afford.

Apart from consumption aspects, role of SIFS in aquaculture cannot be ignored from the production point of view also. Though Indian freshwater aquaculture has grown at a rate of 8 per cent per annum during the last decade, the present production is not enough to meet the increasing demand for food fish in the country. Fish accounts for six per cent of India's food budget as 60 per cent of the country's population eats fish. The national fish consumption will reach 6.3 kg per capita by 2020 from 5.6 kg in 2011. The projected additional demand for 2030 is about 5.41 million tonnes, of which 90 per cent is expected to be met from freshwater sources (World Bank, 2013). But the "Blue Revolution", occurred during last few decades, which initially triggered production of freshwater fish from aquaculture, has been stagnating for years now. Hence, additional demand must be met by diversifying freshwater aquaculture from the present carp-based production management towards introduction of more small indigenous species into small water bodies spread over 2.41 million hectares area all-over the country.

Against this backdrop, it has been found that SIFFS found in the vast inland water resources, provide not only nutrition but also livelihood opportunities and income to a large number of fishers. Significant production of small indigenous fish species of freshwater origin, from culture and capture fisheries, is reported from several water bodies. Studies in India have shown that the profit accruing to fishers is actually higher in the case of SIFFS when compared to those from large cultured species. Although the system of sewage-fed aquaculture in West Bengal had tried in corporating minor indigenous carp species such as *Labeo bata, Labeo fimbriatus, Cirrhinus reba,* and *Amblypharyngodon mola* (Ayyappan & Jena, 2003), there has not been any major effort to integrate these species into carp polyculture systems in India. Before the introduction of hatchery-produced seeds, in the initial years of reservoir fisheries, water bodies were stocked with naturally available seeds (Sugunan, 1992). It has been observed that a variety of indigenous fish species were stocked, for example, in reservoirs of Tamil Nadu and Kerala. After the introduction of hatchery-produced carp seeds, there was a shift in species used for stocking water bodies from indigenous varieties to a combination of *catla, rohu* and *mrigal.* Often small indigenous species were removed as vermin, with negative implications for conservation of biodiversity in freshwater ecosystems. However, recent research in Bangladesh has demonstrated that integration of some of the small indigenous species into polyculture systems—for example, *Amblypharyngodon mola* along with carp species—has increased overall pond fish production (Roos *et al.,* 2007). *Mola* reproduces several times and increases the productivity of the pond and enhances the local availability of fish. It has also been observed that these species command high prices, often higher, for example, than prices for Indian Major Carps (IMCs) (Ahmed, 2009; Saha, 2003), thus providing a source of supplementary income to rural households. Given the local demand for small indigenous fish species of freshwater origin, the FAO (1999) has also indicated the possibility of integrating such indigenous fish species into freshwater culture systems.

1.5 Small is Invisible

Problem is that, such species have received insufficient attention in statistics, inland water fisheries policies and programmes in India, both at the national and State levels. SIFFS are either caught from nearby water bodies or get naturally recruited to homestead/ common village ponds which are then harvested by the pond owner or the local community. Many of these water rich areas are also well known for their fish-*cum*-paddy culture. Naturally, therefore, these species tend to be sold and consumed locally. Perhaps, this could be one of the reasons why they remain invisible in national statistics. Such statistics are largely based on catches reported at large/major landing centres (Halwart, 2008; Roos, 2007). This invisibility in statistics could account for their poor recognition in fisheries and aquaculture development policies.

Also, complex patterns of access rights to such indigenous fish species have not been adequately documented in literature. For example, access to them even in privately-owned paddy fields is often enjoyed by the larger community, including landless people, with related food security and poverty alleviation benefits. This highlights the need to understand the local socio-economic, cultural and institutional context that determines who can access and benefit from fisheries resources from culture fisheries.

1.6 Research Problem

Considering the extent to which small indigenous species of freshwater fish play a role in providing nutrition to the rural poor and in maintaining biodiversity, it is important to consider promoting sustainable use of small indigenous species in culture fishery systems. Eastern India, for example, has a great potential for expanding freshwater aquaculture by integrating small indigenous species of fish into current production systems. Such integration can help better achieve the objectives of increasing fish production, enhancing nutritional security of the rural poor, providing greater employment opportunities, and conserving biodiversity in freshwater ecosystems. These are all objectives of sustainable development as promoted by the Government of India through the Ministry of Agriculture and the Ministry of Environment and Forests. It is, however, important to locate these efforts within specific cultural and socio-economic contexts, looking also at critical issues of ownership and access rights over water bodies, and to formulate relevant strategies, as appropriate. If such factors are taken into consideration, the objectives of nutritional security, promotion of employment and conservation of biodiversity can be better met especially in some of the most disadvantaged areas of Eastern India showing poor human development indicators. There is, therefore, need to throw light on sustainable use of small indigenous fish species, their role in food security, employment, income, poverty alleviation and conservation of biodiversity and also to actively establish the feasibility of polyculture using small indigenous species of fish. In this context, it is important to discuss the developing policy space for sustainable use of small indigenous species in culture and capture fisheries.

1.7 Objectives of Study

India, particularly, West Bengal is blessed with adequate diversity of small indigenous fish species (SIFS). It is usually believed that integration of those fish species in the form of commercial culture, along with present carp based production system can increase the overall efficiency of aquaculture production in the country, as well as, can provide food and nutritional security to the poor fish farmers. There is no denying the fact that such diversification of aquaculture has been started to experience in West Bengal within the ambit of commercial management practices. The Government has recently taken steps for intensifying aquaculture diversification and considerable investment has already been committed. Extension services have been geared at the village level. Training programmes for the fish farmers regarding new commercially viable SIFS have been introduced. Despite all these efforts and enormous potentials for intensified aquaculture diversification, the production level and productivity are still not adequate to meet the large gap between potential and actual yields of fish. Sometimes, recipients of improved technology have been found to follow only a part of adoption strategy as they are generally circumscribed by different socio-economic factors. It is, therefore, important to locate the efforts of aquaculture diversification and its effect on efficiency of overall aquaculture production on more secure foundation of data and methodology. The area of research, which has been proposed here, is basically an attempt to contribute towards policy development in the management of aquaculture diversification by examining the interaction among socio-economic, social-distributional and technological aspects of fish production. The specific objectives of the proposed study will be–

(a) To examine the production management strategies and socio-economic profile of fish farmers in order to identify level and extent of aquaculture diversification as well as structural and operational features of water resources under which production is carried off;
(b) To measure the level of technical efficiencies across farms categorized on the basis of size, ownership pattern, tenural status and adoption level;
(c) To identify various forces at play that determines the level of efficiency of the fish farmers;
(d) To decipher the factors that impede the development of aquaculture diversification in their water resources; and finally
(e) To suggest some policy measures for further development of fish production and enhancement of species diversification in the study area.

1.8 Hypotheses of Study

The present project shall attempt to test the null **hypothesis**—

H_0: The diversification of aquaculture production through introduction of small indigenous species has positive effect on productivity, efficiency and socio-economic improvement of fish farmers; against the alternative hypothesis—

H_{A1}: Adoption of aquaculture diversification without following the recommended package of practices results in efficiency loss causing distress to farmers;

And/or

H_{A2}: Recommendation of aquaculture diversification without providing proper extension activities can affect productivity and efficiency adversely due to underprivileged resource position of the fish farmers.

1.9 Significance of Study

A well-knit and coordinated attempt of aquaculture diversification through introduction of new indigenous species can play several important roles in the sustained economic growth of the fisheries sector in India. On the one hand, it can enhance the probability of eradication of hidden hunger in rural areas by providing protein and micronutrient enriched staple food; and on the other, fish production can be increased manifold in coming future, which is a cause of concern for the policy planners against the background of sluggish growth of production in fisheries sector.

In this sense, the need for economically efficient fish production through introduction of species diversification strategies is self-explanatory. National statistics, however, usually fail to take into account the production and consumption patterns of these species, as production and marketing take place at a very local level, carried out by family members. There is need for better information on the production, marketing and consumption of SIFS.

Again, in order to eliminate gender bias also, successful implementation of aquaculture diversification is required. Present polyculture technologies used by farms in aquaculture practices focused on large carps only. In this way, present strategy is depriving the members of the farming households, especially the children and women, because large carps are grown for cash crop, not for family consumption. Even the large carps seldom used for family consumption often are not distributed evenly in the family, rather the male senior members consume the largest share depriving the women and children (Amilhat *et al.*, 2009; Garaway, 2005). On the contrary, small fish, which are eaten whole and constitute a rich source of vitamins and micronutrients, if available for consumption are distributed evenly among all family members, thereby eliminating gender bias.

Hence, proper knowledge regarding aquaculture diversification strategies followed by local farmers is very much important to contribute a long-term and sustainable developmental policy framework in the field of aquaculture economics.

1.10 Interdisciplinary Relevance of Study

The proposed project falls within the jurisdiction of aquaculture science, which again, crystallized into its present form as a mix of application of Economic theory in the field of Agriculture through the use of tools and technique of Operations Research. The proposed project attempts to deal with some real data in order to test the efficiency of aquaculture diversification. But this requires the application of Operations Research techniques like Data Envelopment Analysis (DEA) to identify best practice farms and Meta-frontier DEA to assess the differences of efficiencies within the sample. Apart from this, the knowledge regarding characteristics and importance of locally available indigenous fish species requires some sort of information of Zoology and Nutritional Science.

1.11 Organization of the Study

The present study consists of eight chapters. The scheme of the study is as follows. In the **chapter one**, an overview of the diversification of aquaculture practices through introduction of small indigenous freshwater fish species (SIFFS) has been sketched. Also, objectives, hypotheses and significance for the present study are also mentioned in this chapter. Overview of aquaculture practices in national and state context has been stated in **chapter two**. In **next chapter**, a comprehensive review of the existing literature on this issue has been dealt with and limitations of those studies have been specified. **Chapter four** explains the general description about the study, that is type of research area and period of study, data description, method of enquiry and analytical framework of the study. **Chapter five** includes the comparative study regarding structural and operational features of diversified and non-diversified aquaculture practices and also the profiles of those fish farmers. **Chapter six** applies a non-parametric Data Envelopment Analysis (DEA) methodology to measure the efficiency of fish farms. Latter, in this chapter, a comparison has been carried out whether level of efficiency varies with level of diversification. In order to identify the reasons behind the level of inefficiency of fish production, if any, a systematic overview of the major constraints faced by the fish cultivators has been explained in **chapter seven**. The **final chapter** contains a brief summary, conclusion and emerging issues for increasing fish production.

2
Potential for Aquaculture Diversification

> Give a man a fish and he eats for one day; teach him how to fish and he eats for a lifetime.
>
> — *Henry David Thoreau*

2.1 Aquaculture in National Perspective

Historically, fishing has been a major source of livelihood for poor communities in India, as well as, a source of healthy food for humanity at large. Now, fisheries and aquaculture are vibrant economic activities, and has been one of the fastest growing food production systems in the country during the last three decades. It is a fact that Indian fisheries and aquaculture sector has been growing at a faster rate than crop and livestock sectors. The average growth rate of over 6 per cent per year in the last two decades is testimony to the potential in the fishery sector. Their significance and contribution towards agricultural (4.6% GDP) and national economies (1.3% GDP), livelihood and nutritional security, employment generation (11 million people) and foreign exchange earnings (over Rs. 8,000 crores) have been enormous though understated so far.

Before modernisation and large scale development of fisheries sector in India, the government viewed fisheries as a source of revenue, and in order to ensure its continuous revenue, measures had been developed to conserve it from 'illegal' and 'destructive' fishing. The Indian Fisheries Act, 1897 became a central legal instrument to achieve this policy objective. Though community and agricultural development were given due priority along with industrialisation, fisheries became an object of 'development' in early 1960s, particularly the mechanisation in marine fisheries sector, followed by growth in aquaculture sector during 1980 and 1990s. However, these developments took place in a policy vacuum as most of the Departments of Fisheries were still mandated and oriented to their revenue generation, regulatory and conservation roles as against the need for using the natural resources for all-round development.

Things began to change for the better since late 1990s. The increasing demand for fish and fish products domestically and in international market; its potential to earn significant foreign exchange, boom and burst of coastal shrimp aquaculture, stagnating marine fish production along with its associated crises, availability of underutilized and unutilized water resources in inland region, etc. have forced the policy-makers to come out with certain interventions, though passive and defensive, in the form of promotional and segmental policies and legislations. In recent years, there has been increasing realization among planners and policy-makers that aquaculture has adequate potential and a tangible opportunity to provide employment and reduce poverty in rural areas by creating sustainable fisheries based livelihoods.

India's contribution in global fisheries development always appears significant. Fish production in the world rose from 23.50 million tonnes in 1950-51 to 156.48 million tonnes in 2011-12. Correspondingly, contribution of India to world fish production is increasing continuously during last six decades. Presently, 5.68 per cent of world fish production has been contributed by India and the corresponding share of inland fish production is more than 10 per cent (Table 2.1).

Table 2.1: Fish Production in World and India for last 60 years

Year	*Contribution of India to World Fish Production*		
	Total	*Marine*	*Inland*
1950	3.83	3.10	9.40
1960	3.27	2.79	6.96
1970	2.69	1.83	11.09
1980	3.40	2.42	11.54
1990	3.89	2.65	10.61
2000	4.45	2.85	9.80
2011	5.68	3.23	10.19

Source: Handbook of Fisheries Statistics, 2014, Government of India.

In the last 60 years, unlike agriculture, the contribution of fisheries sector to Gross GDP continued to grow at a rapid pace because of expansion of culture fisheries enterprise. The share of agriculture and allied activities in the total GDP is constantly declining. It was 34.69 per cent in 1980-81 and declined gradually to become 17.62 per cent in 2004-05. In contrast, the c ›ntribution of fisheries sector to the total GDP has gone up from 0.75 per cent in 1980-81 to 0.92 in 2013-14 (at current prices). Similarly, the share of fisheries in agriculture GDP (AgGDP) has increased robustly from 2.17 per cent in 1980-81 to 5.58 per cent in 2013-14 (Table 2.2). This sector is in fact pushing the agricultural growth upward for the past 5 and half decades.

Table 2.2: Contribution of Fisheries Sector to GDP (at current Prices)

(Rs. in crores)

Year	Total GDP	GDP from Agri, Forestry and Fishing	GDP from Fisheries	GDP from Fisheries as % of	
				Total GDP	GDP from Agri, Forestry and Fishing
2005-06	3390503	637772	31699	0.93	4.97
2006-07	3953276	722984	35182	0.89	4.87
2007-08	4582086	836518	38931	0.85	4.65
2008-09	5303567	943204	44073	0.83	4.67
2009-10	6108903	1083514	50370	0.82	4.65
2010-11	7266967	1306942	57369	0.79	4.39
2011-12	8353495	1465753	65541	0.78	4.47
2012-13	9252051	1668676	78053	0.83	4.75
2013-14	10477140	1881152	96824	0.92	5.58

Source: National Account Statistics, Government of India.

Presently, India is the second largest producing and second largest aquaculture nation in the world. The total fish production during 2014-15 is at 10.16 million tonnes with a contribution of 6.51 million tonnes from inland sectors and 3.65 million tonnes from marine sector. Production has increased from 3.84 million tonnes in 1990-91 and the growth in fish production has shown a cyclical pattern with an increasing long term trend. Recent trends in fish production clearly indicates that marine fish production has almost reached the plateau and there is not much scope to increase production from marine sector. Side by side, aquaculture has been one of the fastest growing agricultural sector in the country. Over the years, contribution of marine fisheries has gone down continuously and at the same time the share of inland fisheries has gone up from 29 to 60 per cent.

Table 2.3: Production (in Lakh tonnes) and Growth (in %) in India

Year	Inland Fish Production		Marine Fish Production		Total Fish Production	
	Inland	Growth	Marine	Growth rate	Total	Growth
1950-51	2.18	—	5.34	—	7.52	—
2004-05	35.26	1.96	27.79	–5.53	63.05	–1.48
2005-06	37.56	6.52	28.16	1.33	65.72	4.23
2006-07	38.45	2.37	30.24	7.39	68.69	4.52
2007-08	42.07	9.41	29.20	–3.44	71.27	3.76
2008-09	46.38	10.24	29.78	1.99	76.16	6.87
2009-10	48.94	5.52	31.04	4.23	79.98	5.02
2010-11	49.81	1.78	32.50	4.70	82.31	2.91
2011-12	52.95	6.29	33.71	3.76	86.66	5.29
2012-13	57.20	8.03	33.20	–1.51	90.40	4.32
2013-14	61.36	7.28	34.43	3.68	95.79	5.96
2014-15	65.77	7.30	34.91	1.40	100.69	5.20

Source: Handbook of Fisheries Statistics, Government of India.

The sector is endowed with present freshwater aquaculture production of about 2.4 tonnes/hectare, which contributes about 95 per cent of the total aquaculture production and accounts for about 40 per cent of the total fish production of the country. This has been possible through phenomenal growth in development of carp farming in small inland water bodies. Within inland fisheries, there is a shift from capture fisheries to aquaculture during the last two and a half decade. Freshwater aquaculture with a share of 34 per cent in inland fisheries in mid-1980s has increased to about 80 per cent in recent years. It has emerged as a major fish producing system in India as a result of initiatives taken by the Government. Fish Farmers Development Agencies (FFDA) were set up in various districts for developing a package of technologies, practices, training and extension and for providing financial assistance to the beneficiaries. So far, about 0.65 million hectare of water area have been brought under fish farming, covering 1.1

million beneficiaries. Currently, the average annual yield is around 3 tonnes/hectare (Figs. 2.1 and 2.2).

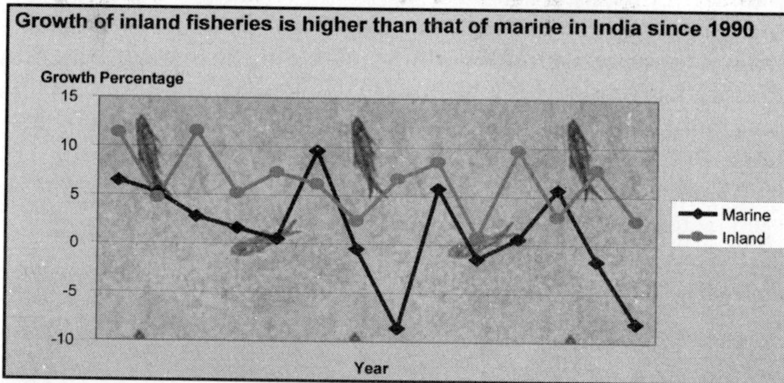

Fig. 2.1: Growth of Inland and Marine Fish Production in India.
Source: Author's computation from *Handbook of Fisheries Statistics*, Fisheries Survey of India, 2017.

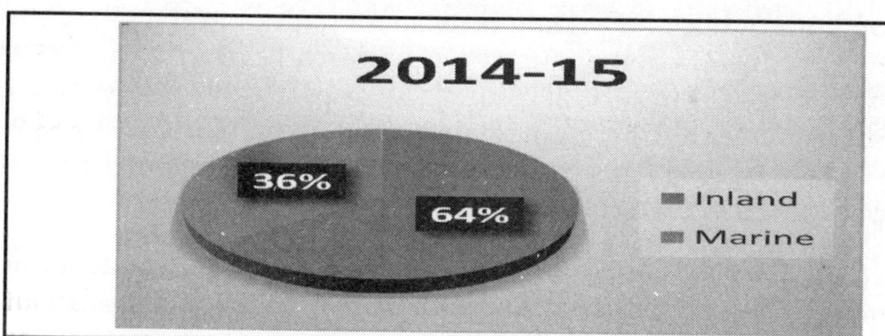

Fig. 2.2: Changing share of inland and marine sector in fish production in India.
Source: Author's computation from *Handbook of Fisheries Statistics*, Fisheries Survey of India, 2017.

Research team of National Centre for Agricultural Economics and Policy Research (NCAEP) led by B. Ganesh Kumar has conducted a project entitled "Exploring Market Opportunities for Fisheries Sector in India" in 2008. They had assessed the trend of fish production in the country using data for the last 25 years (1980-81 to 2005-06). Both linear and non-linear trend analysis was tried in the study and the best equation fitted. Extending the analysis for another 10 years (up to 2015-16) leads to the conclusion that the total fish production in India has been following a linear trend and it is likely proceed further in the same direction. The trend pattern of marine and inland fish production revealed that while the marine sector's production was increasing at a decreasing rate, the inland sector's production was increasing at an increasing rate, the possible reasons for which are that inland aquaculture activities are gaining much importance in some of the states like West Bengal, Uttar Pradesh, Andhra Pradesh, Punjab etc. in recent years. The trend equations for both marine and inland fish production, as well as total fish production are given below:

$$\text{Marine}: Y = -2.5879X^2 + 134.4X + 1061.3$$
$$\text{Inland}: Y = 2.8178X^2 + 36.171X + 914.75$$
$$\text{Total}: Y = 169.5X + 1462.7$$

This trend confirms the characteristics of this sunrise sector in Indian agriculture in days to come. Based on the trend observed in the last 35 years, assuming that the same scenario would prevail on both public and private investment pattern in the sector, the fish production of the country would reach 11.28, 13.17 and 15.24 million tonnes in 2020, 2025 and 2030 respectively (Table 2.4). The share of inland fisheries in total production will increase up to 78 per cent in 2030. This increasing contribution of inland sector, as presumed by the policy planners, will mainly come from aquaculture sector by utilizing the unused and derelict ponds, tanks.

Table 2.4: India's Fish Production Projection *(in million tonnes)*

Year	*Marine*	*Inland*	*Total*
2020	3.50 (31.07)	7.78 (68.93)	**11.28**
2025	3.61 (27.38)	9.56 (72.62)	**13.17**
2030	3.68 (24.17)	11.56 (75.83)	**15.24**

Note: Figures in parentheses indicates percentage of respective total.
Source: Author's computation from data of NCAEPR.

One point of argument in favour of above result is that the strong traditional knowledge base supported by scientific inputs in various aspects of management of inland fish cultivation is one of the factors responsible for growth in inland fish production (Jana and Sena, 2004). Bio-technological application, in the field of genetics, breeding, hormonal application, immunology and disease control will receive attention for increased aquaculture production in particular. Among the inland fisheries resources, freshwater aquaculture, mainly in village tanks and ponds, has shown significantly higher growth rates than those of capture fisheries in the last decade, with the quantity increasing from 1.01 million tonnes in 1990 to 2.10 million tonnes in 2000 and 3.2 million tonnes in 2014. Freshwater aquaculture has continued to form a major share of the aquaculture production, with a contribution of over 95 per cent in terms of quantity. It is only the three Indian major carps, which share as much as 2.1 million tonnes. Freshwater aquaculture in India has made notable strides in recent years with a growth trend similar to that of the world. With an annual growth rate of over 6 per cent during the last decade, the sector possesses higher growth rates than other food producing sectors. The sector has evolved from the stage of a domestic activity in the East Indian states of West Bengal and Odisha to that of an industry in recent years, with states like Andhra Pradesh, Punjab, Haryana and Maharashtra taking up fish culture as a trade. With technological inputs, entrepreneurial initiatives and financial investments, the pond productivity has gone up at a national level from 500-600 kg/ha/yr to over 2000 kg/ha/yr, with several farmers and entrepreneurs achieving higher production levels of 6-8000/ha/yr. Carps is the mainstay of culture practice in the country, which is supported by strong traditional knowledge base and scientific inputs in various aspects of management. Carps contribute 87 per cent of the total aquaculture production. Though the country possesses a large number of potential cultivable carp species, it is only the three Indian major carps; *catla* (*Catla catla*), *rohu* (*Labeo rohita*) and *mrigal* (*Cirrhinus mrigala*), that contribute a lion's share with production (0.654, 0.675 and 0.715 million tonnes, respectively recorded during the year 2006). Scientific interventions in the last five decades have led to the development of a host of carp culture technologies with varied production potentials depending on the type and level of inputs.

The mean national pond productivity has remained at about 2.4 tonnes/ha/yr, despite production levels of 6-8 tonnes/ha/yr being realized by farmers in several parts of the country (Ayyappan *et al.*, 2015). This indicates the enormous scope for both horizontal and vertical expansion of freshwater farming. In this regard, it is necessary that district-wise development plans are made based on the soil fertility, water availability, market structure of the area, investment capacity of the farmers etc. Considering the availability of technological strength and resource potentiality of the Indian farmers, it is feasible to enhance the mean pond productivity to 5 tonnes/ha/yr in the next ten years is feasible. Clearly, therefore, in spite of the existence of the vast resources like water bodies as well as improved technology for aquaculture, the level of production and productivity are not adequate and there remains a large gap between potential and actual yields.

2.2 Aquaculture in State Perspective

Fish and fisheries have been an integral part of the life of the people of West Bengal from time immemorial and play a major role in employment, nutrition, foreign exchange earnings and other aspects of the economy. West Bengal is traditionally a non-vegetarian state, 95 per cent of the state people consume fish. As such fish is a natural complement to rice in Bengali's diet, giving rise to the adage "Machhe-Bhate Bangali" (A Bengali is made of fish and rice).

Since 1950, the state of West Bengal had been consistently occupying the top position in the country in the inland fisheries sector. In the inland sector, almost 30 per cent of the all-India fish production came from West Bengal. While in 1981-82, fish seed, fish production and earning from export from fisheries in West Bengal were 2300 million, 3.78 lakh tonnes and Rs. 32.50 crores respectively; in 2014-15, production of fish seed and total fish production was 16,717 million and 16.17 lakh tonnes respectively and earning from export of fish was to the tune of Rs. 3,688 crore. The state had distinction of being awarded the national productivity award for 14 years in a row. Fisheries sector has a significant role in employment generation, poverty alleviation and socio-economic upliftment in rural areas of the state. Till 2015, the sector has generated non-tax revenue of more than Rs. 62 million, contributing 2.98 per cent of state domestic product at current price. More than 62 million people are engaged in searching their livelihood from this sector. However, in recent years, the state is continuously lagging to maintain its spurt growth behaviour and the evidence is quite clear from Table 2.5. Since 2009-10, not only in marine sector, total fish production of the state has shown a fluctuating trend, leading to decreasing contribution from fisheries in NSDP over the years.

Table 2.5: Production of Fish in West Bengal (*in thousand tonnes*)

Years	*Inland*	*Marine*	*Total*	*Growth in NSDP contribution (%)*
2009-10	13.26	1.79	15.05	1.01
2010-11	12.46	1.97	14.43	0.98
2011-12	12.90	1.82	14.72	1.07
2012-13	13.88	1.52	14.90	1.10
2013-14	13.92	1.88	15.80	4.83
2014-15	14.38	1.79	16.17	3.41

Source: Directorate of Fisheries, Government of West Bengal, 2016.

West Bengal is occupying the leading position in the country in terms of inland fish production, especially carp farming in village tanks and ponds. Research and development efforts in the last five decades have greatly enhanced average fish yields in the state making carp culture in village tanks and ponds an important economic enterprise. The three major Indian carps, namely *catla* (*Catla catla*), *rohu* (*Labeo rohita*) and *mrigal* (*Cirrhinus mrigala*) were the principal species cultured by the farmers in ponds since ages and production from these systems remained significantly low till the introduction of carp polyculture technology. Introduction of exotic species like silver carp, grass carp and common carp into the carp polyculture system during early sixties also added new dimension to the aquaculture development of West Bengal. It is the Pond Culture enhancement initiatives by Government of West Bengal that was responsible for the development and refinement of scientific carp culture in the state through its research in several centres on Composite Fish Culture (CFC) and Fish Seed Production (FSP). With the adoption of technology of carp polyculture or composite carp culture, production levels of 3-5 tonnes/ha/year could be demonstrated in different regions of Bengal. It is the technology of carp polyculture that has revolutionized the freshwater aquaculture sector and brought it from a level of backyard activity to that of a fast growing organized industry.

Research over the years has led to the development, refinement and standardization of a host of technologies with varied production levels depending on the input use. The technology of intensive carp culture has demonstrated higher production levels of 10-15 tonnes/ha/yr (Ayyappan, 2006). The necessity of bringing more species of promise into the carp culture practice is being emphasized. Species like *Labeo calbasu, L. gonius, L. bata, Puntius pulchellus, P. sarana, P. kolus* and *Cirrhinus cirrhosa* are considered by the government to be important candidate species due to their production potential, consumer preference and high market price, and there is a growing research thrust for diversification of carp culture sector.

But it is quite evident that compared to the fisheries development initiatives of other states, West Bengal is lagging behind day by day. The figure relating to the share of various states in the country's total inland fish production for the last two and half decades reveals that West Bengal is fast losing its dominance in this sector to the emerging states like Andhra Pradesh, Uttar Pradesh and Punjab (Table 2.5). Since 2011, state has lost its top position in inland fish production in the country. For the last few years, Andhra Pradesh is showing an aggressive growth pattern in inland fish production and outpaced Bengal, the result of which is that West Bengal is now the second largest producer of fish in the country. Not only Andhra Pradesh, almost all the leading fish producing states in the country are showing higher compound growth rate than West Bengal. The growth rates of fish production were computed for major states of India. Annual growth rate was used to assess production of fish by using the following exponential growth function:

$$Y = a \times b^{t} e$$

Where, Y = Fish production for which growth rate is estimated

a = Intercept

b = Regression coefficient

t = Time period ranging from 1999–2014

e = Error term

Exercise leads to the conclusion that the production of fish has been showing an increasing trend and has registered a positive

Table 2.6: Growth Rate (%) of Fish Production by States, 1990-91 to 2015-16

States	*Inland*	*Total*
West Bengal	4.42* (37.01)	4.01* (29.86)
Andhra Pradesh	13.01* (19.42)	10.03* (16.51)
Bihar	4.88* (9.14)	4.88* (9.14)
Punjab	14.02* (22.34)	14.02* (22.34)
Uttar Pradesh	7.35* (40.30)	7.35* (40.30)

Note: * Significant at 1 per cent, figures in parentheses indicate 't' values.
Sources: Author's calculation from data collected from various sources.

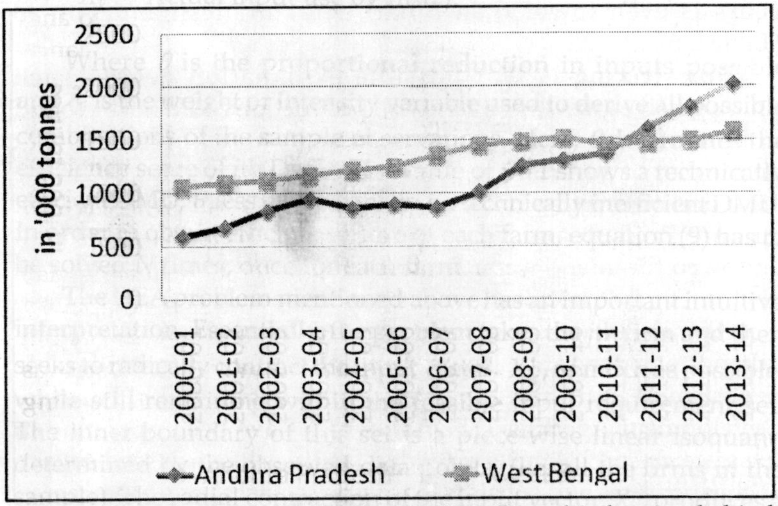

Fig. 2.3: Growth of fish production in West Bengal is lagging behind Andhra Pradesh.

compound growth rate of around 4 per cent per annum. Among the major fish producing states Chhattisgarh has registered the highest annual growth rate of 15 per cent followed by Andhra Pradesh, Uttar Pradesh and Karnataka. In the year 1990-91, the major producing states were West Bengal, Bihar, Andhra Pradesh, Uttar Pradesh and Odisha. They together contributed about 68 per cent to total inland fish production. In the subsequent one and half decades, Andhra Pradesh and Uttar Pradesh had made tremendous progress in its share to total inland production compared to West Bengal. While the other major contributor like Bihar, have decreased in its share, Odisha was maintaining it in total inland production. Another major state, whose contribution is improving rapidly, is Punjab. As a result, from 37 per cent share of India's total inland fish production, West Bengal has lost 8 per cent share to produce mere 29 per cent in 2005-06 and in another 10 years, this share falls down to 21 per cent. While inland fish production in Andhra Pradesh is growing at rate more than 13 per cent per annum, West Bengal is struggling with growth of rate 4.42 per cent only. Even Bihar is growing faster than Bengal in terms of inland fish production. It should also be a matter of concern for the fisheries department of the state that inland fisheries are growing at snail's pace, growth rate for the last 25 years is even lower than Bihar, Uttar Pradesh and Punjab (Table 2.6).

But striking is that possible explanation behind such unimpressive growth of inland fish production could not be found in terms of lack of demand, resource scarcity or lack of commitment on the part of government. There is a huge demand for fish in the state and to meet its demand, the state has to import fish from Andhra Pradesh and Bihar. Side by side, West Bengal is well endowed for inland water fisheries. It is situated in the monsoon belt having 2.76 lakh hectare of tanks and ponds and some others closed water bodies. The government of West Bengal has recently taken steps for intensifying fish culture and a considerable investment has already been committed. Fish Farmers Development Agencies (FFDAs), which have been operating in the state since 1984, have extended facilities like fish seed supply at cheaper rates and subsidy. Extension services have been geared at the village level. Training farmers for the fish farmers has been introduced. Still, the production level and productivity are not adequate to meet the large gap between potential and actual yields.

In search of the reason behind such poor performance, one explanation can be established in terms of the utilization of its water resources. According to data provided by Government of West Bengal, utilization of impounded water bodies is around 79 per cent. In case of tanks, ponds, beels and baors, only 51 per cent of their ultimate fishery potential is being exploited so far. District-wise break-up of resource utilization and production data reveals more interesting result. It is quite clear from Table 2.7 that carp farming is still not popular in North Bengal. And there is huge derelict and semi-derelict areas hole through the Bengal. Burdwan has almost 34 per cent of its total closed water areas, where production has not been carried off. More than 29 per cent of tanks and ponds in Purulia could be brought under scientific pisciculture. Fish culture is completely absent in 13 per cent of closed water resources of South 24-Parganas. Such percentages are quite high for the districts like East Midnapore, Malda, North and South Dinajpur, Jalpaiguri, Coochbehar. Clearly, if all derelict and culturable ponds could be converted into cultured ponds and

Table 2.7: District-wise Nature of Water Area in West Bengal *(in hectare)*

Districts	*Culturable*	*Semi-Derelict*	*Derelict*	*District Total*
Coochbehar	1598.11 (36.98)	1993.76 (46.16)	727.44 (16.86)	**4319.31** **(100)**
Jalpaiguri	386.36 (40.46)	468.00 (49.02)	101.41 (10.62)	**955.77** **(100)**
Dinajpur	9678.66 (68.48)	2173.36 (15.38)	2281.76 (16.14)	**14133.78** **(100)**
Malda	4579.56 (76.49)	900.13 (15.03)	508.23 (8.49)	**5987.92** **(100)**
Murshidabad	16161.76 (96.16)	646.29 (3.84)	0 (0.00)	**16808.05** **(100)**
24-Parganas (N)	8641.45 (86.51)	1068.76 (10.70)	277.80 (2.79)	**9988.01** **(100)**
24-Parganas (S)	11237.79 (86.52)	1389.87 (10.70)	361.28 (2.78)	**12988.94** **(100)**
Howrah	4240.45 (76.35)	415.70 (7.48)	898.51 (16.17)	**5554.66** **(100)**
Hoogly	9224.22 (56.70)	4545.76 (27.94)	2498.03 (15.35)	**16268.01** **(100)**
Midnapur	2886.55 (15.85)	11482.31 (30.867)	3830.27 (63.09)	**18199.13** **(100)**
Bankura	17553.56 (77.33)	3810.75 (16.75)	1332.70 (5.87)	**22697.01** **(100)**
Purulia	50078.06 (70.28)	14229.64 (19.97)	6947.37 (9.75)	**71255.07** **(100)**
Burdwan	20618.79 (66.09)	7386.63 (23.68)	3189.49 (10.22)	**31194.91** **(100)**
Birbhum	15260.63 (88.36)	596.57 (3.45)	413.54 (2.39)	**17270.73** **(100)**

Note: Figures in parentheses indicates percentage of respective total.

Source: Compiled from data of ME and MS Wing, Government of West Bengal, 2007-08.

introduced just semi-intensive method of fish culture with local resources and technology, it would be possible to increase the pond fish production 3 or 4 times the total fish production of the state. Thus, increase in fish production can be realized by trapping resources of rural Bengal and cultivate them with improved fish culture method.

Table 2.8: District-wise Inland Production of Fish in West Bengal, 2014-15

(in tonnes)

Districts	*Fish*	*Prawn*	*Total*
Darjeeling (GTA)	473	—	473
Darjeeling (Siliguri)	1322	—	1322
Jalpaiguri	13638	—	13638
Alipurduar	6818	—	6818
Coochbehar	21280	—	21280
Uttar Dinajpur	28318	—	28318
Dakshin Dinajpur	51512	13	51525
Malda	60751	7	60758
Murshidabad	113062	85	113147
Nadia	98323	96	98329
Birbhum	69748	16	69762
Burdwan	140518	111	140629
Hoogly	96080	100	96180
Howrah	38127	293	38420
North 24-Parganas	144113	50267	194380
South 24-Parganas	149849	29835	179682
Purulia	48522	0	48522
Bankura	49109	0	49109
Paschim Midnapore	66866	7	66873
Purba Midnapore	133724	25575	159298
Total	**1332063**	**106405**	**1438468**

Source: Directorate of Fisheries, Government of West Bengal, 2016.

Resources remain untapped or partially tapped, it means, despite all the effort and enormous potentials for intensified fish farming, the fish farmers may not be economically motivated optimally for fish culture. Improved technology might not yet been disseminated to the level of common fish farmers in the villages. The recipients of technologies might also be greatly circumscribed by different factors. This is quite evident from wide variations in average fish yields in the districts. Comparing Tables 1.6 and 1.7, it is found that using 11,237.56 hectare of culturable water resources; fish farmers in South 24-Parganas are producing 16.09

mt/ha/yr fish on an average. The similar figures for Birbhum, Bankura and Burdwan are 4.42, 2.99 and 4.36 per cent respectively. Such average productivity is measurably low for the districts in North Bengal.

Another point deserves particular mention here. For the development of fisheries sector, Fish Farmer Development Agencies (FFDAs) has been set up in the State. FFDAs have extended facilities like fish seed supply at cheaper rates and subsidy; extension services have been geared at village level and introduced training programme for the fish farmers. So far, 1.18 lakh hectare ponds and tanks have been brought under FFDAs, which is near 50 per cent of the total closed water bodies. Different studies on the performance of FFDAs in West Bengal amply demonstrate that the productivity in water bodies under FFDA programmes is sufficiently higher (10-15 mt/ha/yr) than that in non-FFDA ponds. Thus, it can be considered that the adoption level of modern culture practice is tardy and arbitrary in the state. There is no denying the fact that the Government of West Bengal in recent years has adopted certain policies under FFDA programme. But unfortunately, this package of practices has not been adopted in an appropriate manner by the fish farmers in general. It is true that there is a reasonable scope for augmentation of fish production through adoption of these practices.

According to economists, lower productivity due to wide variations among fish production units along with many other socio-economic factors significantly influenced the demand supply gap in the state. Although, the fish production of West Bengal is increasing over the years, but the productivity of the fishery sector shows a very less increment over the year due to overfishing, lack of quality fish seed in proper ratio, lack of marketing infrastructure, socio-economic and environmental constraints (Roy, 2008) and again the most farmers used to follow traditional technology due to the absence of fishery extension services (Singh, 2001). Breaking up of joint family system, quarrel among legal owners, rivalry, theft, lack of renovation of existing ponds etc. have rendered large numbers of potential water bodies unproductive which could have play an important role in bridging the gap. Farm to farm differences in cultural practices are also considered as important factors contributing to the variations in productivity. There are huge differences in the size of the pond/farm, species cultured, stocking and stocking density, fish seed procurement, nursery management, feed and feeding management, pond fertilization, harvesting frequency, mode of fish marketing, source of information on aquaculture, fishseeds and disease treatment, perception on aquaculture etc. (Abraham *et al.*, 2010; Misra, 2011).

2.3 Potential for Aquaculture Diversification

The policies and development interventions aimed at reducing poverty in less developed countries like India are now closely related with the augmentation of small scale pond aquaculture. These small-scale aquaculture systems are predominantly household based activities and management of these production systems involves household members. Household labour division shows women are actively involved in agricultural production and spend a significant proportion of time in agricultural activities which include aquaculture for fish farming households (Menon, 2000). Involvement of women directly and indirectly in fisheries and aquaculture is an age-old practice in many Asian and African countries. Women perform a range of activities throughout the value chain of aquatic food products (Shaleesha and Stanley, 2000). These activities include fry collection from nature, induced breeding in hatcheries, grow-out production and management, on farm and on shore post-harvest activities, marketing of products and processing of fisheries products (Sharma, 2003; Song, 1999). Over the last three decades, aquaculture has been expanded, diversified, intensified and advanced technologically (Pillay, 2001). As a result, dynamic aquaculture has been developed to become the fastest growing food-producing sector in the world and has significantly contributed to world food security (Jia *et al.*, 2001). While the potential of aquaculture for bridging this gap can be widely recognized from the growth in recent past years, which suggests significant future dynamic growth and contribution to development of the country, this will not be automatically happened only by changing production technologies. A wide range of social and economical issues should be considered simultaneously associated with aquaculture, its development and interactions which are, in fact, closely linked to national, international policies and, institutional features (Muir, 2005). Although, many aquaculture technologies appear to have led to increased yields (Ali, 1996), the development of aquaculture, and the benefits derived, have faced criticism for the lack of clear impacts on the poor and, particularly, the belief that its promotion may further undermine the access of the poorest groups to fish (Thompson *et al.,* 2000). In many cases, the adoption of these technologies and broader impacts on rural livelihoods and benefits to the poorest people remain unclear. Clear understanding of current status of aquaculture as a whole and its impact on livelihoods, particularly in the rural areas, would contribute significantly to effective development of future policy and efficient technologies (Edwards, 1999a).

Poverty alleviation and food security, therefore, should be taken as the strategic starting point through aquaculture intervention. Some see aquaculture as a means of alleviating poverty in developing countries, others naturally see the profit motive as being more attractive (Edwards, 2002). For example, not all of the participants of a World Aquaculture Society (WAS) meeting in 2002 agreed that aquaculture is a appropriate route towards poverty alleviation. It was argued by some of the participants that focus should be given towards creation of wealth (financial, knowledge, health etc.) rather than food for the poor which address the symptoms of poverty but not its causes (Edwards, 2002). This statement might anticipate a shift from low-yield small-scale fish ponds to large-scale, high yielding units. From a macro-economic point of view, it is indeed more attractive to aim at richer rather than poor pond operators (FAO, 2004). However, the World Fish Center considers that the target beneficiaries should be small and subsistence farmers who do not have the resources for intensive, high-value, commercial activities (Kapadia, 2000), though many aquaculture interventions have not always directly addressed the needs of poorest people. Haylor and Bland (2001) proposed that we should "put people first in planning and development, and give special consideration to poor people". Those currently involved in aquaculture may not be very poorest since aquaculture requires resources such as land, ponds, water, credit and other inputs.

If major question is the relative contribution that aquaculture can make to alleviating poverty, some important queries appear relevant. How and in what ways do people benefit from aquaculture ? Can the poor be early adopters of aquaculture technology or can they only gain indirectly ? What sorts of aquaculture technologies and in which contexts can benefits be gained by the poor ? The answers to these complex questions is likely to depend on circumstance, the answers will vary between the areas where aquaculture has tradition and where it is a relatively new practice (Goulet, 1994). Aquaculture certainly contributed towards alleviating poverty in poor rural societies in the past in the few areas of the world in which it is traditional practice *e.g.* China (Hoffmann, 1934), Vietnam (Chevey and Lemasson, 1937) and Indonesia (Ilan and Sarig, 1952) and India (Kumar, 2005). However, even in areas where aquaculture has a long tradition, many small holders culture fish below their potential because of inadequate information (Edwards, 2002). Finally, the adoption and intensification of aquaculture, with the growth of domestic and global markets of high value farmed aquatic products, including farm and non-farm employment are prompting priority need for reviewing impacts on rural livelihoods. An improved understanding of the trend of adoption of aquaculture, particularly small-scale pond aquaculture, and marketing of the products should inform and assist policy development in rural India and allow more meaningful and efficient targeting of poorer people.

One point deserves particular attention here. The economists and policy planners are continuously emphasizing that the need for increasing production as well as maintaining livelihood and nutritional security can be better addressed if aquaculture can be diversified with the introduction of small indigenous freshwater fish species (SIFFS). The present level of commercial aquaculture in India demonstrates that carps are the mainstay of culture practice in the country, as also in West Bengal, which is supported by strong traditional knowledge base and scientific inputs in various aspects of management. Carps contribute 87 per cent of the total aquaculture production (Ayyappan and Jena, 2003). Though the country possesses a large number of potential cultivable carp species, it is only the three Indian major carps; *catla* (*Catla catla*), *rohu* (*Labeo rohita*) and *mrigal* (*Cirrhinus mrigala*), that contribute a lion's share with production (0.654, 0.675 and 0.715 million tonnes, respectively recorded during the year 2014). Scientific interventions in the last five decades have led to the development of a host of carp culture technologies with varied production potentials depending on the type and level of inputs. But, recent research regarding diversification of carp culture has demonstrated that integration of some of the small indigenous fish species (SIFSs) into polyculture systems along with carp species has increased overall pond fish production.

Small indigenous freshwater fish species (SIFFSs) are defined as fishes which grow to the size of 25-30 cm in mature or adult stage of their life cycle. They inhabit in rivers and tributaries, floodplains, ponds and tanks, lakes, beels, streams, lowland areas, wetlands and paddy fields. Although rural population depend highly on indigenous species of fish for nutrition in many parts of India, very little attention has been paid on their role in aquaculture enhancement, nutrition, processing, biology, captive breeding, livelihood security and conservation needs. Consequently, many small indigenous fishes have become threatened and endangered due to pollution, overexploitation coupled with habitat destruction, water abstraction, siltation, channel fragmentation, diseases and introduction of exotic varieties. In order to achieve sustainable utilisation, appropriate planning for conservation and management strategies are of utmost importance. In India, out of 765 native freshwater fish species documented by NBFGR, about 450 may be categorized as small indigenous freshwater fish species. The maximum diversity of the SIFSs has been recorded from the North-East region followed by Western Ghat and Central India. Based on the assessment of NBFGR, of about 450 SIFSs in India about 23 per cent (104 species) are highly important as food and other local significance and also play a significant role in aquarium trade and in providing local livelihood security. Again, of the 104 species, about 62 species have been categorized as food fish while 42 species as ornamental value. Review of literature shows that research efforts on the information on the status of small indigenous fishes and potential utilization in India is very limited. Small scale aquaculture of *A. mola, Puntius sophore, Osteobrama cotio, Cirrihinus reba, Labeo bata, Gudusia chapra* along with Indian major carps have been reported (Ayyappan and Jena, 2003, Roos *et al.* 2003, Jena *et al.*, 2008). Successful captive breeding of several SIFSs have been reported under National Agricultural Technology Project (NATP)-NBFGR projects (Singh and Kapoor, 2004) and also by several workers (Sarkar *et al.*, 2009). Recent trend on pattern, and abundance of SIFSs of the Ganga basin and associated protected areas have been studied by NBFGR (unpublished data) and the results shows that the minnows (*Chela* sp., *Rasbora* sp.

Amblypharyngodon sp., and *Salmophasia* sp.), barbs (*Puntius* sp.), scheilbids (*A. coila* and *Eutropichthys* sp.), clupeids (*Goniolosa manmina* and *G. chapra*) and bagrids (*H. menoda* and *Mystus* sp.) were the dominating groups of fishes.

Among SIFSs, many species are cultivable with high demand, cultivable and can be introduced as a candidate species in freshwater aquaculture system. These are *Amblypharyngdon mola, A. microlepis, Notopterus notopterus, Puntius sarana, Labeo bata, Puntius ticto, Cirrhinus reba, Salmostomaba caila, Nandus nandus, Anabas testudineus, Esomusdan ricus, Puntius chola, P. sarana, Glossogobius giuris, Danio devario,* and *Chanda nama* etc. Other potential species for aquaculture diversification includes *Labeo gonius, L. bata, Labeo boggut, L. dussumeri, L. fimbriatus, Barbodescarna ticus, Puntius pulchellus, P. kolus, P. sarana* and *Cirrhinus cirrhosa*. Some of these species are being cultured at minimum scale, mostly based on wild seed collection. The air-breathing and non-air-breading species, *Channa marulius, C. striatus, C. punctatus, C. gachua, Channa bleheri, C. aurantimaculatata, C. stewartii* have not been taken up for the aquaculture at large scale. With the technology available for seed production and culture of air breading (*Clariusba trachus, Heteropnustes fossilis*), non-airbreading cat fish (*Mystus seenghala, Mystus aor, Horabagrus brachysoma, Notopterus notopterus, Ompok pabda, O. pabo,* and *Ailia coila*), farming needed to be popularized and expanded. Research and policy support for domestication of potential cultivable food and ornamental indigenous fishes as well as value added products from aquatic organisms is also required (*see* Table 2.9 and Photo 2.1).

Table 2.9: Small Indigenous Fishes cultured in ponds and tanks in West Bengal

Species	*Scientific Name*	*Species*	*Scientific Name*
Bata	*Labeo bata*	Mourala	*Amblypharyngdon mola*
Tangra	*Mystus vittatus*	Punti	*Puntius ticto*
Sol	*Channa striatus*	Chanda	*Chanda ranga*
Singhi	*Heteropneustes fossilis*	Pholui	*Notopterus notopterus*
Nandos	*Nandus nandus*	Lata	*Channa punctatus*
Kholse	*Colisa fasciatus*	Pankal	*Mastacembelus pancalus*
Bele	*Glossogobius giuris*	Dheney	*Esomus dandricus*
Techokha	*Panchax panchax*	Kunche	*Amphipnous cuchia*
Pabda	*Ompok pabda*	Bogo	*Xenentodon cancila*
Pangas	*Pangasius sutchi*	Rupchanda	*Pygocentrus nattereri*

Source: West Bengal University of Animal and Fishery Sciences.

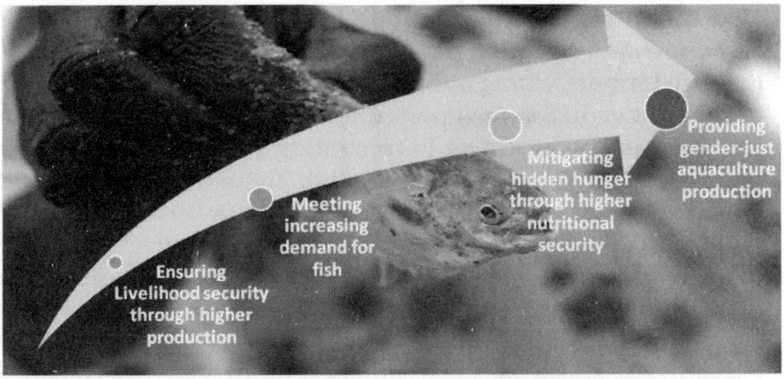

Photo 2.1: Potential benefits for diversified aquaculture production.

It has also been observed that these SIFSs command high prices, often higher than prices for Indian Major Carps, thus providing a source of supplementary income to rural households. Hence, along with the recommended six species of silver carp, grass carp, common carp, and three Indian Major Carps, farmers are also including some Small Indigenous Fish Species (SIFSs) in their carp polyculture practices. As a result, many fish growers are currently culturing more than 10 species in the composite fish culture (Jena *et al.*, 2005; Katiha *et al.*, 2006). Continuous refinement and modification undergone by the research institutes regarding carp culture have led the fish farmers to culture even predatory or weed SIFS like *Channa triatus.* (Sol), *Anabus testudineus* (Koi), *Mystus vittatus* (Tangra) and *Ompok pabda* (Pabda), *Amblypharyngdon mola* (Mourala), *Colisa fasciatus* (Kholse). Rational behind such diversification is that SIFS provide not only nutrition but also livelihood opportunities and income to a large number of fishers (Ahmed, 2009; Roos *et al.*, 2007; Wahab, 2003). Studies in India have already shown that the profit accruing to fishers is actually higher in the case of SIFSs when compared to those from large cultured species. It is imperative, therefore, to intensify scientific research regarding SIFSs to exploit all alternative means to increase production and productivity from natural aquatic resources, including tanks and ponds to their optimum level for sustainable aquaculture.

Side by side, it is also true that, carp culture through SIFSs without any supplementary feed, quality seeds have always been discouraged by scientists (Mazid and Kohinoor, 2003). They have also discouraged introduction of predatory species without recommended adoption package of practices. But stark reality is that fish farmers, caring only for profit, have introduced *mola, bata* or some other SIFS in their polyculture practices without following scientific advice, resulting in frustrating outcome in term of fish production (Neiland and Bene, 2004). Though the nutritive and livelihood importance of local fish species in carp polycultue is widely accepted, therefore, proper package of practice, with seed production technology and supply chains should be developed. Since, natural water bodies (and not government hatcheries) are still the source of SIFS; those resources should be protected and galvanized. Along with these, keeping in view of consumer preferences and market demand, some particular SIFS should be prioritized and government should strengthen their market linkages.

Another point deserves particular mention. The fish farmers practice their own indigenous technology as a common practice through natural resource management. The close and intimate observation of farmers through their age-old practices has developed the expertise of acquiring knowledge and skills possessed by local people can substantially contribute to productive efforts and endeavours. For example, some small farmers, in the study area use to immerse banana logs in their pond by cutting into pieces. According to them, banana plant cell helps in increasing pH of the pond water through their alkaline secretion. Such activity helps to minimize protozoan disease and worm of fish. Some farmers could able to minimize mass mortality of *bata* species in this way. Unfortunately, scientific attitude to these indigenous technologies of the farmers are yet to be exposed. Conventional extension system is no longer able to address effectively these changed grassroots level reality. These calls for different extension approaches like participatory extension approaches including success stories of technology adoption, indigenous innovation by farmers, community based management systems.

3
Review of Existing Literature

> The ideas of economists and political philosophers, both when they are right and when they are wrong, are more powerful than is commonly understood. Indeed the world is ruled by little else. —*John Maynard Keynes*

3.1 Introduction

Aquaculture diversification, which started its journey merely from a small-scale, non-commercial and family based food production system, has now includes large-scale commercial and industrial production of high-value species that are traded at national, regional and international levels. Although production remains predominantly Asian and is still largely based on small-scale operations, there is a wide consensus that diversified aquaculture has the potential to meet the growing global demand for nutritious food fish and to contribute to the growth of national economies, while supporting the sustainable livelihoods of many communities (FAO, 2016). As a result, aquaculture diversification practices in small water bodies, for example, through introduction of small indigenous fish species, are increasingly capturing attention of economists and social scientists. A number of studies related to economics of fish farming have been conducted by eminent social scientists and economists at national level, state level and district level in India. Some of the studies concentrate on the culture practice techniques and farm management details; some emphasized the evidences of structural and operational features under which fish production is practiced in tanks and ponds;

importance of governmental policies and extension system have been highlighted in some research and also, in some cited works, constraints faced by the small fishers has been dealt with. Some other studies concentrate on the potential of aquaculture diversification practices as well as relevance of such diversification on securing food and nutritional security. Few among those studies deserve particular mention.

3.2 Socio-economic Studies in National Perspectives

G.S. Gupta (1983), in his article "Freshwater Fisheries – Present Status, Prospects and Policy Measures" showed that there is an inverse relation between pond size and yield rate. That is, as pond size increases, the productivity decreases. The conclusion was derived from the data, which is based on the new concept of Effective Storage Level (ESL). On the basis of its biological implication, it has brought two other concepts—(i) full storage level, and (ii) dead storage level (DSL). Still, it can be said that the conclusion is not always valid, as it did not consider input output ratio. It may happen that if inputs are increased along with the pond size, rate of fish production increases by the same amount or more than the input growth, depending on whether there is increasing or constant returns to scale in inland fish production.

Srivastava, *et al.* (1984) conducted a study on farm management in the country and observed that there are three types of farmer's income groups (i.e., net income, family labour income and business income). The study revealed that, the yield of an average pond in all India level is 681 kg./hac. The income pattern of different income group of farmers were Rs. 1740, Rs. 2170, and Rs. 2898 for net income group, family labour group and business income group of farmers respectively. The state-wise analysis revealed that, the fish farming achieved good results in West Bengal, Bihar, Madhya Pradesh and Odisha. In another study, Srivastava *et al.* (1984) conducted an experiment on culture practices of fish in different parts of India and reported that, organic fertilizer was used in about 44 per cent of pond and inorganic fertilizer in about 15 per cent of the pond. The data also revealed that, out of total fish production 77.4 per cent share come from Indian Major Carps while 27.6 per cent share for other species of fishes.

Dilip Kumar (1996) emphasized the need for creating the awareness about the emerging advancement in aquaculture technology in the fishermen society. It is necessary to organize short term training for rural youth with emphasis on learning by doing for generation of self-employment opportunities and socio-economic development of fishermen community.

Subrathum (1996) suggested that, integrated fish farming technology with emphasis on participatory approach is required for creating strong and effective linkage between the extension personnel and fish farmers.

S.S. Veerina, *et al.* (1999) in their article "An Analysis of Production factors in Carp Farming in Andhra Pradesh, India", published in Aquaculture Research, used principle component analysis to assess the relationship between farm inputs and fish yields on the basis of data collected from 189 carp farms. They found stocking density as the principle determinants of carp yields. The article has derived an interesting observation that older ponds are more productive. Also, socio-economic variable like age or literacy rates of the farmers has appeared insignificant variable in case of carp yields. It is also important to note that organic fertilization enhance fish production in the study whereas inorganic fertilizers and few feed ingredients have a secondary even tertiary role in production.

Dilip Kumar (2000) reported that, the task of extension becomes more difficult when the technologies to be introduced are developed with the object of long term benefit and sustainability. It is easy to convince them about the benefit of modern technology by demonstrating production and profit but is difficult to make them to understand about long term gain.

P.K. Katiha (2001) in one of his articles "Socio-economic Aspects of Culture-based Fisheries" (CIFRI, Barrackpore, Bulletin, 2001) also observed that the interventions in the forms of the management and institutionalization of the water bodies might be constrained by the wide variety of social considerations. Since the fishery development and management involve and affect primarily the fishers, it is necessary to consider the social aspects involving employment mobility, subsistence orientation of production and income distribution with regard to culture-based fisheries.

Ramchandra Bhatta (2001) has compared the status of inland fishers and fish farmers from six states including West Bengal. He found that household size of fish farmers is as high as 23 in case of Haryana compared to only 7 for West Bengal. The holding size of carp farms is highest in Andhra Pradesh (8.42 ha) follwed by Haryana (7.88 ha), while size is lowest in West Bengal (0.85 ha). Karnataka spends only 17 days for fish farming in a year. Corresponding figure was 75 days for West Bengal. Experience in carp culture is also highest (44.3 years) in West Bengal compared to only 9.75 years for Andhra Pradesh. The share of different sources of income of carp farmers revealed that in Andhra Pradesh the producers are basically fish farmers getting 95 per cent of their income from carp farming, while in Karnataka, Odisha and West Bengal substantial part of the income is generated from agricultural crops. Bhatta found poaching as the most severe problem faced by the farmers followed by disease.

S.K. Bhatnagar (2001) depicted that, the extension plays a major role in popularizing new technologies to be used in fish farming. It has been observed that, there is acute shortage of extension workers in various Government Departments who are supposed to provide extension services in the field to advise the farmers and as such they are not able to play effective role.

S.K. Thade (2002) stated that, growing awareness among the rural people regarding practicing improved Aquaculture that can assure better benefit. Further progress will depend on the successful diffusion of eco-friendly improved technology.

R.K.P. Singh (2003) in his book *"Economics of Aquaculture"* studied the economics of fish production in Bihar. The specific objectives were to examine the culture practices, costs, returns, labour, and employment, marketing practices and constraints in the fish production, on the basis of primary data. They emphasized that, the fish culture is the domain of the economically and socially backward sections of the society. Fish farmers are still using indigenous species of fishes and practicing traditional methods of fish culture. The uses of chemical fertilizer and supplementary feeds have just been introduced in the study area, but the farmers are unaware of the scientific level of their use. The book is actually an improved version of Singh's earlier work on fish production in Hansanpur block of Samastipur district.

Sibranjan Misra (2005), in his book *"Inland Fisheries in India – Issues and Concerns"*, by Concept Publishing Company, New Delhi reveals that poaching acts as a major constraint leading to poor performance of fish production particularly in West Bengal tanks and ponds. Misra, on the basis of data collected from tanks and ponds owners in three districts of West Bengal, arrived at the conclusion that poaching or deliberate poisoning due to rivalry, enmity or jealousy are widespread. Among other problems, lack of proper transport facility, suitable marketing management, non-availability of opportunity for soil and water testing etc. were considered by the poor fishermen as the major inhibiting factors. In consideration to non-adoption of new techniques, he observed that lack of information regarding various improved practices is one of the important factors. The financial difficulties due to bureaucratic delay etc. make the practice of composite fish-farming technologies much more difficult. Other problems emphasized by Misra were erratic and inadequate supply of quality fish seeds or fingerlings in time and at reasonable rate, multiple ownership and adulteration of inputs. Measures suggested by Misra are the utilization of canal irrigation (from which water can be released to the fish ponds in winter season) or rain fed farming on watershed basis, desilting of about to dry-up ponds, long term lease arrangement, Government legislation to evict multiple ownership, development of appropriate technologies (keeping in view the regional, environmental and ecological differences), organized marketing channels, mixed farming etc.

There are several socio-economic and policy variables that influence the adoption behaviour of the fish farmers, practising composite carp culture technologies. On the basis of data collected from Sonitpur district of Assam, **P.K. Talukdar and B.S. Sontaki (2005),** in their article in *Journal of Agricultural Science,* revealed that adoption behaviour of composite fish culture practices is positively influenced by the factors like extension participation (r-value being 0.542 at 5% level of significance), economic motivation (r-value being 0.492 at 5% level of significance) and negatively by the age of the farmers (r-value being –0.295 at 1% level of significance). In view of the above findings, the study recommends that effort should be made by extension agencies to highlight the economic benefits of composite fish culture to promote adoption of this technology.

S. Ghosh and R. Indu (2007) in their study "Inland Culture Fisheries in Village Tanks and Ponds – A Multi-location Study in

India" observed that aquaculture in Village water bodies in India, in general, utilizes poly carp culture and is practised with the utilization of low to moderate levels of inputs, especially organic-based fertilizers and feed. The main problems faced by fish farmers are poaching, water availability and credit. They have also obtained interesting observations. The need for higher investments and the need for building relations to establish ones fishing right have led to the entry of the economically and politically influential people in this profession, who see this as an opportunity for economic gains. But this strengthening of fishing rights of few fishing contractors and increase in production have come at a cost of the traditional fishing communities who have been relegated to providing labour for these fish contractors. The government in many states have formed fisherman co-operatives and given priority rights for fishing in the village water bodies. But the functioning of these co-operatives have been found wanting. The study tries to map the changing institutional structure of the aquaculture sector in India.

S.K. Datta and R. Kundu (2007) in their article in *Journal of Social Science* throw light on the shaded question regarding socio-economic aspects of inland fishermen in West Bengal. According to Datta and Kundu, the unique efforts of fishermen in providing night time labour, source of traditional know-how and sense about the quality of pond water and soil are extremely important for sustainability of fish production in tanks and ponds. Collating data from a case study in Burdwan district in West Bengal, they found that poor family income, low level of literacy, family size etc. coupled with poor financial inputs have left many of the fishermen in unimproved state of economic condition. The fishermen associated with fishing co-operatives are in general rather poor, semi-literate or illiterate and hardly have any other alternative job opportunity to switch over. The little amount that they could possibly save get drained away for buying medicine or for servicing of the nets which for most part of the year remain idle. The authors suggested to counter the trend by ameliorative steps like ensuring access of fishermen in poorer rural cooperatives to credit support, provision of quality seed and feed, or even by spreading distance education through print or electronic media. The believe, human resource development programmes with emphasis on sanitation and health insurance, better training facilities, adoption of small family norms, together with reclamation of hitherto unused wetlands and need based public grants are some of the means that can activate the rural fishers.

In his book, **Jaydev Misra (2011)** has documented the results developed from a primary survey conducted among 360 fish farmers in West Bengal. He found that technologies developed in the government laboratories for commercial aquaculture practices and trainings provided through extension services have either not been adopted by the fish farmers or they are adopting only a part of the recommended package of technology. Actually, the technologies for utilizing the resources need not always be based on intensive commercial operations; rather they should be based on the application of basic aquaculture principles, their adaptation to local knowledge systems and the different social contexts. The deviation from this rationality has compelled the farmers to manipulate their acquired scientific knowledge along with their own conventional wisdom to adopt only a part of the package of practices. As a result, ultimate production has been affected adversely. And therefore, production could be significantly increased through more efficient use of the existing inputs and technology by making extension approach more participatory and farmers-driven so that efficiency in production can percolate widely. In order to improve the efficiency of fish culture, location-specific development strategies, long-term leasing policies, and participatory extension support are suggested to be adopted in West Bengal.

Debnath, *et al.* (2015) in their study focused on gender perspectives in adoption of improved technology in aquaculture practices in Tripura. According to their argument, fisheries like other crops are also a function of adoption level of a technology. Their study is based on a total of 180 fishers consisting 30 women and 30 men respondents that were randomly selected. For each sector, identified fisheries technologies were selected for the study. Factor analysis was carried out for identification of relationships between technologies and multiple regression analysis was performed to identify the factors that determined the adoption level. The study has indicated commonality and divergence in the attitude between women and men fishers in respect of technology adoption. Thus, gender perspective is clearly visible in adoption of technological practices in Tripura.

All these studies leads us to the conclusion that economic information with adequate data and improved methodology on the various aspects of existing aquaculture practices in West Bengal have not been appeared in literature adequately, though much research works have been done in the national perspectives. Also, the studies are not properly co-ordinated with the economic ideas regarding how to improve production and efficiency in this sunrise sector.

3.3 Literature on Efficiency Analysis in Aquaculture

The analysis of socio-economic aspects in fisheries sector now-a-days, starts with its relation with poverty. **Béné (2003)** had showed that the first interpretation of the relationship between fisheries and poverty is that "they are poor because they are fishermen". Fishermen are considered as the poorest of the poor caused by the endogenous and exogenous origin of poverty in fishery. Regarding the exogenous origin, the issue of poverty in the fishery has based on the economic concept of low opportunity income. Small-scale fisheries are usually located in remote areas with very few alternative job opportunities. In other words, the alternative incomes are usually low outside the fisheries sector that keeps fishermen's incomes at low level. Hence, following Béné, it can safely be asserted that policies for enhancement of small scale fisheries must be found out from the sector within. Like, fisheries practice in tanks and ponds must be successful such that poor fish farmers can maintain their livelihood from it.

Now, measurement of success in aquacultural production depends on proper interpretation of cost and revenue structures of enterprises. In this interpretation, financial success can be attributed to enterprises of which the revenues exceed costs. Yet, whether the accounting profits of enterprise is adequate to acknowledge an enterprise as successful is controversial. The enterprises utilize various inputs for production. However, the outcome of input processing is not directly related with the amount and cost of inputs. It is the technical process affecting the final output. Two identical firms having identical input structures may end up with differentiated yields or different cost-revenue structures. Therefore, it is also possible to find out that an enterprise having accounting profits is not efficiently utilising the inputs incorporated or an enterprise which has a negative profit scheme is implementing the best bunch of activities possible. However, the evaluation of success of the enterprise in terms of effective use of inputs (land, labour, seeds, chemicals, water, feed etc. for fish production) and maintenance of a sound cost structure lies in the efficiency analysis of the process (**Burhan Ozkan, *et al.*, 2009**).

There are various methodologies utilized in order to evaluate the efficiency of a production system, in case of aquaculture production. Based on Farrell's innovative article (1957), several approaches to efficiency and productivity assessment have been developed that can be classified into two broad categories: parametric and non-parametric frontier models. The former relies on the specification of an *ad hoc* functional form; imposes certain *a priori* restrictions on the production technology, and estimates the parameters of the production or the cost function statistically. Alternatively, the latter constructs a linear piecewise function from empirical observations of inputs and outputs, thereby avoiding the need to assume functional relationships between inputs and outputs or to make distributional assumptions regarding the residuals in a regression analysis.

The stochastic frontier Analysis (SFA) (**Aigner *et al.*, 1977**) involving econometric methods and data envelopment analysis (DEA) (**Charnes *et al.*, 1978**) involving mathematical programming techniques are the two most popular methods used in efficiency analyses of firms in various industries, including agriculture. The deterministic (i.e., mathematical programming-based) parametric frontier (**Aigner and Chu, 1968**) and probabilistic frontier (**Timmer, 1971**) are other approaches found in the literature. The main advantage of the stochastic frontier model is that it can decompose the deviation from the frontier or best practice into its stochastic noise and technical inefficiency components. The need for imposing a particular functional form for underlying technology is, perhaps, the main weakness of this technique. On the other hand, since DEA is deterministic and attributes all deviations from the frontier to inefficiencies, a frontier estimated by this technique is likely to be sensitive to stochastic noise and other measurement errors in the data.

A great variety of applications of DEA and SFA and have been conducted in many of studies to investigate technical, allocative, cost and scale efficiency by applying input and output oriented models in many different activities in many different contexts in many different countries. There is a number of efficiency studies applying DEA conducted on agricultural sector in many countries. However, DEA applications on aquaculture are relatively low in comparison to the other areas. This section provides recent studies stemming from different methodologies utilized in the field of aquaculture and its implication for future development of the sector since interpretation of efficiency in aquaculture is important as the evolution of fish outputs with respect to diverse range of inputs used has been considered as a critical task within the literature.

The introduction of technical efficiency analysis in fisheries sector dates back to 1996 when **Gunaratne and Leung (1996)** employed the stochastic meta-production frontier approach to examine production characteristics and the levels of technical efficiency among major black tiger shrimp producing countries in Asia. Productive performances of each of the extensive, semi-intensive and intensive shrimp production systems were compared relative to both regional and country-specific production frontiers, followed by an assessment of influence of farm-specific variables on technical efficiency. Based on the meta-production frontier, the mean technical efficiency scores for extensive, semi-intensive, and intensive black tiger shrimp production systems were estimated to be 0.49, 0.60, and 0.57, respectively, with very little variations across countries. However, efficiency scores relative to the country-specific frontiers showed considerable variations. For example, the country-specific mean technical efficiencies for the extensive system varied from 0.35 for Vietnam to 0.61 for India. The corresponding range for the semi-intensive system was 0.37 for Vietnam and 0.69 for Sri Lanka, and that for the intensive system was 0.47 for Taiwan and 0.79 for Sri Lanka. The extensive system in India; semi-intensive and intensive systems in Sri Lanka and Malaysia, and intensive system in the Philippines showed most potential for improvement by adopting the best-practice technology available in the region. Farm-specific variables had a significant influence on efficiency levels in several cases. Farm size had a negative impact on technical efficiency among extensive and semi-intensive farms and a positive effect on intensive farms. In general, farmer's experience was positively associated with technical efficiency, while owner operation was negatively associated.

However, **Gunaratne and Leung (1997)** have contradicted their own result that high intensification of culture practices generates high fish yields. Using samples of intensive and semi-intensive shrimp farms in Malaysia, they conducted a comparative analysis of both parametric stochastic production frontier and the non-parametric data envelopment analysis (DEA) techniques in estimating the farm-level technical, allocative and economic efficiencies. The efficiency estimates from the two approaches were quite similar and showed substantial potential for improving the level of shrimp production in both systems by using existing inputs and technology more efficiently. But, striking is that, in the study, it is found that, on average, technical, allocative and economic efficiencies were similar for the both intensive and semi-intensive systems. This raises questions about the present trend of increased intensification in shrimp production and on the perception that intensification increases production efficiencies.

The result is again in sharp contrast with that developed by **Sharma and Leung (1998)**, who examined the technical efficiency and its determinants for a sample of carp farms from the Tarai region in Nepal using a stochastic production frontier involving the **Battese and Coelli (1995)** model for technical inefficiency effects. They analyzed five inputs (seed, labour, fertilizer, feed and other input) and several farm-specific and management factors, including culture intensity, experience, ownership, farm size, and fish, water and feed management indicators. The overall mean technical efficiency was estimated to be 0.77, with semi-intensive/ intensive farms being more efficient than extensive farms (0.80 *vs.* 0.69). Given the existing technology, the sample farms could increase their production by 23 per cent by using their existing resources more efficiently. Most of these gains would come from the adoption of regular fish, water, and feed management activities. The results also indicated substantial scope for increasing productivity through intensification of carp culture and technological progress, such as increasing fanners' knowledge in modern aquaculture and control of diseases.

Vassdal and Roland (1998) employed the Malmquist index approach to estimate the productivity change in the aquaculture production of Atlantic salmon in Norway for the period from 1992 to 1995. For each producer, the improvement in productivity was decomposed to technical change and change in technical efficiency by solving a series of DEA frontier models. The estimated mean technical efficiency increased from 0.75 in 1992 to 0.85 in 1995. The productivity increased between 15-20 per cent per annum during the study period. Most of this productivity growth was attributed to technological progress rather than the catching-up effect. In fact, about 40 per cent of producers experienced a decline in technical efficiency during 1993-95, although the overall productivity growth was positive, suggesting that they are unable to catch-up with the ongoing technological improvement in the sector.

Technical efficiency estimates of the fishermen involving in carp pond culture in Peninsular Malaysia had been estimated by **Iinuma *et al.* (1999).** The mean technical efficiency for both semi-intensive and intensive carp farms, computed using stochastic frontier model, was estimated to be 0.42, indicating a great potential for increasing carp production in Peninsular Malaysia through improved efficiency. For example, per-hectare carp production could increase up to 3.2 million per hectare if full technical efficiency could be achieved. Since, intensive/semi-intensive system was found to be technically more efficient than the extensive system (0.57 *vs.* 0.24); efforts should be made to promote the intensive/semi-intensive carp culture in Malaysia. However, result developed by the authors is in contrast with that developed by **Gunaratne and Leung**. However, in this study, pond area showed a positive impact and pond age a negative impact on efficiency levels.

Regional variations in efficiency of the fish farmers have been found by **Sharma *et al.* (1999)** in Chinese fish farming system. They applied a non-parametric data envelopment analysis (DEA) technique to measure economic efficiency and its technical and allocative components for a sample of Chinese polyculture fish farms and to derive technically and economically optimal combinations of different fish species for carp culture. In the analysis, four outputs (black carp, grass carp, filter-feeder and other carp species) were being produced using four inputs (seed, feed, labour and other inputs). Smaller farms from the developed regions were found to be relatively more technically and economically efficient in the analysis. The mean technical, allocative and economic efficiencies were estimated to be 0.83, 0.87, and 0.73, respectively. Technical inefficiencies accounted for most of the production inefficiencies in Chinese fish farms. The authors suggested that, on average, farmers should enhance production of grass carp and reduce black carp stocking rates.

To provide a comprehensive comparison of productive performance of carp farming in South Asia, **Sharma and Leung (2000a)** applied the stochastic meta-production frontier model to examine the inter-country differences in levels of technical efficiency of semi-intensive/intensive and extensive carp production systems among the major carp producing countries in South Asia, namely India, Bangladesh, Pakistan and Nepal. Based on the best practice frontier for the region, the mean technical efficiencies for semi-intensive/intensive farms varied from 0.68 for Nepal to 0.79 for India, with an overall average efficiency of 0.75. On average, technical efficiency estimates for extensive farms varied from 0.48 for Bangladesh to 0.62 for Pakistan, with an overall mean of 0.57. Differences in efficiency levels were explained in terms of various farm-specific and country-specific factors by estimating a model for technical inefficiency effects. The adoption of recommended fish, water, and feed management practices was found to be most critical for improved performance of carp producers. For each country, the study also compared the efficiency scores based on its own country-specific production frontier with that obtained from the meta-production frontier. Accordingly, the mean technical efficiency from the country specific frontier ranged from 0.73 for Pakistan to 0.86 for Bangladesh among semi-intensive/intensive farms, and from 0.39 for Bangladesh to 0.77 for Nepal among extensive farms. Semi-intensive/intensive farms from Nepal and Bangladesh showed the most potential for increasing productivity by adopting the best-practice technology in the region. The results indicated that, by operating at full technical efficiency, semi-intensive/intensive farms could, on average, improve their regional yield from 3.2 mt/ha to 4.0 mt/ha, while extensive farms could increase their yield from 2.2 mt/ha to 3.6 mt/ha.

Sharma and Leung (2000b) applied a similar approach to examine the levels and determinants of technical efficiency in carp pond culture in India. The results showed significant technical inefficiencies in carp production in India, especially among the extensive farms. The mean technical efficiencies for semi-intensive/intensive and extensive sample farms were estimated to be 0.81 and 0.66, respectively. By operating at full technical efficiency levels, the semi-intensive/intensive farms could, on average, increase their production from about 3.4 mt/ha to 4.1 mt/ha. Similarly, the extensive farms could increase their production from 1.3 mt/ha to 1.9 mt/ha. Much of these efficiency gains would come from the increased adoption of recommended fish, water and feed management and monitoring practices.

On the basis of primary data collected from Tamil Nadu, India, **Jayaraman (1998)** estimated a probabilistic frontier production function model to determine the productive performance and potential for improvement for a sample of carp farms. More than half of the sample farms (51%) were found inefficient as they were operating below the maximum feasible yield (MFY) and about 49 per cent of the farms were found to have realized the (MFY). The results indicate a substantial potential for increasing carp production given the existing technology. The lack of adoption of recommended practices was identified as the main constraint to reaching the MFY. Jayaraman suggested the need for improvement in extension and research activities to overcome this problem in carp production.

By estimating the stochastic production frontier with a model for the technical inefficiency effects, **Dey, *et al.* (2000)** examined the level of technical efficiency and its determinants of a sample of tilapia grow out operations in the Philippines. The mean technical efficiency was estimated to be 0.83. Farm size as well as farmer's age and education were positively associated with the level of technical efficiency. As farmers have attained a high level of efficiency under existing technology, further improvements in productivity of tilapia fanning will have to come from the promotion of new technology in the region.

Bimbao, *et al.* (2000) also employed the stochastic frontier production function model to analyse the technical efficiency of a sample of tilapia hatchery operations in the Philippines. The mean technical efficiency was estimated to be 0.48. Thus, unlike the grow out operations, the hatchery operations in the Philippines showed a substantial potential for improving production by using the existing technology more efficiently. The results indicated that, by operating at full technical efficiency, the hatchery operations would be able to increase their per-hectare production from 7,48,000 to 15,580,00 fingerlings per production cycle, resulting in a decrease in average cost and improved availability of fingerlings to tilapia grow out fanners.

Efficiency analysis has been conducted by number of researchers for marine aquaculture also. **Boncoeur, *et al.* (2000),** who demonstrated that larger vessels had a greater income potential to the skipper. However, other economic performance indicators (*e.g.* rate of return to capital) suggested just opposite result. In this study, technology had varying impact on efficiency depending on the main gear types employed. Education and training was generally associated with lower levels of efficiency. Formal education in particular was generally negatively related to efficiency in this study. From the SPF model results, potter skippers with formal education were roughly 10 per cent as efficient as their uneducated counterparts, *Ceteris paribus*. However, this is at odds with most studies of efficiency that use formal education as a proxy for skill.

Karagiannis, *et al.* (2000) applied a stochastic production frontier to estimate output-oriented technical efficiency along with the **Kopp and Diewert (1982)** cost decomposition method to compute input-oriented technical efficiency, input allocative efficiency and cost efficiency for a sample of seabass and seabream farms in Greece. Mean output-oriented technical efficiency was estimated to be 0.79, suggesting that by eliminating technical inefficiencies, production may, on average, increase by 21 per cent given the current state of technology and input use. Mean input-oriented technical, allocative and cost efficiencies were estimated to be 0.74, 0.79 and 0.58, respectively. Thus, farms could, on average, reduce their costs by as much as 42 per cent by eliminating production inefficiencies. Improvement in technical efficiency accounted for most of these cost reductions. Based on second-step regression analysis, larger farmers were found to have achieved higher levels of technical and allocative efficiencies. Similarly, specialization in either seabass or seabream production showed a positive impact on technical and cost efficiencies, and utilization of skilled labour seemed to have a positive influence on technical efficiency.

Using a stochastic frontier production model, along with a model for technical inefficiency effects, **Tveteras and Battese (2000)** analysed the factors affecting productive efficiency differences among salmon aquaculture farms from different regions in Norway, with a particular emphasis on the effect of agglomeration externalities on productivity. Regional industry size (measured by total employment) and farm density (measured by number of farms/km) were used in estimating the external economy index. Farm's age was also included in the technical inefficiency model to capture the effects of learning-by doing, capital vintage, quality of marine environment, and adoption of new technologies on technical efficiency. The regional industry size showed a positive relationship with technical efficiency, while the farm density was negatively related with efficiency, indicating the presence of negative biological congestion externalities. Differences in frontier output and technical efficiency levels were significant across regions, perhaps reflecting differences in biophysical conditions and infrastructure.

Chiang, *et al.* (2004) conducted a study in Taiwan which specified a stochastic production frontier function to estimate potential milkfish farm output and efficiency. The study has compared the maximum potential milkfish production per hectare under various pond conditions to provide managers with information on how to increase efficiency. In their paper, published in *Elsevier Journal Aquaculture,* 433 milkfish farms have been surveyed. Both Translog and Cobb—Douglas frontier production models are estimated using the maximum likelihood estimation method. Empirical results show that milkfish farming in Taiwan Tables diminishing returns to scale. To interpret, one per cent increase in all input factors would result in less than one per cent increase in output. This study estimates substitution elasticities to identify which inputs farmers can switch for and to what degree. It also documents complementarity of input factors to provide guidance for milkfish farmers on how to reallocate input resources to achieve production gains. The managerial ability and the pond production conditions, expressed by the type of culture system (mono/polyculture), water source, location, education, and years of experience, explain 90.5 per cent of the difference between actual production and potential production. In other words, the technical inefficiency hampers production by roughly 10 per cent. In another study conducted in India, **Kumar, *et al.* (2004)** determined the technical efficiency of prawn farming to be 69 per cent. Here also, stochastic production frontier approach was used.

Diana Tingley, *et al.* (2005), in their article "Factors affecting technical efficiency in Fisheries: stochastic production frontier *versus* data envelopment analysis approaches" in Aquaculture Research measure technical efficiency of several inputs to the fishing process on open water resources of English Channel using both parametric and non-parametric approaches. In terms of factors influencing efficiency, both approaches were found reasonably consistent. They also found boat size had a generally positive impact on efficiency. Rather than implying that larger vessels are inherently more efficient that smaller vessels, the authors suggests that the more efficient skippers tend to operate on the larger vessels. This is consistent with the finding of **Boncoeur,** *et al.*, who demonstrated that larger vessels had a greater income potential to the skipper, even if other economic performance indicators (*e.g.* rate of return to capital) suggested that smaller vessels were more profitable.

A broader, comprehensive study was carried out by **Dey, *et al.* (2005)** to determine the farm-level fish output efficiencies for selected Asian countries. It presented the estimated levels and determinants of efficiency in freshwater pond polyculture systems in China, India, Thailand and Vietnam. The levels of country-specific TE were estimated for different production intensity levels by estimating stochastic production frontier functions involving the model for technical inefficiency levels.

Using a weight-restricted DEA technique, **Kaliba and Engle (2006)** estimate technical, allocative and cost efficiency of a sample of small- and medium-sized catfish farms in Chicot County, Arkansas. These authors then regress the cost efficiency score in Tobit model on operator characteristics, farm practices, and institutional support services to determine whether these factors lead to a higher level of efficiency. An important finding of this research authors found that higher cost efficiency of catfish farm efficiency in Chicot County, Arkansas, can be achieved by adjusting inputs used in production to optimal levels rather than by adjusting the scale of operation.

Also using a two-step procedure, **Cinemre, *et al.* (2006)** measured the cost efficiency of trout farms and explored determinants of cost inefficiencies in the Black Sea Region, Turkey. The decomposition of the technical efficiency measure showed that pure technical inefficiency was the primary cause of technical inefficiency in the sample of trout farms. Research results also suggested that there were positive relationships between cost efficiency and pond tenure, farm ownership, experiences of the operators, education level of the operators, contact with extension services, off-farm income and credit availability while feeding intensity, pond size, and capital intensity had negative effects on cost efficiency.

Esmaeili, *et al.* (2007) has estimated technical efficiency of fishers located in Hamoon Lake south-eastern of Iran using DEA Approach. Using cross-sectional data that obtained from 74 fishermen, DEA approach is applied in this study to measure technical, allocative and economic efficiencies. On, an average, fishermen are found 82.7 per cent technically efficient in the study. These figures for allocative and economic efficiencies were 75.5 and 62.7 per cent, respectively. Though differences in efficiency among vessels were found small in this study, authors revealed that skippers having no financial difficulties and those who had participated in extension training were more efficient. In addition, technical efficiency scores are positively correlated with the size of vessels in the study.

Ferdous Alam, Murshed-e-Jahan, K. (2008) employed DEA technique in evaluating the resource allocation efficiency of prawn-carp polyculture systems by making use of the data of 105 farmers of Bangladesh. The results showed that 50 per cent of prawn-carp farmers displayed full technical efficiency whereas only 9 per cent were cost efficiency. Technical and allocative efficiencies showed a positive and negative correlation with pond size, respectively. Labour, fingerlings and feed were overused while organic and inorganic fertilizers were underused in general.

Applying a Stochastic Production Frontier to farm-level data from shrimp farmers in West Bengal, **Poulomi Bhattacharya (2008)** examines technical efficiency and its determinants in both scientific and traditional shrimp farming systems. The average technical efficiency of traditional shrimp farming is estimated as 0.49 as against 0.61 for scientific shrimp farming. The estimates suggest that there are high degrees of technical inefficiency among the shrimp farmers culturing shrimp at household levels. The traditional shrimp farmers with higher proportion of leased-in land to their total operational area under shrimp farming have demonstrated higher technical efficiency than shrimp farms with lesser proportion of leased-in land. The higher level of education would help the scientific shrimp farmers to operate at higher levels of technical efficiency. An analysis of the farmers' profile across different levels of technical efficiency in this study reveals that in the case of traditional shrimp farming, majority of the shrimp farmers who belong to the high and moderately high levels of technical efficiency followed the prescribed practice of disease management, regular water checking with the help of trained technicians which is essential for proper shrimp disease management. Moreover, in case of traditional and scientific shrimp farming, the largest size groups of shrimp farmers had higher technical efficiency than the other categories. On the basis of these results derived Bhattacharya calls for more attention towards the smaller shrimp producers on the part of the fisheries department, by providing them with appropriate credit and other extension facilities.

Kehar Singh (2008) in his article published in *Indian Journal of Agricultural Economics* used stochastic efficiency decomposition frontier analysis to estimate the farm specific technical efficiency (TE), allocative efficiency (AE) and economic efficiency (EE) levels. The estimated mean TE, AE and EE found in the study are lying at the levels between 0.65 to 0.68, 0.51 to 0.59 and 0.36 to 0.44 respectively. Small farmers, having less than 0.32 acre of pond area are found relatively more technical and allocatively efficient, thus economic efficient than large farms (having pond area more than 0.32 acre).

Kehar Singh, *et al.* (2009) in their article in *Agricultural Economics Research Review* has estimated technical efficiency of freshwater aquaculture in Tripura and investigated its major determinants. Employing stochastic production frontier approach on the cross-sectional primary data collected from 101 fish farmers, the authors found that seed quality is an important determinant of technical efficiency. The study has relied more on Cobb-Douglas form of stochastic frontier production function rather than of translog form and has revealed wide variations in technical efficiency scores, ranging from 0.21 to 0.96 with mean 0.66. The study has suggested that the Government of Tripura needs to play a role to ascertain the supply of quality fish fingerlings at adequate time and quantity to the farmers. However, the study is regarded as an improvement over earlier studies by **Kehar Singh (2005,**

2008) on the same region as factors affecting efficiencies had not been discussed in those studies.

Biswajit Debnath, *et al.* (2009) in their article, published in **Aquaculture Economics and Management** analyses resource use efficiency and social profitability of an integrated aqua-farm located in Tripura by deriving Resource Cost Ratio (RCR), which is actually a variant of Domestic Resource Cost Ratio (DRCR) propounded by Morris (1990) to analyse comparative advantages between countries. However, the RCR for the integrated farm was found to be – 0.24 in the study. The negative value of RCR shows positive profitability for the integrated farm. The corresponding value for a specialized farm was found to be 0.52. The difference is the greater resource use efficiency of the integrated approach. Private and social profits per unit cost for the integrated farm (0.26 and 0.08, respectively) were higher than for the specialized farm (0.11 and 0.04, respectively). According to them, differences in efficiency of integration stems from the feed mixing plant through which the farm could significantly reduce its feed cost. This study also provides evidence that aqua-farming systems can provide social profitability through efficient resource management by incorporating eco-friendly measures in an integrated farming approach.

In the study undertaken by **Misra and Misra (2014)** in West Bengal, the concept of meta-frontier data envelopment analysis (DEA) has been carried out to examine whether there is any systematic difference in the technical efficiency (TE) of fish farms of different size-classes categorized on various socio-economic conditions. Efforts have also been made to identify the influence of those characteristics on TE score using regression analysis. The study has revealed that on average, the realized fish output can be raised by 37 per cent in the state with the existing technology and resources. More than 60 per cent of the sample farms are operating below the average level of technical efficiency (TE) and this may be due to the mismanagement regarding input mix. Wide variations in TE scores have been found when farms were categorized on the basis of size, region, ownership pattern or proprietorship.

3.4 Studies Related to Aquaculture Diversification

A good number of studies concentrate on nutritional values of small indigenous fish species and their contribution to vitamin, calcium and iron intakes for poor rural communities as well as their potentiality to be integrated with existing aquaculture production. For example, **Vibol, *et al.* (2002)** in their study entitled "Small-scale Fish Culture using indigenous Fish Species in Takeo and Prey Veng Provinces of Cambodia" has tried to investigate whether indigenous fish species can replace or complement exotic species in small-scale aquaculture. Their survey led to conclusion that the growth of *P. hypophthalmus* and *B. gonionotus* was very high when they were stocked together with other indigenous fish species. And high market demand for indigenous species could help farmers to get high profit up to 58 per cent. Hence, they concluded that small-scale fish culture with indigenous fish species is feasible for rural farmers and could possibly be used to replace aquaculture with exotic species.

A study conducted by **Roos, *et al.* (2003)** found that the vitamin A content in SIS varies, from 100 mg to 2,500 mg in *mola* fish. The study addressed the potential of integrating SIS, including *mola,* into existing carp polyculture ponds in Kishoreganj district of Bangladesh. They found that total household fish consumption was positively affected by the domestic aquaculture production. Not only has this, the mean production of carp culture, when integrated with *mola,* shown a positive growth in all the 34 ponds surveyed. Within the range of a total fish production recorded in the 59 trial ponds, there was no indication of a negative correlation between the production of SIS and total carp production.

In another study by **Kohinoor, Thilsted and Wahab (2005),** the possibilities of culturing small indigenous fish species (SIS) in combination with the Indian major carps were explored. So, an experiment in this regard was carried out in the Field Laboratory pond complex of the Faculty of Fisheries, Bangladesh Agricultural University, Mymensingh. Polyculture of Indian major carps with small indigenous fish *mola* (*Amblypharyngdon mola*), *punti* (*Puntius sophore*) and *chela* (*Chela cachius*) was conducted to evaluate the production potential. Five treatments with three replicates were tested. Indian major carps and small indigenous fish were stocked at the rate of 7,500 and 50,000 fish/ha, respectively. The highest production (2103 kg) was obtained in treatment-3 where Indian major carps were cultured with *punti*. It is observed that if partial harvesting is made, polyculture of Indian major carps with small fish is a better proposition in terms of biological production.

In a study conducted by **Kohinoor, Sultana and Hussain (2007)**, an experiment on the polyculture of carps with SIS, *bata (Labeo bata)* was carried out to evaluate their production performance in the on-farm condition. The contribution of *bata* in terms of production was found to be as high as 14.38 per cent in a treatment. Study suggested a profitable production potential of integration of *bata* in the carp polyculture system in Bangladesh.

Nesar Ahmed (2009) in his study focused on the relative profitability and livelihood outcome from SIS integration in carp polyculture system. Results of the study showed that while the potential benefits are great, high production costs, insufficient supply of fish fry, lack of credit facilities and inadequate technical assistance are constraints to the sustainability of fish farming. Moreover, poor livelihood assets, vulnerabilities and weak transforming structures and processes are identified as constraints for sustainable livelihoods of farmers and associated groups. Study, therefore, found necessary to provide institutional, organisational, and government support for sustainable fish farming. According to Ahmed, the present reliance on wild fry limits further expansion of carp-SIS farming and puts pressure on the local environment. The availability of SIS fry has been declining due to destruction of their natural breeding grounds through human encroachment and environmental degradation. It is therefore necessary to explore the possibility of developing SIS hatcheries to reduce wild fry exploitation and increase wild production. In addition, study also found that the development of low-cost quality feed is essential to improve farmer's profit margins.

Sarkar and Lakra (2010), in one of their study, envisaged the significance, conservation and utilization of small indigenous freshwater fish species in India. According to them, it is essential to ban indiscriminate and destructive fishing practices to protect the young and juvenile fish. Catching should also be regulated to conserve the brood stocks of SIF and other fish species. They prescribed the conservation and enhancement of existing gene pools of native fish and SIF's in floodplains, natural depressions, rivers and other related water bodies through establishment and maintenance of fish sanctuaries on fishing areas. Public awareness of the necessity of conservation of indigenous fish diversity and wise management of habitats needs to be created through mass media. In order to ensure this, Sarkar and Lakra advocated to strengthen studies on nutrient analysis, processing and therapeutic properties of SIF's. Economic valuation provide a means for measuring and comparing the various benefits of fisheries and aquatic resource and their ecosystem and can be a powerful tool to aid and improve their wise use and management. Along with these, they found that it is necessary to develop institutional mechanisms to promote culture, consumption and conservation of SIF's.

CIFRI, Barrackpore (2010) has organized a workshop entitled "Small Indigenous Fish Species—Their Role in Poverty alleviation, Food Security and Conservation of Biodiversity", where number of scientists and researchers expressed their views and exchanged ideas on the role of SIFFS in enhancing rural food and livelihood security and in conserving biodiversity. It was also discussed the socio-economic and cultural context for culture and capture of SIFFS with a view to enhancing access, especially of women, to better income, livelihood and nutritional security, and proposed policy spaces for sustainable management of SIFFS. The discussion highlighted the importance of recognizing the role of SIFFS in poverty alleviation, through assessment of their contribution to the economy and nutrition of disadvantaged populations, particularly women and children. Ensuring protection/ management of aquatic habitats, while ensuring that the rights of access of disadvantaged groups to aquatic resources, are also given importance in the workshop discussion. Some scientists advocated the need for improved research and policy to promote the integration of these species into culture-based fisheries and aquaculture systems; and strengthening appropriate community institutions to protect access rights, ensure responsible ecosystem management and equitable economic benefits.

Chand, *et al.* (2012) in their Project report "Aquaculture in Changing Climate of Sundarban" conducted a cross-sectional questionnaire-based survey among the fish farmers of Sagar and Basanti blocks of Indian Sundarban to benchmark the socio-economic profile, current aquaculture practices, climate change pattern and its impact on aquaculture and prevailing coping measures. They found that apart from climate change issues, indiscriminate collection of shrimp seeds from the waters of Sundarban results in biodiversity loss of the region. During survey, people opined the drastic reduction of some native fish species in last thirty years. Few among these are *Ompok pabda, Wallago attu, Anguilla bengalensis, Chitalachi tala* and many others.

In an regional workshop entitled "Production and Conservation of Nutrient-rich Small Fish (SIS) in Ponds and Wetlands for Nutrition Security and Livelihoods in South Asia", held in Dhaka Bangladesh, **Thilsted and Wahab (2014)** presented a paper, where they found that the major challenges of sustainable production and management of inland fisheries resources to meet the requirements of the small fish, especially those micro-nutrient-rich ones, through aquaculture as well as conservation and management of natural resources are: lack of knowledge on the nutritional values of all small fishes, lack of knowledge on their biology, shortage of quality seed, land and water use conflicts, weakness in the implementation of fish acts, lack of alternative income generation for the fishermen, lack of awareness and uncertainty of climate changes. According to them, the policy support of the government for promotion of pond production and wetland production technologies and awareness building will be immensely helpful for increased production and consumption of nutrient-rich small fish by all groups of people, especially women and young children.

On the same event, **Vishnu Bhat (2014)**, the then Fisheries Development Commissioner of Ministry of Agriculture, Government of India focuses on country overview on small indigenous freshwater fishes in our country. According to Bhat, a large diversity of other indigenous species, are found in the water bodies that crisscross the Indian subcontinent. These species are either caught from nearby water bodies or get naturally recruited to homestead/common village ponds which are then harvested by the pond owner or the local community. Before the introduction of hatchery-produced seeds, in the initial years of reservoir fisheries, water bodies were auto stocked with naturally available seeds. However, it has been observed that a variety of indigenous fish species were stocked, for example, in reservoirs of Tamil Nadu and Kerala. But, after the introduction of hatchery-produced carp seeds, there has been a shift in species composition used for stocking water bodies from indigenous varieties to a combination of *catla, rohu* and *mrigal*. Often small indigenous species were removed as vermin, with negative implications for conservation of biodiversity in freshwater ecosystems. Studies undertaken by CIFRI have indicated that traditional fishers in the floodplain wetlands of the Ganga and Brahmaputra rivers basins depend, to a large extent, on small indigenous varieties of fish for their daily earnings, especially during the lean season and fishing holidays. It has been estimated that, on average, almost 30 per cent of daily income comes from sale proceeds of SIFFS, as these species have high market value and are preferred by consumers. Indian local markets, especially in eastern and north-eastern India also experience high consumer demand of small fishes at high price. The Government of India, according to Bhat, is encouraging states for effective utilisation of natural resources for increasing fish production and productivity through special government sponsored schemes like (a) Establishment of National Fisheries Development Board to work towards a blue revolution with a focus on increasing the fish production of the country, to achieve doubling of exports and an additional direct employment to an extent of 3.5 million by extending assistance to various agencies for implementation of activities under Inland, Brackish water and Marine sectors. Further, NFDB is envisaged also to be a platform for public-private partnerships (PPPs) for fisheries and a mechanism for an end-end approach for ensuring efficiency in the process of fish production to consumption in the country; and (b) development of reservoirs and cage culture under National Mission on Protein Supplement.

Kunda, Shah and Mazumder (2014), in a study envisaged the production potential of nutrient rich small indigenous species *Dhela* (*Osteobrama cotio*) in carp polyculture system at Golabgonj, Bangladesh. They found that while survival levels of the carps did not differ significantly for integration of SIFS and *dhela* may be one of the good candidate species for carp polyculture system considering its high nutritional value and having no negative impacts on the growth of carp species. They also found the significant growth in income levels of the farmer practicing diversified aquaculture practices than income of traditional farmers.

Dubey, *et al.* (2015), in their article "Indigenous Freshwater

Piscine Resources of Indian Sundarban Biosphere Reserve: Status and Prospects" focuses on diversity and conservation aspects of freshwater indigenous fish resources of Indian Sundarban Biosphere Reserve. The study revealed the occurrence of 62 ichthyofauna belonging to 45 genera, 28 families and 9 orders. Of these fishes, 6 per cent fish belonged to endangered category and 2 per cent were Vulnerable and Critically Endangered category. This article also addresses the culture potential of the small indigenous fishes as well as threat and conservation issues. Owing various exploitation parametres, sustainable management and artificial propagation might be a suitable process for future protection and conservation of small indigenous fishes as well as food security of local people inhabiting in Sundarban. Among the indigenous fishes, many species have wider potentialities as a candidate species in freshwater aquaculture domain. These are mainly *A. mola, N. notopterus, C. chitala, O. Pabo* and *Puntius* group.

3.5 Conclusion

Most of the studies reviewed here, based especially on parametric stochastic production function approach and non-parametric Data Envelopment Analysis (DEA), has found relatively low production and efficiency levels in existing aquaculture practices. Issues of aquaculture diversification through integration of small indigenous fish species in existing carp culture, though initiated but, not adequately appeared in literature. Also, efficiency estimates using DEA application for such diversification practices is completely absent in case of West Bengal pond aquaculture in particular.

Another observation is that management or farm specific variables had a significant influence on efficiency levels in several cases. But nature of such influences is highly ambiguous to follow. Different conclusions have been derived in different studies based on different methodologies followed, area studied or sample drawn. For example, semi-intensive/intensive carp polyculture farm are found more efficient in Leung's in 1996. But such observation appears insignificant in his next study for Philippines. Again, **Gunaratne and Leung (1996)** found negative impact of farm size on technical efficiency whereas pond area showed a positive impact on efficiency in the study conducted by **Iunuma (1999)** and **Dey, *et al.* (2000)**. As such, conclusions and policy prescriptions regarding the influences of those farms specific and management variables vary widely from literature to literature. Hence, analysis regarding production potential and efficiency estimates in diversified fish culture and determinants of such efficiency must be study specific.

Side by side, a thorough review of the existing literature on the socio-economic, structural or operational issues on aquaculture diversification revealed that no systematic and comprehensive study has been made with regard to the problem that the technology which seems technically attractive has failed to produce substantial results in real world. It is the essential task within the literature to find out exact reasons behind this. On this point, present study is a step forward to investigate the very issue on more secure foundation of data and methodology.

4
Methodology

We must learn truth from facts.

—Mao Je Dong

4.1 Field Area – Indian Sundarban

The Indian Sundarban Biosphere Reserve is a UNESCO declared World Heritage Site, lies on the southern fringes of the West Bengal state of India, where the Gangetic plain meets the Bay of Bengal. The Sundarban, world's largest mangrove ecosystem, is an archipelago of several hundred islands, spread across 9,630 km^2 in India and 16,370 km^2 in Bangladesh. The Indian Sundarban delta comprises of 102 low-lying islands, of which 48 islands are occupied by human habitation in 5,363 km^2 area. On the Indian side, it extends 19 community development blocks over two districts; 13 blocks in South 24-Parganas and 6 blocks in North 24-Parganas districts with total 190 Gram Panchayats and 1064 villages. The freshwater flows from the mainstream rivers and the tidal ingress from the sea result in a gradient of salinity that varies both spatially and temporally within the Biosphere Reserve. In general, the salinity is higher nearer the coast and the water in the inland side boundary of the Sundarban is nearly fresh. Freshwater domains closed to blind rivers, creeks and canals in the Sundarban biosphere are about 891 km^2. The Sundarban biosphere Reserve is endowed with a vast expanse of often inland waters in the form of canals, estuaries, lakes, ponds, tanks, wetlands and paddy fields etc. which always attracted attention for its cosmic aquatic recourses with rich indigenous fish diversity.

Indian Sundarban is the top producer of fish and prawn, with both districts combined producing roughly 31 per cent of the total inland fish/prawn production. Fishery is treated as the backbone of Sundarban economy. Apart from coastal and brackish water aquaculture, freshwater aquaculture is increasing day by day and contributes parallel economy and livelihood security in Sundarban eco-region. Sundarban boasts around 172 species of fishes, 20 species of prawn and 44 species of crabs including two commercial species. Along with these Sundarban acts as the nursery ground for nearly 90 per cent of the aquatic species of eastern coast of India.

Generally, estuary receives abundant supply of nutrients from land drainage and large quantities of organic detritus from mangrove forest which is an important source of energy for a wide variety of estuarine consumers. Further, many commercial estuarine fishes grow to maturity here and make up a large part of the near-shore fishery of the northern Bay of Bengal. Other fishes and prawns that spend most of their lives in freshwater descend annually to the estuary for spawning. Therefore, many marine and freshwater prawn and fish require this environment to complete their life cycle. Aquaculture in Sundarban is based upon both inland and marine fisheries resources. A proper linkage between the two culture systems can change the whole outlook of aquaculture in this area (*see* Fig. 4.1).

Cultivable species in Sundarban includes both freshwater and brackish water species (finfish and shellfish). Freshwater aquaculture is practised mostly in backyard ponds. Villages in the Sundarban have lots of such ponds. Families excavate a portion of their low-lying paddy field to get earth to raise the land and construct dwelling houses and for drinking water. Therefore, almost every household possesses these excavated areas, which, in the monsoon season, store rainwater. These ponds (small water body) are used for freshwater aquaculture. Water of these ponds is also used for household purposes like washing of utensils, bathing and even for drinking purpose. Fish produced in these ponds are mostly used for domestic consumption and excess amount is sold. Apart from this, freshwater aquaculture is also carried out in big ponds (either owned by individuals or few families), land-shaping ponds (mainly excavated for agricultural irrigation purpose) and low-lying inundated paddy fields. Brackish

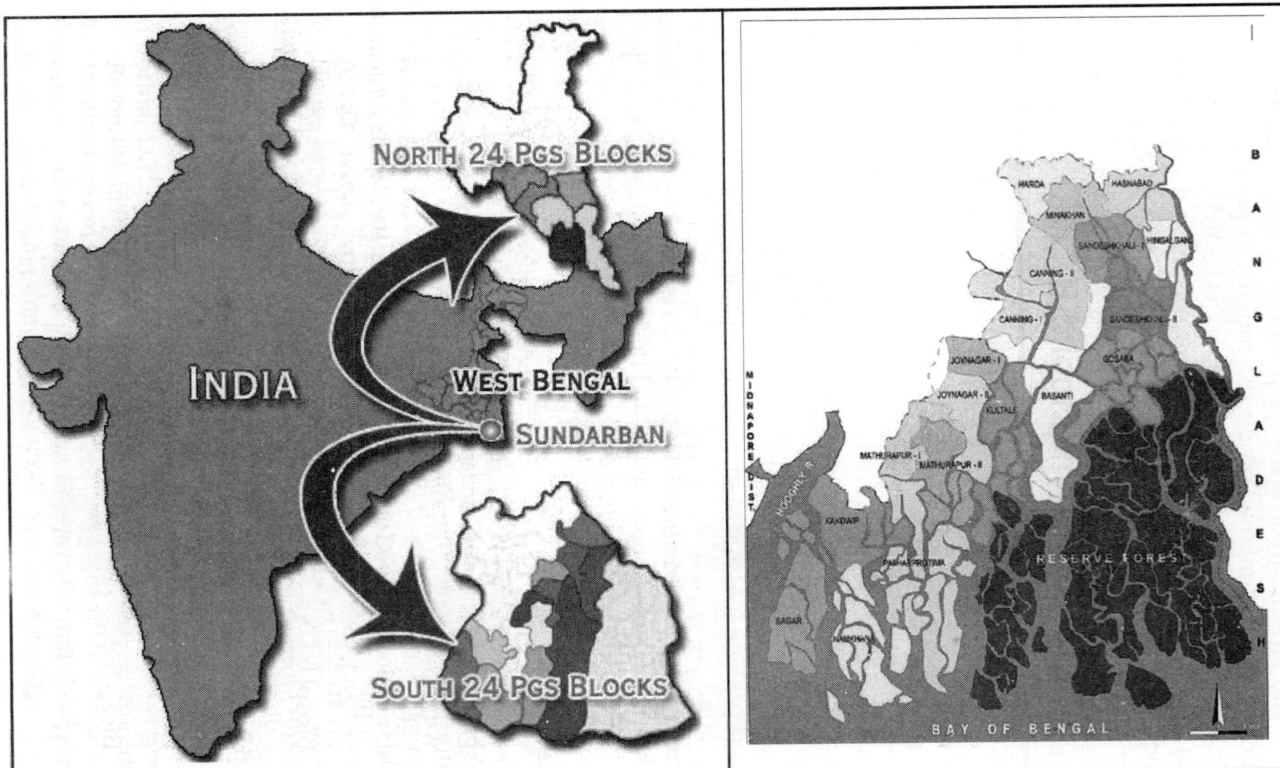

Fig. 4.1: Choice of Study Area – Indian Sundarban.

water aquaculture is practised in large artificial enclosures developed in coastal swamps by erecting earthen dykes, locally called *bheries*. Culture is carried out by taking the tidal saline water in and out through sluices from nearby rivers for commercial pisciculture. A wide varieties of fish species (freshwater and brackish water) are cultured by the farmers of Sundarban.

Subsequently in Indian Sundarban coastal biome, many indigenous fishes have become a major concern due to its constant environmental changes, overexploitation of resources, habitat destruction, pollution, demographic pressure, introduction of exotic varieties, modern agriculture etc. which might be responsible for species turnover. Reductions in freshwater flows to the delta due to upstream diversions of the Ganges and its tributaries and indiscriminate fishing practices are reducing fish populations. Catch data from estuarine fisheries reveal an increase in the yield, but a decrease in the catch per unit effort. The change in freshwater flow in the rivers has led to the change in salinity in the estuarine water and soil, threatening fish species. Population pressures on aquatic resources are a major cause of concern, especially since 14.5 per cent of the 4.5 million people that inhabit the Sundarban engage in fishing, with the majority active in inland fishery zones. Indiscriminate seed collection results in a loss of a variety of other aquatic species.

Thus, knowledge on species and communities can reveal crucial facts necessary to the management of the ecosystems as well as to the identification of important genetic resources. Documentations on indigenous fish resources from West Bengal were carried out by several workers. Various workers explored estuarine, marine piscine resources from water of Indian Sundarban in a scattered way. However, detail documentations on freshwater indigenous fish resources of Indian Sundarban biosphere are really scanty. In continuation to the fact, production potentiality and efficiency in commercial practices regarding inclusion of these indigenous fishes in traditional carp culture have seldom appeared in literature of the researchers working on Sundarban. The present work is an effort to explore available freshwater indigenous fish fauna from Indian Sundarban Biosphere on the basis of production and efficiency.

4.2 Method of Sample Selection

Indian Sundarban spreads over 5 sub-divisions and comprises of 19 Community Development blocks, of which 6 in North and 13 in South 24-Parganas districts with total 190 Gram Panchayats (GPs) and 1064 villages (Table 4.1). A cross-sectional interview-based survey was carried out at freshwater aquaculture dominated island blocks selected through proper sampling design. This survey was conducted during the months of July to December 2015, using random sampling technique. First of all, pilot survey has been conducted in Chunakhali GP of Basanti block in order to acquire proper understanding of diversified aquaculture practices in Indian Sundarban. Local NGO, like Joygopalpur Gram Vikash Kendra for Basanti block were engaged during this pilot survey. Then, for the purpose of sampling design, two out of 4 sub-divisions of South 24-Parganas, and Basirhat sub-division of North 24-Parganas have been purposively chosen for field survey. But accurate freshwater aquaculture mapping for Indian Sundarban is still unavailable on government front. However, GPS mapping of brackish water aquaculture farms in Sundarban and adjacent area has been made by Mr. Sourabh Kumar Dubey of University of Animal and Fishery Science, West Bengal. Following this map, the present study locates the freshwater aquaculture farms on those selected sub-divisions, as shown in Fig. 4.1.

On the second stage, from each subdivision, two community development blocks of freshwater aquaculture region of Sundarban have been randomly selected. At the final stage, a comprehensive list of pond or tank owners from each GPs in the selected blocks has been prepared and then those villages in which farmers are growing SIFS with carp polyculture have been purposively chosen. In case of non-fulfilment of this condition in a particular village, a nucleus of villages with two or more contiguous villages was constituted. From each village, ten fish farmers have been randomly selected. In this way, the total number of 30 household pond owners from each block has been chosen. The number of sample pond owner from each sub-division is 60 and the total number of ultimate unit of analysis for the Sundarban area as a whole is, therefore, 180. The resultant sampling tree has been depicted in Fig. 4.3.

It has been found that among those 180 fish farmers

Table 4.1: Administrative Profile of Sundarban Region

Districts	*Sub-Division*	*Blocks*	*No. of GP*
South 24-Parganas	Kakdwip	Sagar, Namkhana, Kakdwip, Patharpratima	42
	Diamond Harbar	Mathurapur-I, Mathurapur-II	21
	Baruipur	Kultali, Joynagar-I, Joynagar-II	31
	Canning	Canning-I, Canning-II, Basanti, Gosaba	46
North 24-Parganas	Bashirhat	Hingalganj, Hasnabad, Sandeshkhali-I, Sandeshkhali-II, Haroa, Minakhan	50
Total	**5**	**19**	**190**

Source: West Bengal University of Animal and Fishery Science, West Bengal.

interviewed, only 78 have introduced SIFS along with carp polyculture, details of which have been presented in Table 4.2. In this study, fish farmers practising SIFS culture along with carp are termed as "progressive" farmers. Those, who are culturing only carps (not diversifying with SIFS) are termed as "traditional" farmers.

The study has been performed on the basis of an open-ended and exploratory research design. Observations are made according to the administered pre-designed structured questionnaires to all the fish farmers selected. The quasi-participant method was also used as and when necessary. Farmers were interviewed directly at his/her house/farm. For entire data collection process, 12 numbers of surveyors were engaged. The filled-up questionnaires were checked by Principal Investigator for entry and recording errors, missing data, and consistency before analysis. The purpose of the survey is to benchmark the socio-economic profile, current nature of aquaculture practices and various constraints and challenges faced in relation to diversified aquaculture practices in Indian Sundarban.

The study is designed to highlight the existing environment of small-scale fish farmers with emphasis on freshwater culture along with productivity, nature and extent of integration of small indigenous fish species in carp polyculture practices of those blocks of Indian Sundarban. The outcome of the survey has been utilized in designing the experiments for developing diversified aquaculture strategies for better adaptation of nutrient-rich fish

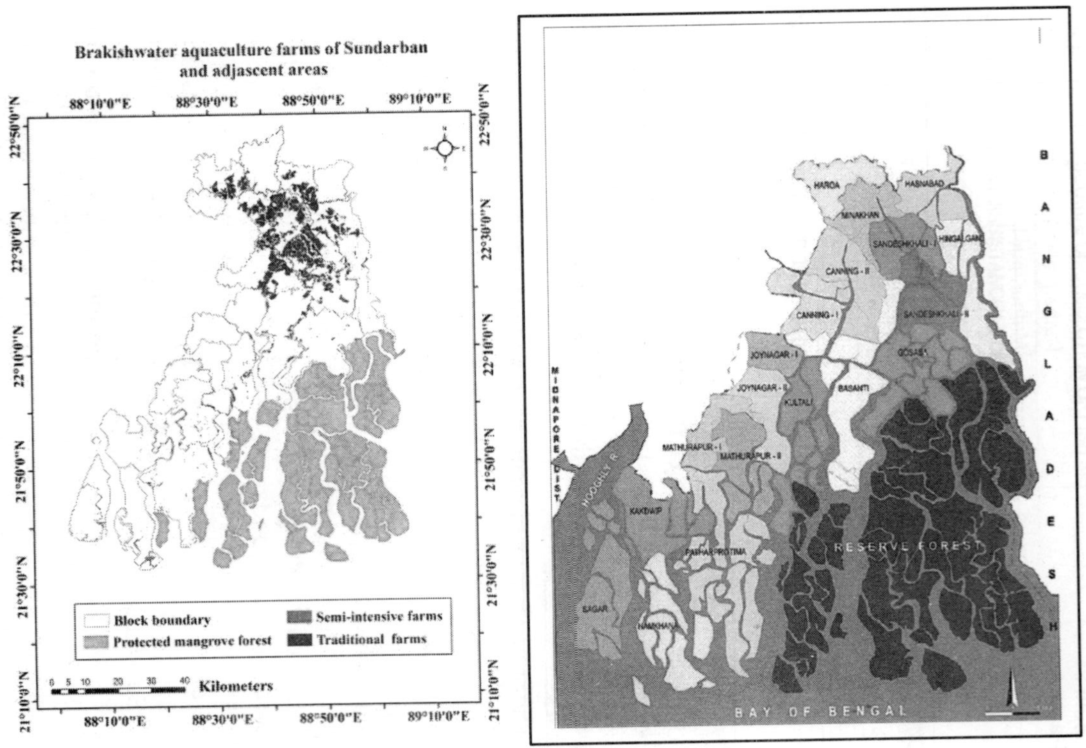

Fig. 4.2: Location Study of Field Survey.
Source: Extracted from GPS mapping done by West Bengal University of Animal and Fisheries Science, Kolkata.

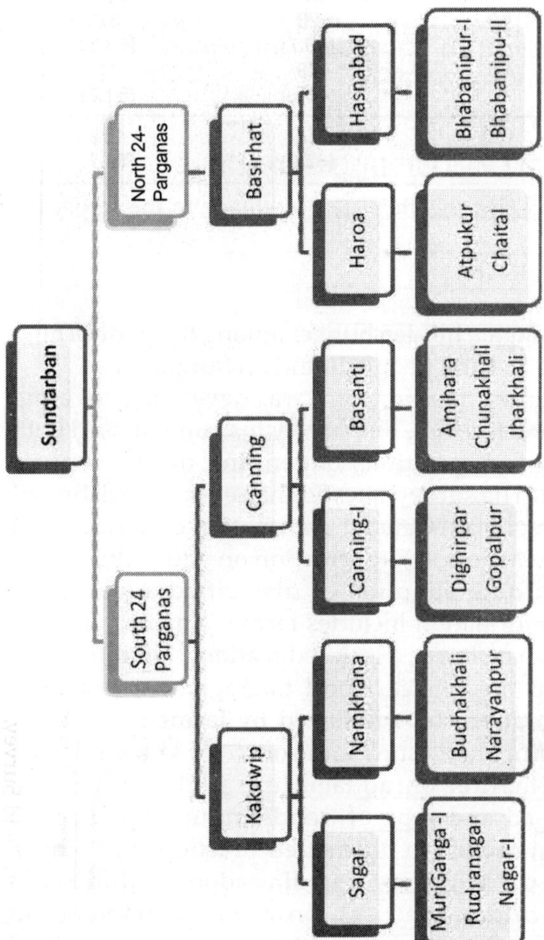

Fig. 4.3: Sampling Tree of Present Study in Indian Sundarban.
Source: Pilot Survey, 2015-16.

Table 4.2: Sample Farmers practicing carp culture with or without SIFS

Sub-Division	*Sample Size*	*Progressive Farmers*	*Traditional Farmers*
Kakdwip	60	21 (35.0)	39 (65.0)
Canning	60	28 (46.7)	32 (53.3)
Basirhat	60	29 (48.3)	31 (51.7)
Total	**180**	**78** **(43.3)**	**102** **(56.7)**

Note: Figures in the parentheses indicate percentage to the respective totals.

Source: Field Survey, 2015-16.

culture in order to mitigate hidden hunger among the poor fishing communities as well as rural people in Indian Sundarban.

A multi-layer survey questionnaire was developed covering all aqua farming characteristics. The survey instrument used both closed and open-ended questions depending on the type of information desired. The survey questionnaire was consisting of four major categories, i.e. (a) General information on farmers, (b) pond management practices, (c) information on aquaculture, and (d) constraints regarding adoption of diversified aquaculture practices. General information includes farmer's name, age, sex, caste, village, gram panchayat, block, educational qualification, family size and income source. Pond management practices include pond preparation steps followed by farmers, stocking, supplementary feeding, harvesting and source of knowledge on aquaculture. Information on aquaculture includes type of aquaculture practised and type of ponds, number of species cultured, proportion of SIFS in diversified practices and others. Farmers also expressed their views regarding adoption difficulties of diversified aquaculture practices, problems encountered in species mix, indigenous knowledge about possible impacts of SIFS integration, name of few threatened fish species, awareness on possible environmental impacts of SIFS seed catch from river, and status of natural breeding of small indigenous fish. The collected data were recorded and analysed and reports on socio-economic profile, aquaculture practices, and farmers' opinions about aquaculture diversification were generated.

4.3 Description of Data and Variables

Fish polyculture typically involves the production of several fish species or outputs using several inputs, including seed or fingerlings, feed, manure and fertilizers, labour, land etc. In practice, fish farmers produce different types of fish species using seeds of different species. Here, fish output (or seed input) is expressed as the aggregated nominal value of total fish output (or total seed inputs) of all species taken together, instead of each species individually. Aggregation has been done because of the inability or unwillingness on the part of the fish farmers to provide detailed information about the use of different species of fish seed or fish output. Hence,

Output (Y) represents the aggregate value of all fish species (Indian Major Carps, Chinese Carps and SIFS) produced, measured in kilogram per acre. Similarly, the inputs involved in fish polyculture are also aggregated into seven categories, which have been found to be used by farmers on regular basis. All the inputs are expressed on annual basis, as follows:

Seed (X_1) represents the total amount of seeds fingerlings of all species released to the pond, measured in kilogram per acre;

Feed (X_2) denotes the total dry weight of feed, measured in quintal per acre. Feed includes:

Fertilizer (X_3) represents, on the one hand, the nominal value of green aquatic plants and phytoplankton, cow-dung, measured in quintal per acre. Manure in the study denotes organic fertilization. The aggregated nominal value of urea, single super phosphate, measured in kilogram per acre is also included as inorganic fertilizer.

Labour (X_4) represents the total expenses for family and hired labour used in fish farming, measured in man-days per acre.

Others (X_5) represent the toxicants used for pond preparation, measured in kilogram per acre and the medicine or lime used in pond, measured in kilogram per acre.

There are some other variables that affect the input-output structure of the farmers, such as marketing and harvesting cost, cost on depreciation, interest and land-use. But, in course of analysis, it has been found that all the variables are not functioning enough separately to affect the production structure significantly. Hence, number of such variables has sometimes been aggregated as "other variable".

Here, output for carp and SIFS is expressed as the aggregated nominal value of total fish output, of each category, of all species taken together, instead of each species from the group individually. Aggregation has been done because of the inability or unwillingness on the part of the fish farmers to provide detailed information about the use of different species of fish seed or fish output of carps and SIFS.

4.4 Theoretical Framework

Objective-wise different analytical and statistical techniques have been followed. Economic and operational conditions of the fish farms have been explained through tabular analysis of the data collected through the socio-economic survey. The average and percentage analyses were used to examine the structure of farms; water spread area, stocking density, output obtained and price received. Some other descriptive statistical measures, like correlation coefficient, test of association like χ^2 (chi square) test were also used as and when needed. To receive an idea about costs and returns of fish farming in the study area, benefit cost ratio has been computed. Efficiency of the fish farms was assessed with the help of non-parametric Data Envelopment Analysis (DEA). Though logit model have been used to assess the determinants of the adoption practices, DEA remains the principle theoretical framework of the study. Based on the objectives of the study two different DEA models have been used – one measures technical efficiency and analyses input use efficiency of the fish farms; while another, usually called as meta-frontier DEA model, helps to differentiate technical efficiency of a farm on the basis of socio-economic or farm-specific subgroups. Before proceeding to the models, non-parametric methodology needs to be discussed.

4.4.1 Non-Parametric Methodology

Economic theory asserts that the goal for efficient management is the optimal utilization of inputs to produce outputs in such a manner that maximizes economic returns. Based on Farrell's innovative article (1957), several approaches to efficiency and productivity assessment have been developed that can be classified into two broad categories: parametric and non-parametric frontier models. The former relies on the specification of an *ad hoc* functional form; imposes certain *a priori* restrictions on the production technology, and estimates the parametres of the production or the cost function statistically. Alternatively, the latter constructs a linear piece-wise function from empirical observations of inputs and outputs, thereby avoiding the need to assume functional relationships between inputs and outputs or to make distributional assumptions regarding the residuals in a regression analysis.

Most of the non-parametric applications are based on the Data Envelopment Analysis (DEA) model as proposed by **Charnes, Cooper and Rhodes (CCR)** in **1978**. In recent years, DEA has become a central technique in productivity and efficiency analysis, applied in different aspects of economics and management sciences. DEA has been used in comparing organizations. In agriculture, DEA has also been applied to studies of various products ranging from horticulture and cotton to aquaculture.

DEA models operationalizes the concept of efficiency in the context of linear programming problems that calculates the frontier production function of a set of Decision-Making Units (DMUs) and evaluate the relative technical efficiency of each unit, thereby allowing a distinction to be made between efficient and inefficient DMUs. Those identified as "best practice units" (i.e., those determining the frontier) are given a rating of one, whereas the degree of technical inefficiency of the rest is calculated on the basis of the Euclidian distance of their input–output ratio from the frontier **(Coelli *et al.*, 1998)**.

According to **Farrell (1957)**, technical efficiency (TE) represents the ability of a DMU to produce maximum output given a set of inputs and technology (output-oriented) or, alternatively, to achieve maximum feasible reductions in input quantities given input prices and output (input-oriented). The choice between input- and output-oriented measures is a matter of concern, and selection may vary according to the unique characteristics of the set of DMUs under study. In this study, input-oriented DEA seems more appropriate, given that it is more reasonable to argue that in the agricultural and its allied sector a farmer has more control over inputs rather than output levels, which may often be exogenously bounded. In addition, the inelastic demand of most agricultural products renders cost reduction a better means of increasing profitability than output growth (**Coelli, 1996**). Also, from utility-maximization point of view, most of poor farmers tend to be risk averse in nature. Their predominant goal is economic survival. They really do trade of lower risk against higher profit or the disutility of increasing risk. Adequate stability of output and income and the avoidance of major short-term losses take precedence over profit maximization. As a result, rational use of inputs, rather than output maximization, appears more rational strategy for the fish farmers. Again, since both input- and output-oriented measure give the same numerical figure for technical efficiency score, the same interpretation will follow the result.

4.4.2 Model I: DEA to Measure Input Use Efficiency in Aquaculture

Assumptions

In the non-parametric DEA method, one makes a number of fairly general assumptions about the technology, but leaves the functional form unspecified. Typically, it is assumed that the production possibility set is convex and both inputs and outputs are freely disposable. We consider an economy producing outputs from n inputs. An input-output bundle (x, y) is considered feasible when the output bundle y can be produced from the input bundle x. The technology faced by the firms in the industry can be described by the production possibility set

$$T = [(x, y)\text{: } y \text{ can be produced from } x] \quad \text{... (1)}$$

In the single output case, one can conceptualize the production function

$$f(x) = \max y\text{:}(x, y) \in T \quad \text{... (2)}$$

In the multiple output case, frontier of the production possibility set is the production correspondence

$$F\,(x, y) = 1 \quad \text{... (3)}$$

The method of Data Envelopment Analysis introduced by **Charnes, Cooper, and Rhodes (CCR) (1978)** and further extended to non-constant returns technologies by **Banker, Charnes, and**

Cooper (BCC) (1984) provides a way to construct the production possibility set from an observed data set of input-output bundles.

Suppose that (X^j, Y^j) is the input-output bundle observed for firm j $(j = 1, 2, \ldots, N)$. Now, we make the following assumptions about the technology –

(I) All observed input-output bundle are feasible. Thus,

$$(X^j, Y^j) \in T \qquad \ldots (4)$$

(II) The production possibility set is convex. Hence, if $(X^1, Y^1) \in T$ and $(X^2, Y^2) \in T$, then

$$[X^1 + (1-\lambda)X^2, \lambda Y^1 + (1-\lambda)Y^2] \in T, 0 \le \lambda \le 1 \qquad \ldots (5)$$

In other words, weighted averages of feasible input-output combinations are also feasible.

(III) Inputs are freely disposable. Hence, if $(X^0, Y^0) \in T$ and $X^1 \geq X^0$, then

$$(X^1, Y^0) \in T \qquad \ldots (6)$$

This rules out the negative marginal productivities of inputs.

(IV) Output is freely disposable. Hence, if $(X^0, Y^0) \in T$ and $Y^1 \geq Y^0$, then

$$(X^1, Y^0) \in T \qquad \ldots (7)$$

Then the smallest production possibility set satisfying the assumptions of convexity and free disposability that includes these observed bundles is

$$S = [(X, Y): X \geq \sum_1^N \lambda_j X_j,$$

$$Y \leq \sum_1^N \lambda_j Y_j; \sum_1^N \lambda_j = 1; \lambda_j \geq 0, j = 1, 2, \ldots\ldots N] \qquad \ldots (8)$$

The set S is also known as the free disposal convex hull of the observed input-output bundles. One can obtain various measures of efficiency of a firm using the set S as the reference technology.

Now, the output-bundle of the firm may be treated as an assigned task and the efficiency of the firm is judged by the maximum equi-proportionate reduction in all of its inputs without compromising the feasibility of the target output.

Variables Used

We consider one output-four input Variable Returns to Scale DEA model. The analysis is based on cross-sectional pond-wise per acre value of output (dependent variable, Y) and the values of all the four independent variables explained as follows:

X_1 = Fish fingerlings used as seed (kg/acre)
X_2 = Supplementary fish feed (kg/acre)
X_3 = Fertilizers, both organic and inorganic, used (kg/acre)
X_4 = Labour (man days/acre)
X_5 = Others i.e. aggregated value of oil Cake, liming and pre-stocking manuring (quintal/acre)

Here, number of inputs has been reduced to four due to two reasons. First, according to the importance of the inputs from the production point of view, fish seed (fingerlings) comes first, followed by fish feed, fertilizers, labour, and others (inputs like oil cake, lime etc.). Second, use of more inputs in DEA model, increases the number of constraints which will in turn increase the efficiency scores of the sample farms as frontier becomes tighter when there are number of constraints.

Mathematical Presentation

We consider the situation with 180 fish farms or decision-making units (DMUs), each producing output Y from a bundle of 4 inputs. The *j*th DMU ($j = 1, 2, \ldots, 180$) uses X_k^j units of *k*th input in the production of Y^j units. A separate linear programming (LP) problem is solved for each of the *j* DMUs ($j = 1, 2, \ldots, 180$) in the sample. The input based technical and scale efficiency for the *j*th DMU can be obtained by solving the following LP problem:

$$\underset{\lambda^j, \theta^j}{Minimize}\ \theta^j$$

Subject to –

$$\sum_{j=1}^{180} \lambda^j Y^j \geq Y_0^j \text{ (output constraints)}$$

$$\sum_{j=1}^{180} \lambda^j X_k^j \leq \theta^j X_k^0 \text{ (inputs constraints, } k = 1, 2, 3, 4, 5)$$

$$\sum_{j=1}^{180} \lambda^j = 1$$

$$\lambda^j \geq 0, j = 1,2,...,180$$

Where, θ^j is the dual of the variable indicating proportional increase in output possible by firm *j*;

λ^j = weight or intensity variable (or, shadow price) used to derive all possible linear combinations of the sample observations.

Y_0^j = Actual output produced by firm *j*.

X_k^0 = Actual input use by firm *j*.

Where θ is the proportional reduction in inputs possible and λ_j is the weight or intensity variable used to derive all possible combinations of the sample observations. Here, θ determines the efficiency score of *j*th DMU. The value of θ= 1 shows a technically efficient DMU; θ less than one shows a technically inefficient DMU. In order to obtain efficiency score of each farm, equation (9) has to be solved *N* times, once for each farm.

The DEA problem mentioned above has an important intuitive interpretation. Essentially, the problem takes the *j*th firm and then seeks to radically contract the input vector, X_k^j, as much as possible, while still remaining within the feasible input requirement set. The inner boundary of this set is a piece-wise linear isoquant, determined by the observed data points, (i.e. all the firms in the sample). The radial contraction of the input vector, X_k, produces a projected point, $\left(X_k^j\lambda^j, Y^j\lambda^j\right)$, on the surface of this technology. This projected point is a linear combination of this observed data points. The constraints in the above LP problem ensure that this projected point cannot lie outside the feasible set.

One interesting point to note here is that a technically efficient DMU may still be over- or under-producing if it is found that altering the size of the farm towards optimal size increases (or decreases) the efficiency of that farm. It does mean that the DMU is not scale efficient. To analyse the performance of a farm, it is important to take care of this information since the magnitude of scale efficiency will tell us how much productivity gain would be feasible if that DMU can be moved to its optimal size. Scale efficiency of a particular DMU can be determined by running the CRS and the VRS models (the VRS model includes one more constraints that weighted value of the intensity variable, λ_j, must be equals to one) on the same data. A difference between these two scores indicates the scale efficiency of the DMU. Hence, scale efficiency (SE) is TE^{CRS}/TE^{VRS}.

Once θ and λ_j can be determined it is easy to find out the optimal value of the input from the above LP equation. A comparison of the actual quantity of input used with the corresponding optimal quantity of that input reveals whether a particular DMU is using too much or too little of that input. Hence, for any particular input I, input use efficiency can be calculated by the ratio –

$$\alpha^i = \frac{L_0^i}{L_*^i}$$

A value of α^i greater (less) than unity implies over (under) use of that input.

In the present study, technical and scale efficiency score has been determined by solving those LP problems with the use of DEAP 2.1 (**Coelli, 1996**). The software also gives us the optimal use of each inputs, which will help to find out the input use efficiency.

Graphical Interpretation

The DEA methodology can also be shown through the Fig. 4.4.

In this diagram, six firms, A, B, C, D, E and F are producing output with two input X_1 and X_2. Among them, A, C, D and F are best practice firms, which determine the DEA frontier. In those four points, inputs are optimally used. But, firm B and E are using more input than required. They can produce even the same output even by reducing inputs radically to the point B/ and E/, where weighted average productivities are much higher than B and E respectively. Hence, technical efficiency at each of the points A, C, D and F is one but at points B and E, technical efficiency must be less than one, because

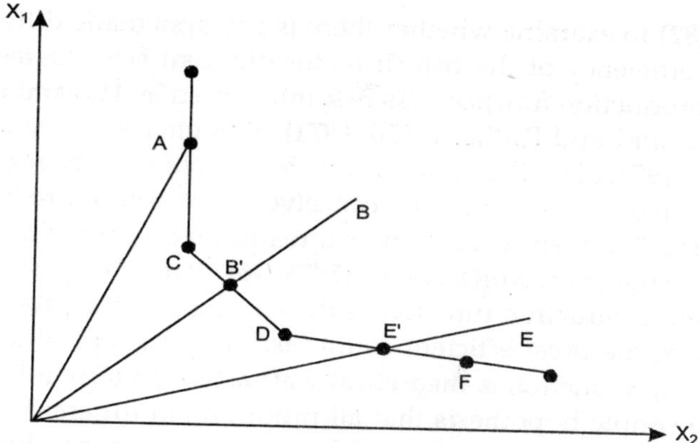

Fig. 4.4: Radial Movements and Input Slacks in DEA Model.
Source: Adapted from Ray, S.C. (2004): Data Envelopment Analysis – Theory and Techniques for Economics and Operations Research, Cambridge University Press, UK.

$$TE_B = \frac{AP^B}{AP^*}$$

where, numerator is the weighted average productivity at point B and denominator is that at point B/, i.e. at the corresponding point on the frontier.

4.4.2 Model 3: Meta-frontier DEA to Measure Group Efficiency

One point deserves particular mention here. The efficiency of a firm depends not only on the inputs it uses, but also on several other factors (such as infrastructural facilities, region, level of education and technical knowledge, work culture, size etc.). It is very difficult to incorporate those factors into a production frontier to examine their effects on efficiency, though important. Hence, group-efficiency analysis might reveal more concrete results if it is carried on separately for different group. Also, a definite conclusion can be drawn if it is found that a particular group of farmers are efficient with respect to all the farmers taken together. For that it is important to calculate the group efficiency to reach to the final conclusion.

In this section, the concept of meta-frontier production function has been employed, defined by **Hayami and Ruttan**

(1971: 82) to examine whether there is any systematic difference in the efficiency of the fish firms for different size classes. The meta-production function was first introduced by **Hayami (1969)** and **Hayami and Ruttan (1970, 1971)**. As stated by Hayami and Ruttan (1971: 82), "The meta-production function can be regarded as the envelope of commonly conceived neoclassical production functions." In their discussion of agricultural productivity across various countries, **Ruttan *et al.* (1978: 46)** state, "We now define the meta-production function as the envelope of the production points of the most efficient countries." The concept of a meta-production function is theoretically attractive because it is based on the simple hypothesis that all producers in different groups (size, regions, etc.) have potential access to the same technology. Following the seminal work of **Hayami and Ruttan (1970)**, some other authors like **Mundlak and Hellinghausen (1982)** and **Lau and Yotopoulos (1989)** also employed the methodology to compare agricultural productivity across countries.

Meta-Frontier Methodology

In Meta-Frontier analysis, the performance of each individual fish firm in the sample is measured against two different frontiers—one based on firms from all the different groups in the sample and the other based only on firms from the group (based on size, intensification of adoption of improved culture or region) to which it belongs. The first can be regarded as the national or *grand* frontier and the other as the *group* frontier. The grand and the group frontiers can be defined as follows. Define the index set $I = [1,2,....,N]$ where each observed data point is an element of I. Now consider a partition $I = \cup\ I_r$ where I_r includes only observations from group r. Then, under the standard assumptions of convexity and free disposability of inputs (x) and outputs (y) the empirically constructed group and grand production

$$S^r = [(x,y) : x \geq \sum_{j \in I_r} \lambda_j x^j;\ y \leq \sum_{j \in I_r} \lambda_j y^j;\ \sum_{j = I_r} \lambda_j = 1\ ;\ \lambda_j \geq 0\ \ (j \in I_r)]$$

(for group r)

And

$$S^G = [(x,y) : x \geq \sum_{j \in \cup I_r} \lambda_j x^j;\ y \leq \sum_{j \in \cup I_r} \lambda_j x^j;\ \sum_{j \in \cup I_r} \lambda_j = 1;\ \lambda_j \geq 0;\ (j \in \cup I_r)]$$

possibility sets are respectively. It may be noted that while each S^r is a subset of S^G, the latter is bigger than the union of the individual group production possibility sets. This is illustrated in Fig. 4.5 for a 1-input, 1-output 2-group example.

Let the points P_1 through P_4 show the input-output bundles of four firms from group *P*. Similarly, Q_1 *through* Q_4 *are* the input-output bundles of firms from group *Q*. The group frontiers are shown by the broken lines $AP_1P_3P_4C$ for group *P* and by $BQ_1Q_2Q_3D$ for group *Q*. By contrast, the grand frontier is the outer envelope of the two frontiers shown by the broken line $AP_1P_3Q_2Q_3D$.

Note that points in the area P_3EQ_2 lie above both group frontiers, but (by virtue of convexity) are below the grand frontier. While judged against their own group frontier the technical efficiency of each the points Q_1, Q_2, and Q_3 *equals* unity while the corresponding efficiency of Q_4 *is* $\frac{JQ_4}{JK}$. When judged against the grand frontier, Q_2 *and* Q_3 *remain* efficient. On the other hand, the efficiency of Q_1 *falls* from unity to $\frac{BQ_1}{BN}$ while the efficiency of Q_4 *does* not change. Thus, the *group efficiency* of the group *Q* measured at the points Q_1, Q_2, and Q_3 *equals* unity (even though point Q_4 *is* inefficient) while at the point Q_1, the group efficiency, measured

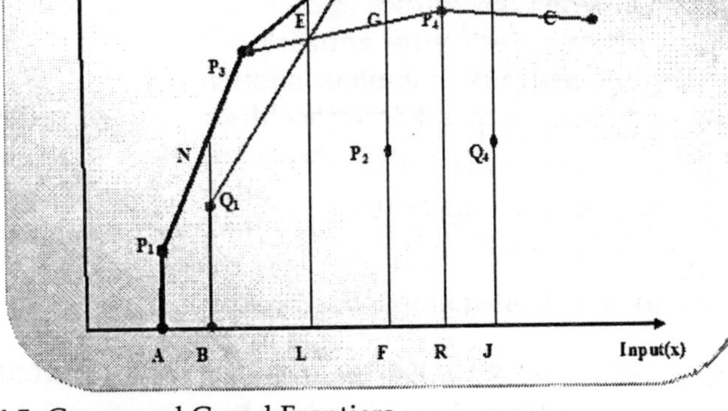

Fig. 4.5: Group and Grand Frontiers.

Source: Ray, S.C. (2012): Data Envelopment Analysis, Publishing House, UK.

with respect to grand frontier, is $\frac{BQ_1}{BN}$. The geometric mean of the group efficiency measures at these different points may be used as an overall index of the *group efficiency* of Q. From group P, the points P_1 and P_2 lie both on the group and the grand frontier. The point P_4 is on the group frontier but has technical efficiency $\frac{RP_4}{RS}$. In the case of point P_2 technical efficiency is $\frac{FP_2}{FG}$ relative to the group frontier and $\frac{FP_2}{FH}$ when measured against the grand frontier. Thus, at this point a measure of group efficiency is $\frac{FG}{FH}$. It is interesting to note that point E lies on both of the group frontiers but not on the grand frontier. Thus, at this point both groups would have the same level of group (in) efficiency.

Mathematical Presentation

For the overall or grand efficiency of the fish farms in the sample, we solve the following LP problem, including all 180 farms from all size classes as –

$$\underset{\lambda^j,\theta^j}{Minimize}\ \theta_G^j$$

Subject to –

$$\sum_{j=1}^{180} \lambda^j Y^j \geq Y_0^j \text{ (output constraints)}$$

$$\sum_{j=1}^{180} \lambda^j X_k^j \leq \theta_G^j\ X_k^0 \text{ (inputs constraints, k = 1, 2, 3, 4, 5)}$$

$$\sum_{j=1}^{180} \lambda^j = 1$$

$$\lambda^j \geq 0, j = 1, 2, ..., 180$$

Where, θ_G^j is the dual of the variable indicating proportional increase in output possible by firm j; or Grand technical efficiency, TE_G^j.

λ^j = weight or intensity variable (or, shadow price) used to derive all possible linear combinations of the sample observations.

Y_0^j = Actual output produced by firm j.

X_k^0 = Actual input use by firm j.

Similarly, the relevant DEA model for size-class r with Nr (= 78) fish farms in the sample, specified as 'progressive' farmers, is –

$$\underset{\lambda^j, \theta^j}{Minimize}\ \theta_r^j$$

Subject to –

$$\sum_{j=1}^{78} \lambda^j Y^j \geq Y_0^j \text{ (output constraints)}$$

$$\sum_{j=1}^{78} \lambda^j X_k^j \leq \theta_r^j X_k^0 \text{ (inputs constraints, k = 1,2,3,4,5)}$$

$$\sum_{j=1}^{78} \lambda^j = 1,\ \lambda^j \geq 0, j = 1, 2, ..., 78$$

Where, θ_r^j is the dual of the variable indicating proportional increase in output possible by firm j; or the group technical efficiency, TE_r^j.

A point-wise measure of technical efficiency of group r relative to the grand frontier evaluated at the input-output data of farm j is –

$$\beta_r^j = \frac{TE_G^j}{TE_r^j}$$

An overall measure of the efficiency of group r is –

$$TE(r) = (\prod_{j \in r} \beta_r^j)^{1/N r}$$

where N^r (= 78) is the number of farms in group r.

Clearly, for any fish farms j in a group r, TE_G^j is a measure of its performance relative to other farms within the same group. On the other hand,. β is a measure of its performance compared to all groups in the study. Similar group performance of the fish farmers can also be assessed for traditional (Nr = 102) farmers.

4.5 Limitations of the Study

But as with all similar studies, the study suffers from certain general limitations. **Firstly**, the duration of the reference period is short. So, what one gets is a cross-sectional picture at a point of time. **Secondly**, lack of specialized enumerations, the unwillingness or inability of the fish-farmers to provide detailed information, the widely scattered location of production units and areas are some of the main problems. It is true that estimates of catch with a reasonable degree of precision can be obtained at a very high cost. For inland waters, the areas are scattered with unorganized and irregular catch operation. Incidentally, the maintenance of the accounts by operators is not in evidence in the study area. Hence, the study suffers from these drawbacks.

5
Socio-Economic Features

No one saves us but ourselves. No one can and no one may. We ourselves must walk the path. — *Buddha*

Pond fish production and its diversification depend upon various inputs used, the nature of production practices, types and size of water bodies and also upon varying socio-economic status of fish farmers. Socio-economic characteristics of the fish pond owners generally influence the extent of utilization of their ponds and thereby production. Complex structural and operational features of the production process, under different diversification strategies, sometimes impede the optimal utilization of water resources. Different management and technological factors drive the amount of production differently. Clearly, production practices and input uses depends on technology, socio-economic environment and management policies on the production area. They are together responsible for affecting pond fish production in the study area. In this section of the study, the main thrust is to examine those forces at play, which are classified into four different categories – (a) Social factors signifying profile of fish farmers; (b) structural characteristics of the fish ponds; and (c) operational and management environment signifying input-output structure in the production area.

5.1 Social Factors Behind Aquaculture Diversification

5.1.1 Age-structure

Pond owners under study were grouped in three age categories, that is, young farmers (below 30 years), matured farmers (30-50 years) and old farmers (50 years and above) for two specified categories of ponds, namely progressive and traditional, which are presented in Table 5.1:

Table 5.1: Age-wise distribution of sample Fish farmers (*units in number*)

Age Group	*Traditional*	*Progressive*	*Overall*
Young Farmers	25	33	58
(Below 30 years)	(24.5)	(42.3)	(32.2)
Matured Farmers	48	28	76
(30-50 years)	(47.1)	(35.9)	(42.2)
Old Farmers	29	17	46
(50 years and Above)	(28.4)	(21.8)	(25.6)
Total	**102**	**78**	**180**
	(100.0)	**(100.0)**	**(100.0)**

Note: Figures in the parentheses indicate percentage of the respective total.

Source: Field Survey, 2015-16.

It may be observed from Table 5.1 that more than 42 per cent of the pond owners belonged to matured age category and 25.6 per cent belonged to old age category. Striking is that, considerable number of rural youth has been found to enter into aquaculture business and their representation accounts for 32.2 per cent of the total sample. However, such proportion is different for different category of ponds. Comparatively higher proportion of young farmers (42.3%) and less proportion of matured and old farmers (35.9 and 21.8% respectively) were found operating in progressive ponds. It was therefore quite evident that young family members of the fishing community are more keen to diversify aquaculture practices and generate more income from their aquaculture business. Traditional practices, on the other hand, still depend on the managerial skill and long experience of the matured and old fish farmers. It may further be observed that the comparatively less proportion of progressive tanks and pond owners belonged to old age category (21.8%). It was mainly due to poor health status of old farmers who were generally toiling below poverty line and withdrew themselves from work due to more strenuous jobs in diversified fish culture. The result confronts that was derived by Bhatta (2001) and Katiha (2005).

5.1.2 Educational Status

Educational level of fish farmers has been examined since it affects the knowledge level, skill development, exposure to production technology and marketing practices and adoption level of improved technology in aquaculture practices. To assess the educational level of fish farmers under investigation, they are categorized into different groups like that below secondary, secondary and above secondary which are presented in Table 5.2:

Table 5.2: Educational level of pond owners operating different categories of ponds (*units in number*)

Educational Status	*Traditional*	*Progressive*	*Overall*
Illiterate	11 (10.8)	5 (6.4)	16 (8.9)
Literate (Below Secondary)	37 (36.3)	27 (34.6)	64 (35.6)
Secondary	34 (33.3)	37 (47.4)	71 (39.4)
Above Secondary	20 (19.6)	9 (11.5)	29 (16.1)
Total	**102 (100.0)**	**78 (100.0)**	**180 (100.0)**

Note: Diagrams in the parentheses indicate percentage of the respective total.
Source: Field Survey, 2015-16.

It may be observed from Table 5.2 that only 8.9 per cent of farmers under investigation were illiterate and 75 per cent went to school up to secondary level. Rate of illiteracy decreases with the increase in the level of diversification of aquaculture. However, almost reverse trend was observed in case of fish farmers having educational level above the secondary level. Almost 20 per cent of traditional pond owners belonged to education level of graduation and above whereas such percentage is as low as 11.5 for progressive farmers. The result does not confront that of previous study. Bhatta (2001) revealed that fish farmers in West Bengal have at most six years of education, but in our study, it is found that more than 46 per cent of the farmers go beyond secondary level of formal education.

5.1.3 Family Size

The family size has been examined to have an idea about the supply of human labours for fishing activities. The comparatively larger size of family is supposed to take care of fishing activities through family labour. Fish farmers were categorized in three family size groups that is, small (<5 members), medium (5–8 members) and large family (8 and above members) which are presented in Table 5.3:

Table 5.3: Pond Category-Wise Family Size of Fish Farmers

(units in number)

Family Size	Traditional	Progressive	Overall
Small (< 5 members)	22 (21.5)	27 (34.6)	49 (27.3)
Medium (5 – 8 members)	49 (48.0)	33 (42.3)	82 (45.6)
Large (> 8 members)	21 (20.5)	18 (23.1)	39 (21.7)
Total	**92 (100.0)**	**78 (100.0)**	**170 (100.0)**

Note: Figures in the parentheses indicate percentage of the respective total.

Source: Field Survey, 2015-16.

It may be observed from Table 5.3 that about 27 per cent of fish farmers had small family, 45.6 per cent had medium family and 21.7 per cent had large family. It may be noted that all the category of tanks and pond owners had almost identical proportion of size of family. Most of the pond owners are of medium family size, that is, having 5 to 8 members in family. It may further be observed that the larger proportion of progressive farmers (34.6%) has relatively small family whereas the comparatively higher proportion of traditional pond operators (48%) had medium family size. The trend is in order of other studies. The traditional pond operators are in the business of fish culture for a long period of time and have generally larger size of family because the assets in general, and land in particular, keep family members united whereas progressive households have meager asset and family members disintegrate and prefer to live independently since these families do not have asset which could attract them to live together in joint family (*see* Figures 5.1 to 5.6).

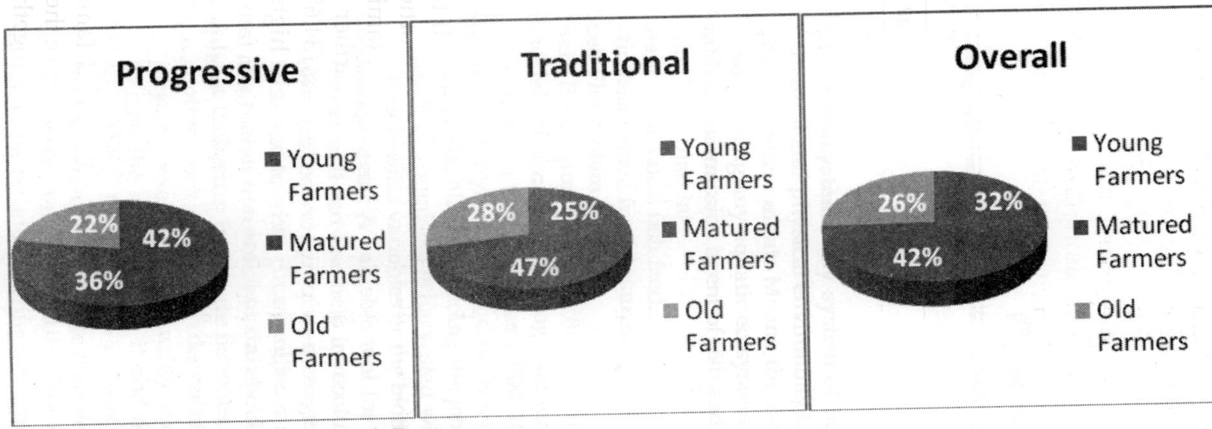

Fig. 5.1: Age Structure of Sample Fish Farmers.
Source: Field Survey, 2015-16.

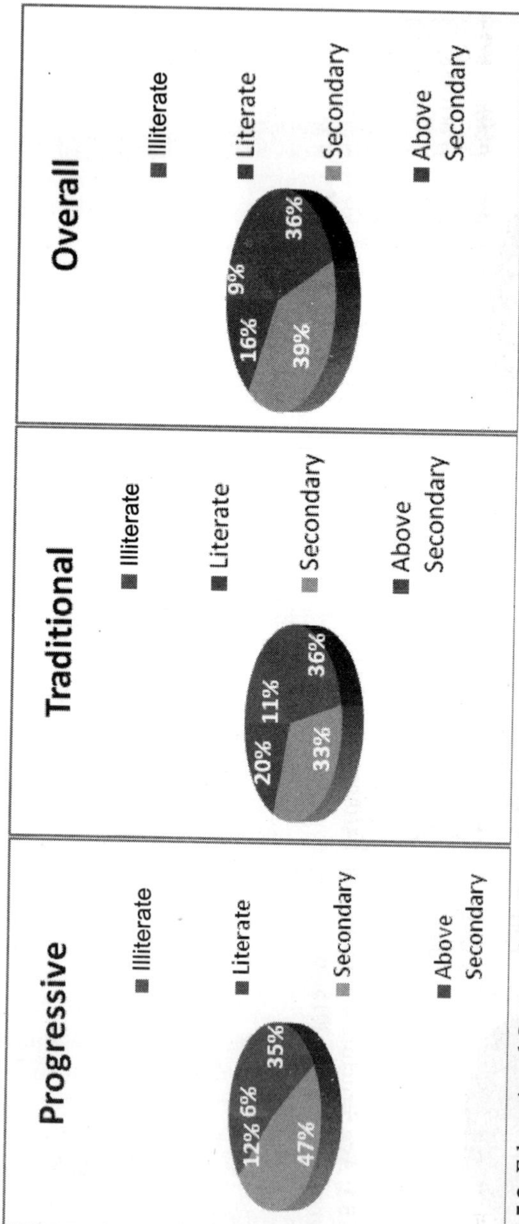

Fig. 5.2: Educational Status of the Sample Farmers.
Source: Field Survey, 2015-16.

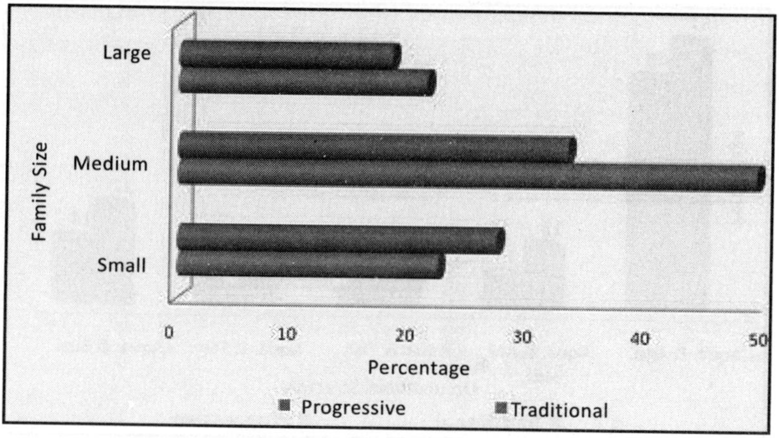

Fig. 5.3: Family Size of Sample Fish Farmers.
Source: Field Survey, 2015-16.

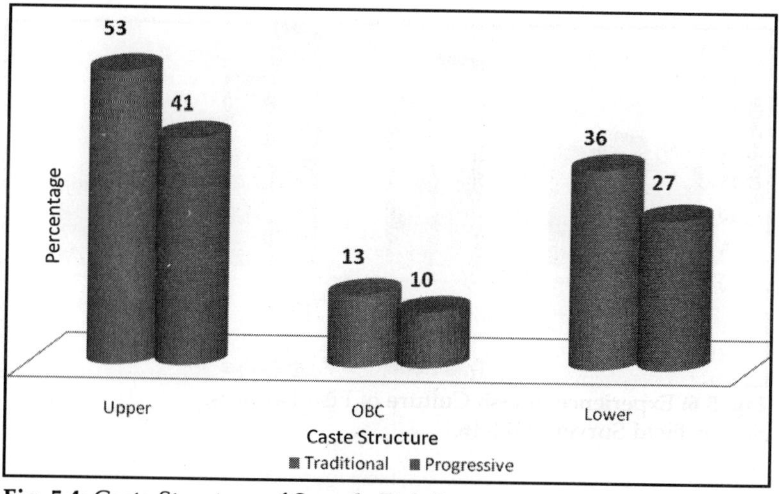

Fig. 5.4: Caste Structure of Sample Fish Farmers.
Source: Field Survey, 2015-16.

5.1.4 Caste Structure

Caste is one of the important factors of taking fisheries as occupation, and possession of skill in different rural economic activities and the observation holds more accurate in West Bengal because the state experienced slow change in rural economy.

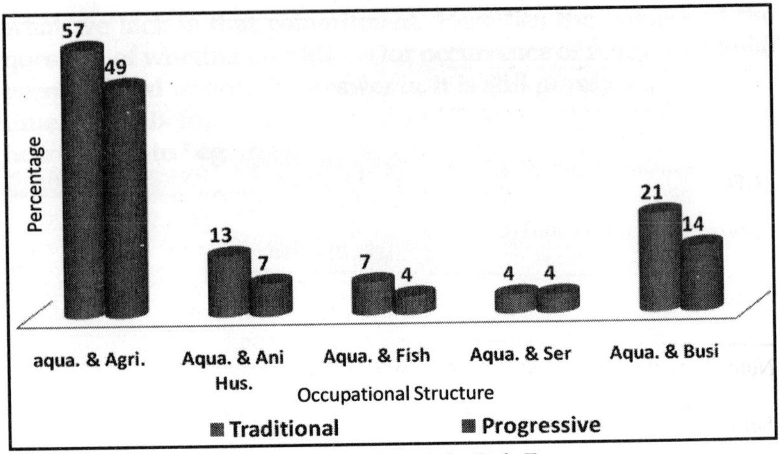

Fig. 5.5: Occupational Structure of Sample Fish Farmers.
Source: Field Survey, 2015-16.

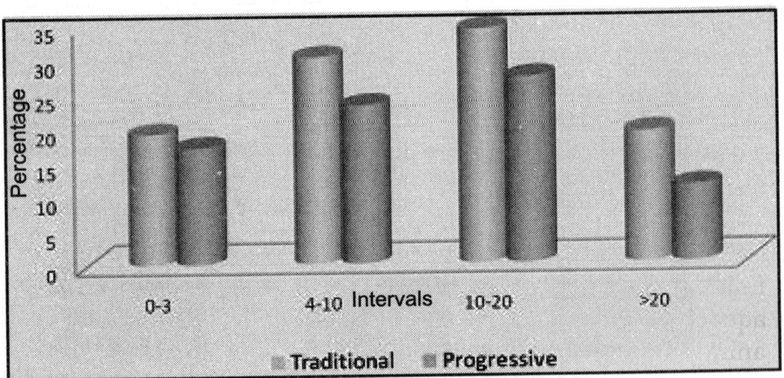

Fig. 5.6: Experience in Fish Culture of Fish Farmers.
Source: Field Survey, 2015-16.

Keeping this in view, the caste structure of fish farmers under study has been categories in three caste groups that is, upper caste (General Caste), OBC and lower caste (Schedule Castes and Tribes) which are presented in Table 5.4.

Table 5.4 revealed that more than half of sample (52.2%) of the family belonged to General Caste, only 12.8 per cent to OBC category and 35 per cent to Scheduled Caste and Schedule Tribes. Caste structure is almost similar for both traditional and

Table 5.4: Caste structure of sample Fish farmers *(units in number)*

Caste	Traditional	Progressive	Overall
Upper Caste (General)	53 (51.9)	41 (52.6)	94 (52.2)
OBC	13 (12.7)	10 (12.8)	23 (12.8)
Lower Caste (SCs and STs)	36 (35.3)	27 (34.6)	63 (35.0)
Total	**102 (100.0)**	**78 (100.0)**	**180 (100.0)**

Note: Figures in the parentheses indicate percentage of the respective total.

Source: Field Survey, 2015-16.

progressive fish farmers. Another observation is that distribution of fish farmers among different caste categories are in line of the distribution of the same among the population of Sundarban as a whole.

5.1.5 Occupational Structure

All the fish farmers under study were, no doubt, engaged in fish production, but all of them did not have fish farming as only occupation. Respondent farmers had varied type of occupations either as main or subsidiary. All the occupations of respondent fish farmers were categorized in four groups. Other than aquaculture, they have occupations like fishing, crop farming, animal husbandry, business and others. The occupation which generated either comparatively more employment or more income was considered as main occupation or primary occupation and second important occupation in the order was considered as secondary occupation. Occupations of traditional and progressive aquaculture firms were computed which are presented in Table 5.5.

It may be observed from Table 5.5 that the majority of responded fish-farmers (61.1%) had crop farming as secondary occupation and 11.1 per cent had adopted animal husbandry for alternative business. 17.8 per cent of the sample farmers, practicing aquaculture are involved in different kind of business. Public or private employees are still reluctant to engage in aquaculture business. Only 3.9 per cent of total sample has been found in any kind of services. However, the comparatively larger proportion

Table 5.5: Occupational Structure of sample fish farmers (*units in number*)

Categories of Ponds	*Aquaculture along with...*					
	Agriculture	*Animal Husbandry*	*Fishing*	*Service*	*Business*	*All*
Traditional	57 (55.9)	13 (12.7)	7 (06.9)	4 (03.9)	21 (20.6)	102 (100.0)
Progressive	49 (62.8)	7 (9.1)	4 (5.1)	4 (5.1)	14 (17.9)	78 (100.0)
Overall	**106** **(61.1)**	**20** **(11.1)**	**11** **(06.1)**	**8** **(03.9)**	**35** **(17.8)**	**180** **(100.0)**

Note: Figures in the parentheses indicate percentage of the total number of fish farmers under respective category of pond size group.

Source: Field Survey, 2015-16.

of progressive pond owner (62.8%) has crop farming was the second important main occupation. Only few sample farmers were engaged in open fishing related activities.

5.1.6 Experience in Carp Culture

The farming experiences in fish culture on the other hand extended up to 32 years for the traditional farm owners with a minimum of 2 years experience for some of the progressive pond owners in our study area. Experience level of fish farmers are almost equally distributed among progressive and traditional farmers in our study (*see* Table 5.6). More than 62 per cent of the sample fish farmers had experience in aquaculture more than 4 years and less than 20

Table 5.6: Experience in carp culture of sample fish farmers

(*units in number*)

Categories of Ponds	*Experience in Fish Culture (in years)*				
	0-3	*4-10*	*11-20*	*>20*	*All*
Traditional	19 (18.6)	30 (29.4)	34 (33.4)	19 (18.6)	102 (100.0)
Progressive	17 (21.8)	23 (29.5)	27 (34.6)	11 (14.1)	78 (100.0)
Overall	**36** **(20.0)**	**53** **(29.4)**	**61** **(33.9)**	**30** **(16.7)**	**180** **(100.0)**

Note: Figures in the parentheses indicate percentage of the total number of fish farmers under respective category of pond size group.

Source: Field Survey, 2015-16.

years. About 16 per cent of them had experience more than 20 years. Larger culture experiences of those fish farmers signify the fact that Sundarban has uniqueness regarding culture experience since the backyard pond system has been in existence for many years. It can be mentioned in this regard that Andhra Pradesh has less than one year of experience in fish culture while all-India average of fish farming experience except West Bengal is not more than 8 years (Bhatta, 2001).

5.2 Structural Features of Water Units

5.2.1 Size of Water Units

Based upon the total pond area the farmers were divided into four categories, i.e. farmers having total pond area of less than or equal to 0.5 *bigha;* area between 0.6–2.0 *bigha;* area between 2.1 and 5.0 *bigha* and water units of size more than 5 *bigha*. It has been found from Table 5.7 that the progressive farmers were operating on relatively large size of ponds compared to traditional farmers. Almost 54 per cent of the sample ponds under progressive farming were of size more than 2 *bigha*. Traditional farms were operating more on medium ponds of size between 0.5 and 2 *bigha*. Large sized ponds were relatively less in number. Only 23 out of 180

Table 5.7: Size of Sample Water Units

(*units in number*)

Size Class (bigha)	*Traditional*	*Progressive*	*Overall*
≤0.5	11 (10.8)	7 (08.9)	18 (10.0)
>0.5 – 2.0	46 (45.1)	19 (24.4)	65 (36.1)
>2.0 – 5.0	32 (31.4)	42 (53.9)	74 (41.1)
> 5.0	13 (12.7)	10 (12.8)	23 (12.8)
Total	**102** **(100.0)**	**78** **(100.0)**	**180** **(100.0)**

Note: Figures in the parentheses indicate percentage of the respective total.

1 *bigha* of land is equal to 0.13 ha.

Source: Field Survey, 2015-16.

ponds (12.8%) had size more than 5 *bigha*. In various other studies, it has been found that average size of ponds in West Bengal is less than 1 hectare (Bhalla, 2001; Kumar, 2005). A study carried out by Central Inland Fisheries Research Institute (CIFRI, Barrackpore, West Bengal) during 1978-81 in 24-Parganas, revealed that ponds of size less than 0.4 hectare are predominant with an average size of 0.1 hectare, quoted in "Scope for Scientific and Commercial Fish Farming in West Bengal" by Sri A.V. Natarajan. Present study of Sundarban area also satisfies the fact. Average size of ponds in this study was about 0.91 hectare.

5.2.2 Distribution of Ownership and Proprietorship

Size-group-wise ownership and extent of proprietorship of ponds and tanks were estimated and shown in Tables 5.8 and 5.9. It was found that in the study area, the water units (ponds and tanks) were either owned or leased-in through different sources. The water units were operated either as sole proprietorship or by the multiple of operators as partners. From Table 5.8, it is evident that 106 (58.9%) of the total sample water units were cultivated by the owner-operators; whereas 74 units (41.1%) of the total sample units were leased-in. Such distribution of owned and leased-in ponds is almost identical for traditional and progressive farmers.

Table 5.8: Size Group-wise Distribution of Ownership of Water Units

Pond Category	*No. of Ponds*	*Ownership Status*	
		Owned	*Leased*
Traditional	102 (100.0)	60 (58.8)	42 (41.2)
Progressive	78 (100.0)	46 (58.9)	32 (41.1)
Overall	**180** **(100.0)**	**106** **(58.9)**	**74** **(41.1)**

Note: Percentages in parentheses indicate the respective percentages.
Source: Field Survey, 2015-16.

During the course of investigation, it was observed that the preponderance of the owner-operators and relatively less importance attached to leasing out system, especially to small pond owners might be accounted for by two reasons. One, with the advent of new technology of composite intensive fish culture, self-cultivation is being considered by the owners a paying proposition; and two, because of a series of tenancy legislations in recent years giving more rights to the tenants, the owners have become more apprehensive of losing the occupancy rights in their leased out water units.

It can be mentioned that water units in the study area were found to be usually operated by different agencies like individuals, either singly or jointly, co-operatives or local bodies. Joint private operations and solo private operations were found to be the major agencies. From Table 5.9, it is evident that quite a significant proportion of the water bodies were found to be operated by more than two partners, particularly in the cases of traditional water units (54.9%) as compared to 39.7 per cent for progressive farmers. Single operation of water units is also high in percentage for traditionally managed firms (35.3% as compared to 28.2% for progressive farmers). It is important to note that quite a good proportion of progressively managed water units are cultivated by a large number of operators. Such percentage is as high as 32.1 per cent for progressive farmers as compared to only 9 per cent in case of traditionally managed firms. Unlike other States in India, it had been found in our study area, in Sundarban, the preponderance of multiple ownerships of water units, irrespective of size-classes.

As we have already mentioned in Table 5.8 that in our study area, 41.1 per cent of all the ponds surveyed were leased-in. Three

Table 5.9: Size Group-wise Distribution of Proprietorship of Water Units

Category of Ponds	*No. Ponds*	*Extent of Proprietorship*		
		Sole	*Only 2 Partners*	*More than 2 Partners*
Traditional	102 (100.0)	36 (35.3)	56 (54.9)	10 (09.8)
Progressive	78 (100.0)	22 (28.2)	31 (39.7)	25 (32.1)
Overall	**180** **(100.0)**	**58** **(32.2)**	**87** **(48.3)**	**35** **(19.4)**

Note: Percentages in parentheses indicate the respective percentages.
Source: Field Survey, 2015-16.

distinct sources were mainly identified with which lease agreements were made—they were private owners, public bodies and others like Panchayat, Zilla Parishad, trust or institutions like schools etc. The duration of lease was of various time period ranging from one year to ten years.

5.2.3 Duration of Lease and Means of Acquisition

It may further be observed from Table 5.10 that majority of the water units (i.e. 66 out of 74 ponds or 89.2%) were leased-in for a short duration, i.e. up to 4 years; whereas only 10.8 per cent of the water units surveyed were leased in for long period of time. However, for both categories of ponds, majority of the leased-in water units are of the duration between 2 to 4 years. However, no significant variation has been found in the characteristics of leased duration among traditional and progressive water units.

Table 5.10: Size group-wise leased-in ponds along with their lease duration

Category of Ponds	*Leased-in Ponds*	*Lease Duration*		
		One Year	*2-4 Years*	*More than 4 Years*
Traditional	42 (100.0)	11 (26.2í)	27 (64.3)	4 (09.5)
Progressive	32 (100.0)	7 (21.9)	21 (65.6)	4 (12.5)
Overall	**74** **(100.0)**	**18** **(24.3)**	**48** **(64.9)**	**8** **(10.8)**

Note: Percentages in parentheses indicate the respective percentages.
Source: Field Survey, 2015-16.

Table 5.11 brings out the fact that most of the water units (57.8%) were acquired through inheritance and only 1.7 per cent of total water units were purchased. Only single water unit has been newly constructed in the study sample, whereas 41.1 per cent of the total units were acquired through leasing arrangements. Another interesting observation is that though percentage of leasing arrangement as means of acquisition was high in case of progressively managed firms, inheritance as a mean of acquisition was almost same in case of both traditional

Table 5.11: Percentage distribution of water units by means of acquisition

Means of Acquisition	*Lease Duration*		
	Traditional	*Progressive*	*Total*
Lease	42 (26.2)	32 (64.3)	74 (41.1)
Inheritance	58 (56.9)	46 (58.9)	104 (57.8)
Construction	00 (00.0)	01 (01.3)	01 (00.6)
Purchase	02 (01.9)	01 (01.3)	03 (01.7)
Overall	**102** **(56.7)**	**80** **(43.3)**	**182** **(100.0)**

Note: Percentages in parentheses indicate the respective percentages.
Source: Field Survey, 2015-16.

as well as progressive firms. It should be stated that it is the inheritance factor which is mainly responsible for fragmentation of ownership (that is, multiple ownership). It is quite imperative here to mention that Hindu laws of inheritance, "Mitaksara" and "Dayabhaga", the dominance of which continued uninterrupted in the countryside played a very important role in subdivision and fragmentation of lands and ponds in India. This is eloquently explained in Pronoy Roy's "Subdivision of Land Soil Quality Biases: A Study of Property Rights in Indian Agriculture" (*Indian Journal of Agricultural Economics*, June 1983: 193). It is sometime stated that *zamindari* abolition in some States has resulted in multiple ownership.

5.2.4 Water Depth and Location of Ponds

The minimum water retention level during dry and wet season is one of the major factors, which affects the growth of fish. Progressive farmers maintain maximum level of water in both dry and wet season (6.67 metres and 8.97 metres respectively). Traditional farmers suffer from lack of water during summer season, because many of the ponds are village ponds where the water during the dry season is being utilized for other household and irrigation activities and due to seepage problems (Table 4.12). Water retention

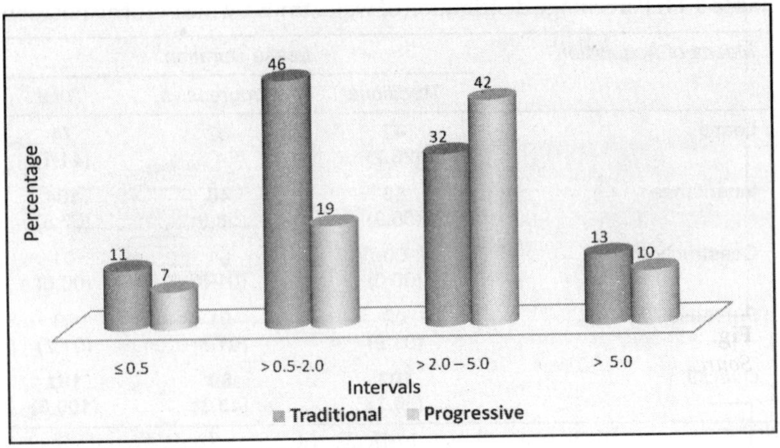

Fig. 5.7: Size of Sample Water Units.
Source: Field Survey, 2015-16.

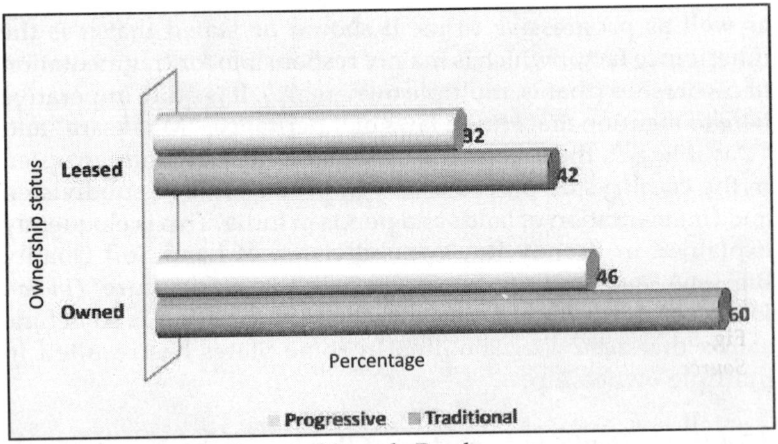

Fig. 5.8: Ownership Status of Sample Ponds.
Source: Field Survey, 2015-16.

level in monsoon is also low (8.09 metres) in case of traditional ponds compared to progressively managed ponds (8.97 metres). However, no water bodies in the study region are maintaining the recommended level of water retention level. Specially, traditional ponds are going far from the recommendation in the post-winter season. If water depth could not be managed up to recommended level, farmers will be bound to harvest juvenile uneconomic varieties belonging to different size class.

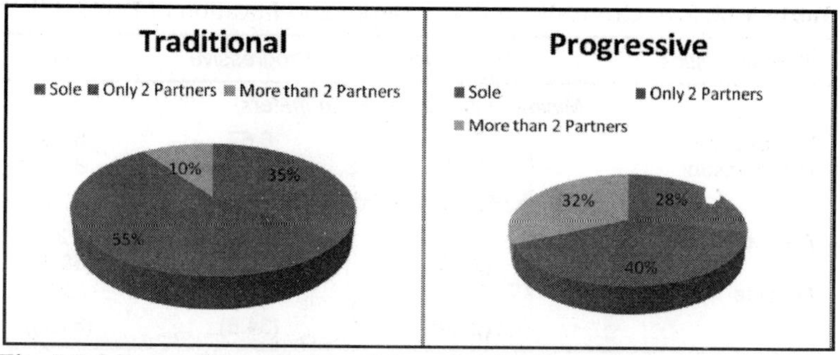

Fig. 5.9: Means of Acquisition of Sample Fish Farmers.
Source: Field Survey, 2015-16.

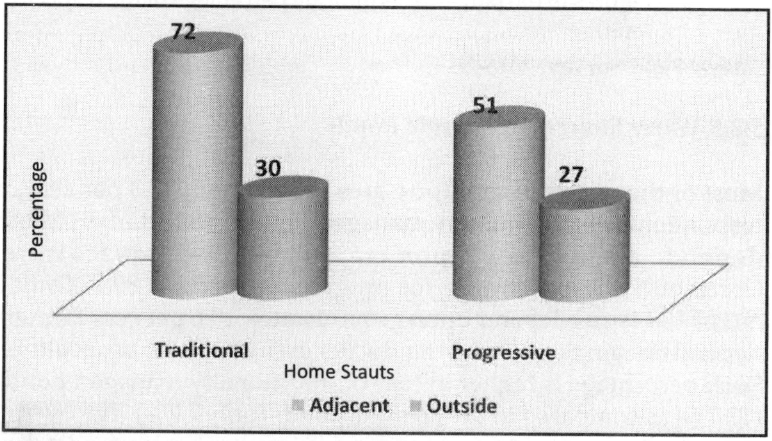

Fig. 5.10: Distance of Ponds from Home.
Source: Field Survey, 2015-16.

It is also evident from Table 5.12 that large percentages of farmers (68.3%) do not need to travel across to get access their pond. In most of the cases, fish farmers are residing within the radius of 1 to 2 kms from their home for both categories of ponds. About 30 per cent of traditional ponds are located outside the homestead, sometimes ponds are 8 to 10 kms away from their house. But higher the distance of ponds from house higher will be the cost of supervision and watch and ward. Clearly, such cost appears much lower for homestead ponds.

Table 5.12: Size Group-Wise Water Depth and Location of Ponds

Characteristics	*Traditional*	*Progressive*	*Overall*
	Minimum Water Depth (in meters)		
Dry Season	5.12	6.67	5.89
Wet Season	8.09	8.97	8.53
	Distance of Pond site from Homestead		
Adjacent	72 (70.6)	51 (65.4)	123 (68.3)
Outside	30 (29.4)	27 (34.6)	57 (31.7)

Note: 1. Recommended level of water depth is 7 meters and 9 meters in dry season and wet season respectively.
2. Figures in the parenthesis indicate percentage of the respective total.

Source: Field Survey, 2015-16.

5.2.5 *Water Sources of Sample Ponds*

Most of the ponds in the study area are rain fed. 87.3 per cent of respondents of traditionally managed ponds in Sundarban island depend exclusively upon rainwater for aquaculture. Corresponding percentage for progressive farms is 89.7. Only 2 out of 180 farms depend upon groundwater. 10.6 per cent farmers depend on rain as well as groundwater exclusively for aquaculture. Such percentage is higher in case of traditionally managed ponds (12.7%) as compared to progressive ponds (only 7.7%). The overall data also indicate that 46 per cent farmers maintained inlet and outlet in their ponds and 54 per cent farmers do not have proper inlet and outlet in their ponds. The percentage is almost equally distributed among progressive and traditional ponds in the study area. From this it is evident that ponds in the region are not scientifically designed. It is also found from the study that some ponds and tanks are seasonal irrigational tanks only (*see* Table 5.13). The demand for water from these ponds for irrigation purpose is heavy, resulting, in many cases, in complete draw-down. In these water units, it is only a put and take fishery because of limited period of water storage. A study carried out by CIFRI during 1978-81 in 24-Parganas revealed that only 33 per cent of the water area covered by ponds is used exclusively for fish cultivation, while 64 per cent of ponds (by area) are used for different purposes

Table 5.13: Source of water on the ponds under study

Water Source	*Traditional*	*Progressive*	*Overall*
Rainwater Only	89 (87.3)	70 (89.7)	159 (88.3)
Groundwater Only	0 (00.0)	2 (02.6)	2 (01.1)
Rain and Groundwater	13 (12.7)	6 (07.7)	19 (10.6)
Total	**102** **(100.0)**	**78** **(100.0)**	**180** **(100.0)**

Note: Figures in parentheses indicate percentage of respective total.

Source: Field Survey, 2015-16.

including fish cultivation, while three per cent are remaining fallow.

5.3 Operational and Management Environment

The research and development efforts during last five decades have greatly enhanced average fish yields in the study area making aquaculture an important economic enterprise. It has grown in geographical coverage, diversification of culture species and methods, besides intensification of farming systems. The three Indian major carps, *viz.*, *catla* (*Catla catla*), *rohu* (*Labeo rohita*) and *mrigal* (*Cirrhinus mrigala*) were the principal species cultured by the farmers in ponds since ages and production from these systems remained significantly low till the introduction of carp polyculture technology. Other freshwater carp species being cultured are *Bata (Labeo bata)*, and *Kalbaus (Labeo calbasu)*. The introduction of exotic species like silver carp (*Hypophthalmichthys molitrix*), grass carp (*Ctenopharyngodon idella*) and common carp (*Cyprinus carpio*), Bighead *(Aristichthys nobilis)*, Japani punti *(Puntius javanicus)*, Pangus *(Pangasius hypothalamus)*, Rupchanda *(Pygocentrus nattereri)*, Tilapia (*Oreochromismossam bicus*) into the carp polyculture system added new dimension to the aquaculture development of the study area. Among Small Indigenous Fishes (SIFSs), many species were reported to be cultivated throughout the Island. These are *Amblypharyngdon mola, Notopterus* sp, *Puntius sarana, Puntius ticto, Cirrhinus reba, Nandus nandus, Anabas testudineus, Puntius chola, Glossogobius giuris, Chanda nama* etc.

With the adoption of technology of composite carp culture, production levels has increased several folds since last few years and brought Sundarban fishery from a level of backyard activity to that of a fast growing and well organized industry and placed the island on the threshold of blue revolution. Traditional farms in our study are those farms, which concentrate on the culture of Indian major carps and silver carps. Those who are practicing diversified aquaculture farming by culturing at least 6 varieties of fish species along with SIFSs, are termed as progressive farmers. However, adoption level of modern technology has been with several modifications depending on the market demand and resource availability. As a result, wide variations have been observed in the amount of input uses and level of culture techniques adopted by the fish farmers in the study area, which needs to be examined.

5.3.1 Use of Water units in the Study Area

The range of uses of water units is very large and includes uses like irrigation, duck rearing, cattle watering, and aquaculture field drainage and also for crop production for both cattle and human being. Figure 5.11 demonstrates that almost 87 per cent

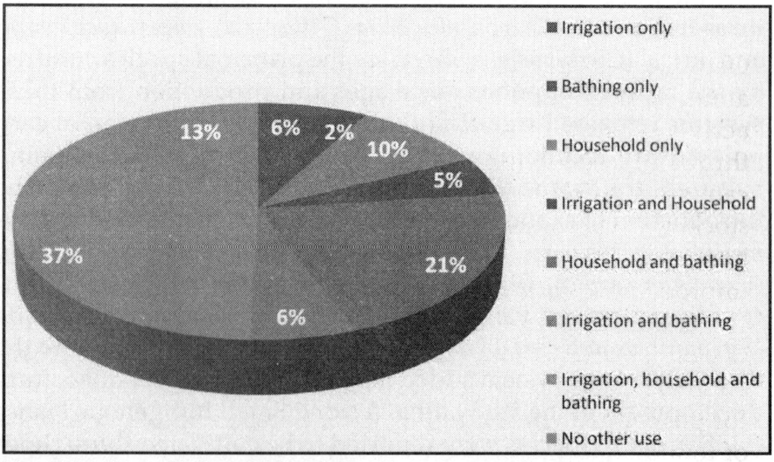

Fig. 5.11: Use of Water Units other than Aquaculture.

Note: Percentages are reporting this use of water units.

Source: Field Survey, 2015-16.

water units are used for multipurpose with a wide variety of combination of uses. "Household uses" in our case include dishwashing, cloth-washing, supply of water for cooking etc. 10 per cent of the water units are used, other than aquaculture, for household purpose solely but along with bathing and irrigation, this percentage has increased up to 36 per cent. 11 per cent of the ponds and tanks are also used for irrigation purposes solely along with household activities. There are inlet and outlet channels indicating that the units may be used for drainage and irrigation also. It can also be pointed out that the water units sometimes provide both water and space for growing vegetables. Dried out parts of the ponds are sometimes used for winter (Boro) paddy cultivation—either for nursery seedbeds or for transplanting the paddy itself. But field irrigation, household activities and bathing is major part of sub-use sector of fish ponds. The use of ponds for other activities generally hinders its optimal usage for composite culture.

5.3.2 *Culture Practices Followed by Fish Farmers*

The livelihoods of a large number of farmers are associated with fish farming in the study area. The peak fish farming season is from April to December, a culture period of around nine months. Fish fry are stocked in April to June and harvested primarily from October to December. Culture period is limited to one crop annually. Fish Culture practices in the study area include all activities from pre-stocking operations to harvesting of fish through human efforts. Their cultural practices may simply be categorized on the basis of major operations like pre-stocking, stocking input application, application of supplementary feeds and harvesting. Table 5.14 explains the various levels of adoption of improved fish culture methodology.

Pre-stocking operation in the area studied includes cleaning of ponds, eradication of plant weeds, insects, predatory fishes and frogs, netting. This would facilitate the better environment for proper growth and movement of fingerlings. Less than half of total fish farmers have undertaken pre-stocking activities in our study area. Such activity is quite high for progressive pond owners (66.7%) and relatively low for traditional farmers (47.1%).

Table 5.14: Information regarding adoption of Appropriate Culture Practices

Questions	*Traditional*	*Progressive*	*Overall*
Pre-stocking	48 (47.1)	52 (66.7)	100 (55.6)
Recommended stocking	39 (38.2)	46 (58.9)	85 (47.2)
Seed testing	23 (22.5)	32 (41.0)	55 (30.6)
Liming and intoxication	55 (53.9)	47 (60.3)	102 (56.7)
Inorganic fertilization	72 (70.6)	39 (50.0)	111 (61.7)
Supplementary feeding	49 (48.0)	61 (78.2)	110 (61.1)

Note: Figures in the parentheses indicate standard deviation values.
Source: Field Survey, 2015-16.

Stocking refers to applications of external fish seeds into the ponds for the purpose of raising them up to the marketable size. The average size of fingerlings was 5.36 cm in length and 11.8 gms in weight. Farmers did not attempt to stock any specific ratio of different species. Even, recommended schedule of stocking have not been followed by more than half of the farmers (95 out of 180 farmers studied). For almost 61 per cent of traditional operators, stocking density is far from recommendation. The highest average stocking density was maintained by progressive farmers (9237 per acre). However, it is also evident from the standard deviation figures of Table 5.14 that there are wide variations in stocking density among the farmers, especially for traditional pond operators. However, along with carp, farmers also stocking small indigenous species, like *mola* (*Amblypharyngodon mola*), *puti* (*Puntius sophore*), *koi* (*Anabas testudineus*), in their ponds to enhance total fish production. Usually, fingerlings were stocked from local *aratdars* (26.9%), or hatchery (71.1%). Natural sources, such as old perennial ponds, floodplains and rice fields are also the sources of seed collection. But considerable number of progressive farmers (14.1%) generally use seed from their own sources. Traditional farmers bank heavily on hatchary based fish seeds (Table 5.15).

Fish thrives well in alkaline water. Lime is used in a pond to maintain the appropriate alkaline nature of the fishponds.

Table 5.15: Size Class-wise Sources of Fish Seed in the Study Area

Pond Category	Hatchery	Local Aratdar	Natural Source	Both Hatchery and Natural Source
Traditional	76 (74.5)	15 (14.7)	3 (02.9)	8 (07.8)
Progressive	52 (66.7)	6 (07.7)	11 (14.1)	9 (11.5)
Overall	**128** **(71.1)**	**21** **(26.9)**	**14** **(07.8)**	**17** **(09.4)**

Note: Figures in the parentheses indicate standard deviation values.
Source: Field Survey, 2015-16.

Toxicants are the substances which are used to eradicate predatory fish, insects and frogs from the ponds. The most common toxicant is *mohua* oil cake. Usage of lime and other toxicants by the farmers in the region studied vary marginally, from 53.9 per cent for traditional pond operators to 60.3 per cent for progressive farmers.

Manures are not directly consumed by fish. It, in fact, enhances the vegetative growth of green aquatic plants and phytoplankton which are ultimately consumed by fish. Dung is the most commonly used manure. Apart from such organic fertilization, inorganic fertilizers, like urea, single super phosphate are also used by operators in the study area. It also facilitates the growth of micro- and macro-vegetative plants in the ponds. But such use of inorganic fertilizer is abruptly low for progressive farmers (50%) and they often expressed their awareness regarding enhancement of death of SIFS due to indiscriminate use of inorganic fertilization. However, about 70 per cent of traditional farmers had used those fertilizers in their ponds.

Another critical input necessary for better and vast growth of fish is the use of commercially manufactured improved supplementary feed like Azolla, soybean flour and fish meal. Rice bran, white bran, mustard oil cakes are most common among the supplementary feeding applied by the farmers. In almost all the ponds, upon enquiry, it was revealed that very few farmers use supplementary feeds as per recommended schedule, rather hit and trial method followed. Sixty per cent of the medium sized farmers generally employed commercially manufactured pelleted feeds. Surprisingly, more than half of traditional farmers are not using supplementary diets. Feeds consisting of a mixture of locally available feed ingredients such as rice bran, wheat bran and oil cake or farm-made aqua feed comprising rice bran, wheat bran, oil cake, fish meal, flour, dried fish, salt and vitamins are more common feeding practices in the study region. The most common feeding frequency in extensive farming system was once per day, while all large and 62 per cent of medium farmers reported twice per day feeding. Use of supplementary feeding is satisfactorily high (78.2%) for progressive farmers (*see* Figs. 5.12 and 5.13).

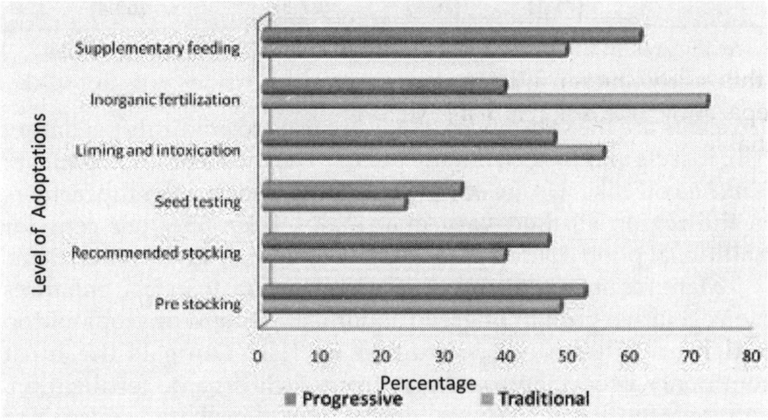

Fig. 5.12: Level of Adoption of Scientific Culture.

Source: Field Survey, 2015-16.

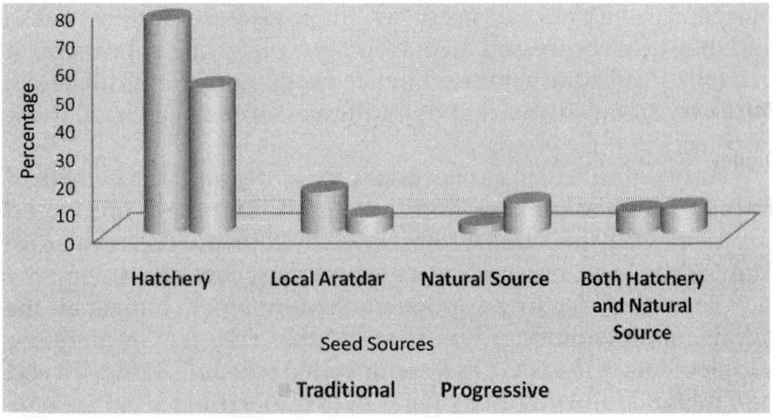

Fig. 5.13: Seed Sources of Scientific Culture.

Source: Field Survey, 2015-16.

Overall, in most cases, culture practices have been found not according to the recommended schedule. The composition of different steps was mismatched to the recommendation. A large number of sample farmers expressed their complete unawareness about scientific culture practices. Sometimes, acquired knowledge from government extension services have been modified by the farmers to fit with their own constraints.

5.3.3 Input Output Structure of Aquaculture in Study Area

In this study, the sample focused on the different aspects of pond preparation like silt removal, weed removal of predatory fishes, initial liming. However, information on the farmers' effort regarding such pre-stocking activities has been captured in the inputs like labour or land-use. The pattern of seed stocking by the sample fish farmers has been shown in Table 5.16. Average stocking density per acre was 7583 fingerlings for carp species and 21145 SIFS. There was a significant difference (P<0.05) in such density between different category of ponds. Table 5.16 also indicates the position of

Table 5.16: Input-output Structure of Aquaculture in Study Area

Input Characteristics	*Traditional*	*Progressive*	*Overall*
Stocking Density (quantity/acre/yr)			
Carp	9237 (893)	5929 (714)	7583 (791)
SIFS	—	13145 (3292)	13145 (3292)
Fish Feed (Kg/acre/yr)	1712 (781)	1686 (423)	1699 (598)
Organic Fertilizer (Kg/acre/yr)	889 (164)	734 (171)	811 (167)
Inorganic Fertilizer (Kg/acre/yr)	816 (167)	391 (49)	603
Duration of Rearing (month)	8	10	—
Labour used (number/acre/yr)	264 (32)	168 (28)	216 (30)
Fish yield (Kg/acre/yr)			
Carp	2017 (324)	1846 (167)	1931 (246)
SIFS	—	498 (91)	498 (91)

Note: Figures in the parentheses indicate standard deviation values.
Source: Field Survey, 2015-16.

the farmers regarding use of feed. It is quite clear that the proportion of traditional farmers using feed was higher than that of progressive farmers. As much as 96 per cent of the pond area held by progressive farmers was covered by the use of feed, while the corresponding proportion for the traditional farmers was close to cent per cent. Surprising to note that there is wide variation in the use of feed among the traditional farmers (standard deviation figure is as high as 781). On an average sample farmers were using 1699 kg of fish feed per acre in a single production year.

Farmers used fertilizers mainly in the form of cow dung, urea and triple super phosphate (TSP) at varying rates. The use of organic manure like cow dung is widespread among the traditional farmers due to relatively cheap and wide availability of it in the study area. But uses of inorganic fertilization like urea or single super phosphate was relatively low (391 kg per acre) for progressive farmers. Only 35 per cent of small farmers used fertilizer. Lack of technical knowledge and poor economic returns were two major reasons behind such low rate of use. All medium and large farmers used inorganic fertilizers for fish farming. There was a significant difference ($P<0.05$) in fertilizer use between different size class of farming systems.

There are two types of labour inputs used in fish production—family labour and hired labour. Apart from the use of labour inputs in netting, fish catch and disbursement of fish, seed and manure; labour was also used by the farmers for supervision in order to prohibit unauthorized stealing and deliberate poisoning. Table 5.16 gives overall pattern of use of labour input by the sample fish farmers. There are not much differences in the use of labour, though traditional farmer's labour cost is higher than that of progressive farmers. It is interesting to note that traditional farmers, though using more labour than that of progressive farmers, usually employ family labour in higher proportion. The use of average family labour was 193 days and average hired labour 71 days for traditional farms. The proportion of hired labour in total labour input has increased for progressive farms, though they had used only 168 labour days of labour in one production year.

For measuring the overall production level of ponds, the output of all carp species is taken together and aggregate yield of SIFS has been estimated separately. Regardless of farming category, the average annual yields of carp were estimated at 1931 kg/acre

(Table 5.16). There was a significant difference ($P<0.05$) in fish yields between different categories of ponds with a higher mean value in traditional farming system (2017 kg/acre) followed by progressive farming (1846 kg/acre). This was mainly due to a combination of larger ponds and higher inputs of fish seed, feed and fertilizer used in larger size of ponds. The variation in input use, discussed earlier, brought about significant variation in the average yield rates per acre. However, a number of interdependent factors might also affect growth rate and productivity of fish, including environmental factors, water quality and other aspects of pond management.

5.3.4 Costs and Returns of Aquaculture in Study Area

Only physical parameter of input and output of fish production may not bring out managerial efficiency. Hence, given the physical quantities of inputs, the annual cost of operating the pond aquaculture is also computed. Table 5.16 shows that total annual costs of fish farming over all sample farmers averaged Rs. 23,316 acre, ranging from Rs. 21,728 in progressive ponds farming to Rs. 23,808/acre in traditional class of farming. There was a significant difference ($P<0.05$) in total costs between different category of ponds. Regardless of farm category, the average annual variable costs and fixed costs were Rs. 20,041 (85.9%) and Rs. 3,275/acre (14.1%) per acre, respectively. Among the variable costs, seed dominated all other costs representing 43.2 per cent of total variable costs. Feed also constituted a major share of total cost (41%) with progressive farmers were incurring higher cost (43.2%) than traditional farms. Under fixed costs, the average annual depreciation cost (i.e. water pump, nets and feed machines), interest on operating capital and land use cost or lease money were estimated at Rs. 2828 and Rs. 3176 respectively for traditional and progressive farmers. Fixed cost was relatively high for progressive farmers (16.4% of total cost), mainly due to the higher land use cost (44.7% of total fixed cost) and interest cost (35.5% of total fixed cost). The result has strong implication because leased in pond percentage in progressive farm category is relatively high. So, rental charges can be established as a reason for higher interest cost. It may be due to the fact that progressive farmers usually operate their ponds by lending money from moneylenders, their rates of interest are quite high (*see* Fig. 5.14).

Table 5.17: Costs and Returns of Pond Aquaculture in Study Area

Cost and Return (Rs/acre/yr)	*Traditional*	*Progressive*	*Overall*
Variable Cost			
Seed	8932 (42.6)	8179 (45.0)	8653 (43.2)
Feed	8196 (39.1)	7858 (43.2)	8224 (41.0)
Fertilizer	1423 (06.7)	831 (04.6)	1278 (06.4)
Labour	1865 (08.9)	928 (05.1)	1427 (07.1)
Marketing and Harvesting	564 (02.7)	378 (02.1)	459 (02.3)
Total Variable Cost (TVC)	**20980 (88.1)**	**18174 (83.6)**	**20041 (85.9)**
Fixed Cost			
Land Use	1718 (60.7)	1421 (44.7)	1623 (49.6)
Interest	392 (13.9)	1127 (35.5)	974 (29.7)
Depreciation	718 (25.4)	628 (19.8)	678 (20.7)
Total Fixed Cost (TFC)	**2828 (11.9)**	**3176 (16.4)**	**3275 (14.1)**
Total Cost (TC = TVC + TFC)	23808 (100.0)	21728 (100.0)	23316
Gross Revenue (GR)	44928	47763	45932
Net return (NR)	21120	26035	22616
Benefit Cost Ration (B:C:R) (GR/TC)	**1.89**	**2.19**	**1.97**

Notes: 1. Figures in the parentheses indicate percentage of sub cost with respect to total cost incurred.

2. Depreciation cost = (purchase price - salvage value) / economic life.
3. Interest cost = Interest on operating capital at 15 per cent per annum.
4. Valuation of land was at its rental price.
5. Gross Revenue = Productivity × farm-gate price.

Source: Field Survey, 2015-16.

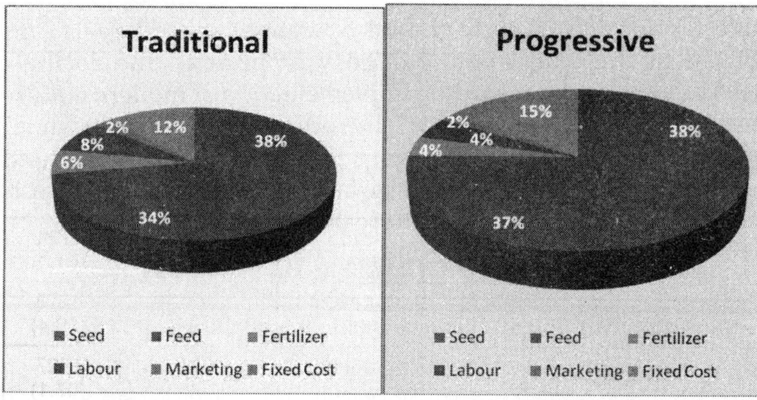

Fig. 5.14: Distribution of Input Cost Structure of Sample Ponds.
Source: Field Survey, 2015-16.

The average annual gross revenue was estimated at Rs. 45,932 per acre, varying from Rs. 44,928 per acre in traditional categories of farming to Rs. 47,763 for progressive farmers (Table 5.16). The highest average gross revenue was reported by progressive farmers due to relatively high production of carp as well as SIFS. As reported by the respondents, small indigenous fishes could grab commendable prices in the market, which enhanced the revenue of progressive farmers. Despite higher production costs per acre, the average annual net return was not highest in traditional farms. In terms of net returns (gross returns minus total cost), progressive farmers have appeared most efficient (Rs. 26,035 per acre) compared to traditional (Rs. 21,120 per acre). There was a significant difference ($P<0.05$) in net return between the different farming systems.

A benefit-cost ratio (BCR) or profitability index of one means that the operation is at break-even position. The BCR values were 1.89 and 2.19 for traditional and progressive farmers. The findings showed the progressive farmers are recovering Rs. 2.14 by investing one rupee while such return were Rs. 1.89 for traditional farmers. Highest net return along with highest benefit-cost ratio for progressive farmers indicate that such farmers were putting more efforts into maintaining their fish ponds, feeding and monitoring of culture practices. As a result, they tend to be more efficient. The farmer's ability to follow this regular activity decreases in case of traditional farms. The result also indicates that traditional farmers had failed to capitalize the economies of scale (economies of scale should operate as more large farms belong to the traditional category of ponds) due to their lackadaisical nature regarding implementation of modern culture practices. On the other hand, introduction of various small indigenous fish species in the carp polyculture system, without increase in cost, helped progressive farmers to capture higher cost-benefit ratio and make aquaculture business more lucrative.

6
Efficiency in Aquaculture

> Efficiency is doing things right; effectiveness is doing the right things.
>
> — *Peter Drucker*

6.1 Introduction

In previous chapter, cost and revenue structures of the sample fish farms have been properly interpreted and benefit cost ratio (B:C:R) have been calculated. In the interpretation, financial success has been attributed to those farms whose revenues exceed costs and therefore B:C:R became high. In course of observation, it has been found that progressive farmers could gain highest such financial success followed by traditional farms.

However, sometimes, it appears controversial whether the accounting profits of fish farms are adequate to acknowledge those farms as successful. A farm can also increase its revenue by better marketing management or through distributional facilities. Some specific farms can also reduce their input costs with respect to others by buying those from their friends or relatives. The outcome of input processing may not be directly related with the amount and costs of inputs. Two identical farms having identical input structures may end up with differentiated yields or different costs revenue structures. Therefore, it is possible to find out that a fish farm having accounting profits is not efficiently utilizing the inputs incorporated or a farm which has a negative profit scheme, is implementing the best bunch of activities possible. Hence, the evaluation of success of the fish farms in terms of effective use of inputs and maintenance of a sound cost structure lies in the efficiency analysis of the process. It is the technical process affecting final output. In this chapter, technical efficiency of sample fish farms have been evaluated on the basis of non-parametric data envelopment analysis (DEA), the methodology of which has been explained in chapter 4.

As mentioned earlier, technical efficiency (TE) represents the ability of a fish farm to produce maximum fish given a set of inputs (fingerlings, feeds, fertilizers, labour etc.) and technology and *vice versa*. DEA operationalises these efficiency concepts in the context of a set of linear programming problems. It calculates the frontier production function of a set of decision-making units (DMUs) and evaluates the relative technical efficiency of each unit, thereby allowing a distinction to be made between efficient and inefficient farms. Those identified as "best practice units" (i.e., those determining the frontier) are given a rating of one, whereas the degree of technical inefficiency of the rest is calculated on the basis of the Euclidian distance of their input-output ratio from the frontier. That is, if efficiency score of a particular farm appears to be 0.5, say, it implies that she is 50 per cent efficient and can reduce half of its input use.

6.2 Distribution of Technical and Scale Efficiency Scores

The DEA model for computing input-oriented technical and scale efficiency was solved by using software DEAP 2.1 (Coelli, 1996). The estimated value of technical efficiency (TE) and scale efficiency (SE) are shown in Tables 6.1 and 6.2 and Figs. 6.1 and 6.2. Estimates of mean technical and scale efficiencies of the sample farms have revealed some interesting facts. The estimated technical efficiency score under CRS technology for the sample farms varies from 0.32 to 1.0, with a sample average of 0.636 (Table 6.2). It implies, on the one hand, that on an average, the farms can reduce 36.4 per cent of input use and can still produce the same output. A good number of farms are operating below potential and there are significant possibilities to increase the TE level of carp producers. The number of farms whose technical inefficiency is greater than 50 per cent (TE score is less than 0.5); that is, the number of farms which can contract more than half of their input use on an average, is 55 (30.6%). The number of farms who are carrying fish production optimally is only 11, which is only 6 per cent of the total sample.

Table 6.1: Distribution of Efficiency Score of Fish Farms

Efficiency Score	*TE*		*SE*	
	Number	*Percentages*	*Number*	*Percentages*
0.00 to 0.26	00	00	00	00
0.27 to 0.49	49	27.2	56	31.1
0.50 to 0.69	76	42.2	71	39.4
0.70 to 0.89	38	21.1	42	23.3
0.90 to 1.00	17	09.4	11	06.1

Note: Figures are based on author's calculation.
Source: Computed from data received through field survey, 2015-16.

Table 6.2: Summary Efficiency Score of Sample Farms

Characteristics	*TECRS*	*TEVRS*	*SE*
Overall Sample Mean	0.636	0.659	0.732
Maximum efficiency	1.0	1.0	1.0
Minimum Efficiency	0.32	0.34	0.42
No and percentages of farms showing efficiency score less than average	109 (60.6)	95 (52.8)	67 (37.22)
No of "Best Practice" farms (TE = 1)	**11 (06.1)**	**13 (07.2)**	**22 (12.2)**

Note: Figures are based on author's calculation.
Source: Computed from data received through field survey, 2015-16.

The difference between maximum and minimum TE score indicates that there is wide variation in the efficiency of the farms.

This difference has another important implication. The worst performing farm (having technical efficiency score of 0.32) can increase its efficacy regarding input use up to 68 per cent (and thereby can reach to the optimum TE score on one) just by sharing their own experience and implementing the input management strategy of best practice farms, without begging arms for institutional support. Thus, the way to eliminate technical inefficiency in aquaculture in Sundarban would be to adopt the best practices strategies and input application management of efficient farms. Distribution of efficiency scores show that TE concentration was more in the sixtieth percentiles (49%). Rests have, more or less, equal division between lower and upper area of mean technical efficiency scores.

The interpretation of scale efficiency scores allow for some interesting remarks. Mean scale efficiency scores 0.732, implying that the average size of sample fish farms is far from optimal size. Assuming no other constraining factor, an additional of 26.8 per cent productivity gain would be feasible, provided they adjusted their farm operation to an optimal scale. Only 22 (12.2%) farms are actually operating at the most productive scale where CRS apply and scale efficiency equals one. The majority of the scale-inefficient fish farms, 99 (55%) are operating under increasing returns to scale (i.e. at a point corresponding to the downward portion of the average long run cost curve) and the remaining 59 (32.2%) are under decreasing returns to scale. This means that the largest increase in technical efficiency could be obtained by eliminating the problem of increasing returns to scale. This implies that, if production efficiency of aquaculture in Sundarban is to be improved, two options such as increasing pond size or decreasing input applications can assure it. Efficiency analysis theory suggests that the former are obviously small farms that need to increase their size in order to achieve cost savings, whereas the latter are larger farms that have expanded more than necessary and thus would be better off by reducing their size (*see* Figs. 6.1 and 6.2).

6.3 Actual *Versus* Technically Efficient Input Applications

In course of explaining the methodologies of DEA, it has been mentioned that θ is the proportional reduction in inputs possible and λ_j is the weight or intensity variable used to derive all possible combinations of the sample observations. Here, θ determines the efficiency score of *j*th DMU. The value of $\theta = 1$ shows a technically efficient DMU; θ less than one shows a technically inefficient DMU. In order to obtain efficiency score of each farm, LP equations have to be solved once for each farm. Once θ and λ_j can be determined it is easy to find out the optimal value of the input from the above LP equation. A comparison of the actual quantity of input used with the corresponding optimal quantity of that input reveals whether a particular DMU is using too much or too little of that input. Hence, for any particular input I, an index of input use efficiency can be calculated by the ratio –

$$\alpha^i = \frac{L_0^i}{L_*^i}$$

where, L^i_0 is actual amount of a specific input used and L^i_* is potential input ought to be used in order to reach in full efficiency.

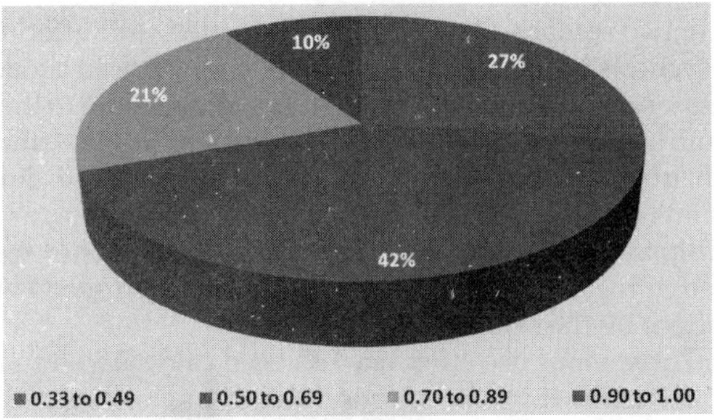

Fig. 6.1: Technical Efficiency Score of Sample Farms.
Source: Computed from data received through field survey, 2015-16.

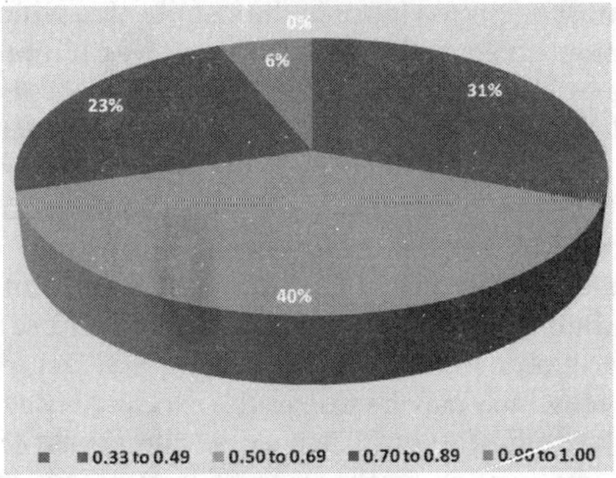

Fig. 6.2: Scale Efficiency Score of Sample Farms.
Source: Computed from data received through field survey, 2015-16.

Now, a value of α^j greater (less) than unity implies over (under) use of that input.

Table 6.3 presents information on actual (observed) and technically efficient (potential) quantities of input applications and output (fish) per acre according to the size of farms. Average actual usage of majority of inputs was lower than the theoretical TE levels. Actual use of carp fingerling should be increased by 18.3 per cent, on an average, in order to stay in best practice level. The progressive and traditional farmers should increase it by 30.7 and 13.6 per cent respectively, which clearly indicates that progressive farmers are more reluctant regarding optimal use of carp seeds. This might be due to two reasons. One, progressive farmers are suffering from "fear psychosis" of incurring loss by investing more on aquaculture business; and two, introduction of SIFS allowed them to think that use of more carp species in polyculture system might dampen the growth of SIFS. Those farmers might have faced financial constraints for its low use of most important input but, as regard to traditional farmers, they had shown lack of proper technical knowledge regarding fingerling use. Overall, fish seed had been undershoot by the sample farmers.

Similarly, input use efficiency has been calculated for all other principle inputs. It has been found that farmers in general have underutilized feed massively, whereas labour and fertilizers have been overused. Accordingly, feed use should be increased by more than 67 per cent in order to achieve full efficiency. This implies that fish feed is the most neglected input in the sample area which affects the fish production adversely. Undershooting of feed is more prominent for traditional farmers (70.4%) compared to progressive farmers (62.6%). Side by side, fertilizer and labour had been overshooting by the farmers. Though slight increase in the use of fertilizer (only 1.5%) is required to be best practice farm, farmers should reduce its labour use by almost 15 per cent. However, interesting to note that progressive farmers had used fertilizers less than what is required, whereas traditional farmers should reduce fertilizer use by almost 17 per cent. Traditional fish farmers were using fertilizer more than the potential level which may be due to the excessive usage of organic fertilizers like domestically available cow dung or oil cake. Another significant observation is that use of labour is more than the recommended (optimal) level irrespective of the categories of ponds. This might be due to the fact that, for the farmers involved in pond fish culture, extent of family cooperation is quite significant. Fish is grown for home consumption using family labour, supplemented with some hired labour for intensive harvesting. Usually, family labour is used for fish farming during the off-agricultural season, in which case there would be minimal costs for pond preparation. As labour cost become minimal due to the use of family and off-agricultural based labour, farmers were overshooting the input without concerning its adverse impact on production. It has also been found that farmers in Basanti block and especially progressive farmers were more profitable because they can take advantage of management with reduced cost of labour inputs.

Table 6.3: Mean Actual versus Technically Efficient Input-output Applications

Input-Output	*Size of Farm (Acre)*		
	Progressive	*Traditional*	*All*
Actual Use of Carp Seeds (number/acre)	5929	9237	6315
Optimum Use of Inputs (number/acre)	7217	8128	7733
Change Required	**1822 (30.7)**	**1109 (13.6)**	**1417 (18.3)**
Actual Use of SIFS Seeds (number/acre)	13145	—	13145
Optimum Use of SIFS Seeds (number/acre)	16716	—	16716
Change Required	**3571 (27.2)**	**—**	**3571 (27.2)**
Actual Use of Feed (kg/acre)	1686	1712	1699
Potential Use of Feed (kg/acre)	2742	2918	2841
Change Required	**1056 (62.6)**	**1206 (70.4)**	**1142 (67.2)**
Actual Use of Fertilizers	1125	1705	1453
Potential Use of Fertilizers	1247	1573	1431
Change Required	**122 (10.8)**	**(–) 132 (– 07.7)**	**(–) 22 (– 01.51)**
Actual Use of Labour	168	264	216
Potential Use of Labour	141	219	185
Change Required	**(–) 27 (– 16.1)**	**(–) 45 (– 17.1)**	**(–) 31 (– 14.4)**
Actual Amount of Carp Produced	1846	2017	1943
Potential Amount of Carp Output	2852	3318	3116
Change Required	**1006 (54.5)**	**1301 (64.5)**	**1173 (60.4)**
Actual Amount of SIFS Produced	498	—	498
Potential Amount of SIFS Output	612	—	612
Change Required	**114 (22.9)**	**—**	**114 (22.9)**

Note: Figures in the parenthesis indicate percentage of the respective total.
Source: Data Envelopment Analysis (DEA), results of data received through field survey, 2015-16.

Theoretically efficient quantity of carp fish production per acre appeared to be 3116 kg as against 1943 kg of actual production. Clearly, actual production was significantly lower. The theoretical optimum suggests that production of fish could be increased by 1173 kg (60.4% of the actual production) had the technically efficient input quantities been applied by the farmers. To investigate the percentage of required changes in outputs across different pond size groups, Table 5.3 shows that the operators of the progressive ponds could have increased fish production by 54.5 per cent with the TE inputs level. The traditional pond operators were able to match actual fish production with the optimum, requiring highest change of 64.5 per cent of the actual production. However, progressive farms could also increase their production of SIFS up to 22.9 per cent by following the theoretical level of input structure. Hence, overall, progressive farmers could enhance productivity more than that of traditional farmers.

All these facts signify that, despite continuing growth in aquaculture in the study area, most of the present production techniques are quite rudimentary when compared with fully developed aquaculture practices. As a result, potential for growth in aquaculture, as well as the potential for aquaculture diversification through introduction of SIFS in carp polyculture system, in the Sundarban region is still far from exhausted. Reliance on unimproved breeds, seed collection from the wild, tardy nature of current practices, modification and manipulation of the proper adoption practices are manifestations of its unsophisticated nature. It is not that sample farmers have no knowledge about proper culture practices. Consultation with government officials has revealed that a good number of times extension services had been geared at the village level. The attendance rates of the adopters were also high. Still, production was far from expectation. Actually, technologies for utilizing such resources need not always be based on intensive commercial operations; rather they will be based on the application of basic aquaculture principles, their adaptation to local knowledge systems, and the different political and cultural contexts. The deviation from this rationality had compelled the farmers to manipulate their acquired scientific knowledge along with their own conventional wisdom to adopt only a part of the package of practice. As a result, ultimate production would adversely be affected. Production can therefore be significantly increased through more efficient use of farmers' resources and of existing inputs and technology.

6.4 Meta Frontier DEA of Aquaculture Diversification

Wide variation in technical efficiency scores of the sample farmers in the study area, derived in previous section, clearly reveals the facts that there is no "one rule fits all" model for diversification of aquaculture development. Sometimes, it is found that farmers are not making efficient use of existing technologies and therefore, technical efficiency score is considerably low. In that case cost effective approach should be adopted. Sometimes, farmers are reasonably efficient and technical efficiency score is high. In that case the second option of technology development and transfer would seem more appropriate. Intensification of culture practices would be a feasible option only if farmers are using inputs below economically and environmentally optimal levels. Hence, everything depends on local environmental and socio-economic constraints, as well as the degree of control over inputs and outputs afforded by intensification. Since present study concentrates on the effect of diversification strategy on the productivity and efficiency of aquaculture practices in Sundarbans, effort has been made in this section to examine whether there is any significant difference in TE score among progressive and traditional farmers.

Actually, the efficiency of a farm depends not only on the inputs it uses, but also on several other factors (such as infrastructural facilities, region, level of education and technical knowledge, work culture, pond size etc.). It is very difficult to incorporate those factors into a production frontier to examine their effects on efficiency, though important. Hence, group-efficiency analysis might reveal more concrete results if it is carried on separately for different group. Also, a definite conclusion can be drawn if it is found that a particular group of farmers is efficient with respect to all the farmers taken together. For that it is important to calculate the group efficiency to reach to the final conclusion regarding the effects of different farm specific variables on technical efficiency score.

However, it is common practice to use production frontiers to assess the level of efficiency of production units or farms. But while technical efficiencies of farms that are measured with respect to a given frontier are comparable, this is not normally the case among farms that operate under different technologies. Such problems arise when comparisons of farms from different groups are involved. In this section, attempts has been made to find out difference in group-productivity relation in diversified aquaculture farming across the region to measure the group efficiency relative to its grand frontier. For this, meta-frontier Data Envelopment Analysis (DEA) has been used, the detailed methodology of which has been discussed in the chapter 4.

At the farm level, the technical efficiency has a mixed relationship with aquaculture diversification strategy of the farmers. While the progressive farmers practicing carp culture along with SIFS recorded slightly more technical efficiency, both on the basis of group and grand frontier; farmers culturing only carp have been found as slightly inefficient. This is evident from Table 6.4. Taking all observation into consideration, grand technical efficiency has been found as 0.651 and 0.642 for progressive and traditional farmers respectively. Implication is that, progressive farmers can able to minimize its input use by 34.9 per cent and can still produce the same output. Alternatively speaking, progressive farmers can enhance its production by 34.9 per cent by using its existing inputs optimally. Side by side, using existing inputs, traditional farmers can increase fish production by 35.8 per cent. Hence, traditional farmers are 0.9 per cent less efficient than progressive farmers.

Taking ratio of the geometric means of group and grand frontier, intensification efficiency of diversification has been calculated. The index of intensification-efficiency (signifying farmers' capability to cultivate fish in appropriate manner) of the "progressive" farms (practicing SIFS with carp) is 0.723, which is higher than that of "traditional" farms (0.714). From the analysis, it is quite evident that introduction of various small indigenous fishes in carp polyculture system increases the efficiency of aquaculture business. In this analysis, such increase is only marginal, the reasons for which can be examined further. But, there is no denying the fact that, such diversification strategy has enough potential to make aquaculture lucrative in Sundarban.

Table 6.4: Mean Technical Efficiency of Fish Farms Across Different Culture Practices

Diversification Group	*No. of Fish Farms*	*Technical Efficiency Score*		*Index of intensification Efficiency*
		Based on Grand Frontier	*Based on Group Frontier*	
Progressive	78	0.651	0.742	0.723
Traditional	102	0.642	0.727	0.714
Total	**180**	**0.646**	**0.734**	**0.178**

Source: Data Envelopment Analysis (DEA), results of data received through field survey, 2015-16.

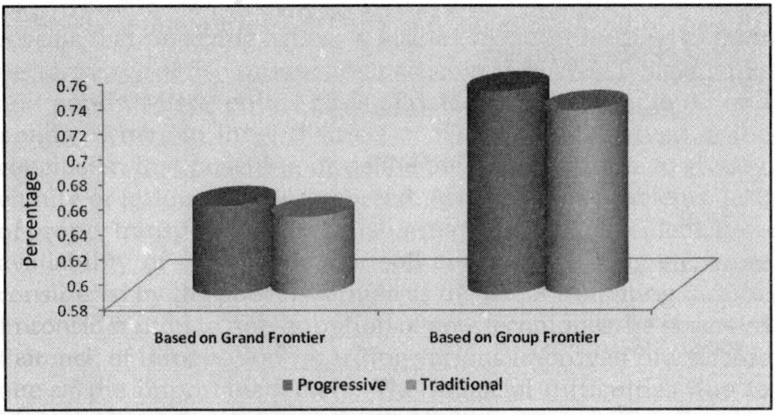

Fig. 6.3: Group and Grand Technical Efficiency Score of Sample Farms.
Source: Field Survey, 2015-16.

Another interesting observation revealed from the analysis is that grand technical efficiency scores are low for both categories of ponds comparative to group technical efficiency score. Grand TE is calculated on the basis of all observations taken together, whereas group TE disaggregated data according to groups specified. Hence, it can safely be asserted that there is little scope to enhance the efficiency of the farms within the group rather to find out policy prescriptions outside the groups. Constraints behind low efficiency are not inherent within the diversification strategy as such; rather effort must have to be made to craft such diversification much more worthwhile for the poor aquaculture farmers in Sundarban region.

In order to find out regional variations in such kind of efficiency, if any, average technical efficiency score has been computed for each sub-division and depicted in Table 6.5. Table 6.5 also incorporates measures of area efficiency which broadly reflects the impact of the social, economic and cultural factors in a particular area on the technical efficiency of a branch. While achievement of high overall efficiency becomes a target for whole Sundarban, the issues relating to area efficiency call for actions at particular sub-division. The result, in this case, appeared ambiguous. In case of Kadwip and Canning (South 24-Parganas is the representative district), the results are the same as derived earlier. That is, intensification of carp culture through introduction of SIFS has increased technical efficiency of the farms. But, the

Table 6.5: Mean Technical Efficiency of Different Culture Strategy for Different Region

Regions	Criterion	*Class culturing Carp*	
		With SIFS	*Without SIFS*
Kakdwip (South 24-Parganas)	% of farms	35.0	65.0
	Grand TE	0.657	0.632
	Group TE	0.752	0.734
	CV (in %)	35.25	56.23
Canning (South 24-Parganas)	% of farms	46.7	53.3
	Grand TE	0.705	0.711
	Group TE	0.797	0.736
	CV (in %)	154.20	44.0
Basirhat (Noth 24-Parganas)	% of farms	48.3	51.7
	Grand TE	0.577	0.631
	Group TE	0.713	0.767
	CV (in %)	81.36	24.35
Overall	**% of farms**	**43.3**	**56.7**
	Grand TE	**0.651**	**0.642**
	Group TE	**0.742**	**0.734**

* CV indicates coefficient of variation in individual technical efficiency score within the respective group.

Source: Data Envelopment Analysis (DEA), results of data received through field survey, 2015-16.

"traditional" farmers, producing only carps, in Basirhat (representative district is North 24-Parganas) is found more technically efficient than "progressive" farmers.

Also, judging by coefficient of variation (CV) in the group efficiency levels, progressive farmers of Canning had much higher degree of variation (more than 154%) than other. Highest mean along with highest variability in the levels of efficiency, the progressive fishers in Canning did not necessarily appear to have performed in superior fashion. It may be, few of the progressive farmers had outperformed in this region, which uplift their group technical efficiency. On the other side, traditional farmers in the district of Basirhat had the mean group technical efficiency level 0.767 with variability of only 24 per cent. Highest mean along with lowest variability in the levels of efficiency, the traditional fishers in Basirhat appear to have performed in superior fashion.

Table 6.6: Regression Results Explaining (Grand) Technical Efficiency Score using Diversification Dummies

Independent Variables	*Regression coefficient*
Diversification dummies	0.212* (–1.015)
Constant	122.08
R^2	0.472
F	12.990*

Note: Figures in the parentheses are *t* values.
* indicates one per cent level of significance.
Source: Regression results on technical efficiency scores of Data Envelopment Analysis (DEA).

Clearly, the relationship between diversification of aquaculture through SIFS and technical efficiency has been found to be more complex than what is normally believed. Rather than a direct and positive relationship, where productivity increases along with diversification, mixed relationship had been found. Hence, in order to find out the effect of diversification on the technical efficiency score, regression analysis has been adopted.

The dependent variable is the measured level of (grand) technical efficiency of an individual farm. Diversification as dummies has then been regressed on the technical efficiency score. Those who adopted local species along with carp (thus diversified their culture) have been given the value of 1, while other has been valued as 0. The relationship between diversification and technical efficiency appeared as positive and significant. The result is depicted in Table 6.5. The model is significant because of high F value. The high value of R^2 shows that the independent variables together account for 47 per cent variations in the technical efficiency score. The regression coefficient for diversification through SIFS is 0.212 and it is positive and statistically significant at one per cent probability level. The inference is that the (grand) technical efficiency score increases by 11.41 per cent when there is one per cent increase in SIFS in carp polyculture.

Overall, an ambiguous relationship between technical efficiency and diversification strategy through SIFS has been found. While, Meta frontier DEA model, used in this study are drawing no concrete conclusion, regression results are suggesting for introduction of SIFS in polyculture system to enhance productivity and efficiency. More sophisticated economic models may suggest a different set of explanatory variables which may in turn give different results. Also, influence of some other dummies in the regression model may reveal clear picture. Nevertheless, the theoretical and empirical results in the paper show that ambiguity is always a part of the efficiency-diversification puzzle.

6.5 Determinants of Technical Efficiency Diversified

Aquaculture – Multiple Regression Results

It is evident from the discussion so far that there are significant differences across groups when farms are classified by any single criterion (Diversification category or region) without controlling the other factors. But exclusive focus on a single criterion may hide the consequences of variations in any other characteristics. For an example, it is not obvious from Table 6.5 that the superior performance of fish farms from Canning Sub-division in Sundarban is due to their location only. The partial effect of differences in anyone category can be accurately measured only within a multiple regression model incorporating all the relevant explanatory variables. Hence, in this section, the influence of socio-economic and farm characteristics are examined by regressing them on the (grand) technical efficiency score of progressive farmers practicing carp culture along with SIFS.

The dependent variable is the measured level of (grand) technical efficiency of an individual fish farm under progressive farm category. The dummy variables 'Kakdwip' (KDP), 'Basirhat' (BSR) are the locational dummies. The category 'Canning' (CNG) is treated as the reference group. In the tenure classification, owned (OWN) is the dummy variable for aquaculture in owned ponds whereas leased (LEASED) in ponds are reference category. In the organization type category, the dummy variables identify farms as individual proprietorship (PROP 1) and more than two partners (PROP 2). Farms of proprietorship of more than two partners (PROP MORE) constitute the reference group. Apart from various categorical variables, size of ponds, age, education and experience of the farmers are also included as regressors. Size is measured by the nominal value of acre. Age is measured in years. Experience of the farmers is measured in number of years in fish farming and number of years in school is the measure for education level of the farmers. The (grand) technical efficiency scores of progressive farms generated from meta-frontier DEA model are regressed on the above mentioned variables as follows –

$$TE_i = \alpha_0 + \alpha_1(CSZ) + \alpha_2(OAR) + \alpha_3(RLZ) + \alpha_4(OWNED) + \alpha_5(PROP\ 1) + \alpha_6(PROP\ 2) + \alpha_7(SIZE) + \alpha_8(EDU) + \alpha_9(EXP) + \alpha_{10}(AGE) + e_i$$

where, α_0 is constant and is the $\mathbf{e}_i$ error term.

Table 6.7: Description of Variables used in Multiple Regression Analysis

Type of Independent Variables	*Operational Definition*
Location Dummies	Canning = 0, Kakdwip = 1, Basirhat = 2
Tenure Dummy	Leased = 0, Owned = 1
Proprietorship Dummies	More than 2 partners = 0, Individual = 1, Two partners = 2
Pond Size	Area of pond (Acre)
Education	Number of years in schooling
Experience of Farmers	Number of years in fish farming
Age of farmers	Number of years

Source: Author's calculation.

Regression estimates for different locational and farm-specific variables are given in Table 6.5. Out of nine variables estimated, 3, have appeared significant at 5 per cent (or lower) levels and 2 are at 1 per cent level. However, further insights beyond what is obtained from meta-frontier analysis can be gained from a careful perusal of the regressions reported in Table 6.5. For an example, let consider the case of Basirhat (BSR). In Table 6.5, it has the lowest average level of (grand) technical efficiency exceeding the corresponding measure for overall by 0.074. In the regression analysis reported in Table 6.8, the coefficient BSR dummy variable is highest between locational dummies and corresponding value becomes 0.3966. Moreover, it is statistically significant at one per cent level of probability and standard error value is as low as 0.00026. By contrast, for the same year, average grand TE value for Kakdwip (KDP) is higher than average grand TE score, but the

Table 6.8: Regression Results Explaining (Grand) Technical Efficiency Scores of Progressive Farms using Different Variables

Independent Variables	*Estimated Coefficient*	*Standard Error*
KDP	0.045	0.00342
BSR	0.396***	0.00065
OWNED	0.183**	0.00022
PROP 1	0.117***	0.01630
PROP 2	– 0.033**	0.00300
SIZE (106)	0.003*	0.00016
EDU (102)	0.017	0.00007
EXP (102)	0.087*	0.00453
AGE (102)	– 0.049**	0.02458
Constant	0.238***	0.04783
R^2 (in %)	26.24	
Adjusted R^2 (in %)	24.46	
F-test	54.24**	

Note: *, ** and *** indicates significant at 10, 5 and 1 per cent level respectively in atwo-tailed test.

Source: Regression results on technical efficeicny scores of Data Envelopments Analysis (DEA).

estimated coefficient of the RLZ dummy variable in Table 6.5 is only 0.045, and not statistically significant. This shows that controlling for other factors sometimes (though not always) could portray a different picture about technological differences across region.

The owned farmers has positive and significant coefficient (0.183), indicating that technical efficiency is high on owned operated farms. In other words, leased in farms are less efficient than owned farms. The result is in confrontation with some other studies (Kumar, *et al.*, 2004). Actually, most of the tenure arrangement under progressive farming in our study area is oral and bipartite matter mainly on short-term duration. Eviction of lessees is quite frequent. Absence of long term leasing policy is a genuine hindrance. The uncertainty attached with short duration normally dampens the fish farmer's motivation and not congenial for aquaculture diversification.

Effect of extent of proprietorship on technical efficiency has shown an interesting result. Culture operation by single proprietorship has significantly influenced technical efficiency in the study. Corresponding coefficient is 0.117 and it is significant at one per cent level of probability. However, in case of joint operation, influence became significantly negative (–0.033). Hence, it is safe to assert that technical efficiency has a negative relationship with number of ownership, that is, multiple ownership are affecting efficiency of aquaculture diversification adversely in our study area. It is obvious, because multiple ownerships put constraints on fish culture as the partners use face problems to receive the final conclusion. Taking unique decision regarding crucial investment plan is also a problem for multiple ownership.

Experience in diversified aquaculture farming has a positive influence in technical efficiency and it is significant at 10 per cent probability level. But estimated coefficient for education is 0.017 and it is not even statistically significant. Striking is that age has a negative influence on technical efficiency and it is statistically significant, indicating that old farmers are congenial for higher productivity. The result has crucial implication on the human resource development strategy. No doubt, formal education is always important for any kind of job to be adopted in future, helping in better management decisions, placing the farmers in an advantageous position to acquire information and other extension services in a cost effective manner. But this is not sufficient to ensure a success in diversified farming. Endogenous knowledge acquired through experience in carp farming helps the farmers a lot to enhance their productivity. But it should also be taken into consideration that mere spending days in farming could not enhance endogenous knowledge (as age has a negative impact). The result is in, some points, contradiction with the well documented role of human in improving the efficiency in aquaculture (Dey, *et al.*, 2004; Kumar, *et al.*, 2004). Human Capital should be developed by appropriate and comprehensive extension and research strategies.

The association between farm size and technical efficiency in diversified aquaculture farming is positive and significant, but association is found week as estimated coefficient is only 0.003 and it has also no adequate statistical significance. The result implies that large farms are more efficient, but the fact is not always true. Actually, majority of the fish farms in Sundarban Island are small and often lack capital to invest for enhancing yield. They need policy support in term of credit, technical knowledge and extension. But at certain stage, large differences in (grand) technical efficiency across farms as well as regions call for exchange of expertise and experience to improve and strengthen the diversified aquaculture activity.

Overall, superior performance of owned fish farms rather than leased in farms suggests that owner operation should be encouraged as a preferred organizational form of aquaculture diversification through introduction of SIFS. Also, consolidation of smaller farms into larger entities would enhance efficiency to certain extent, but not always. Our measures of technical efficiency suggest considerable room for increasing output without requiring any additional inputs. Hence, even without an increase in allocative efficiency through appropriately changing the input mix, average cost of production in the progressive farming could be lowered significantly – often by 30 per cent or more. This would greatly help the competitive position of diversified aquaculture farming in downtrodden areas of Sundarban.

7
Adoption of Aquaculture Diversification Practices

For the things we have to learn before we can do them, we learn by doing them. — *Aristotle*

7.1 Adopting New Technology in Aquaculture

Wide variation in technical efficiency scores and low level of production, revealed in previous chapter, clearly brings us to the fore that improved fish culture technologies has not been adopted by sample farmers uniformly. No doubt, in recent years, Government of West Bengal has been extending several facilities for expansion of culture fisheries and diversification of aquaculture, such as fish seed supply at cheaper rate, training programme for farmers, subsidy for renovation of tanks as also some welfare measures like Group Personal Accident Insurance, saving-*cum*-relief scheme, social fishery, river ranching etc. Along with these, institutions like FFDA, CIFRI, CIFA have been established to help the fish farmers with necessary financial, technological and extension support in order to increase fish production in tanks and ponds by composite fish culture practices. The focus is basically on creating a demonstration effect through individuals where success of one fish farmer could motivate others to take up fish farming. Despite all these facts, low productivity of fish clearly leads us to conclude that technologies developed in government laboratories and training services provided by extension personnel were either not producing the desired result or not being adopted by the farmers. In any case, these two facts are mutually correlated. Because, rejection of a particular technology, after being practiced would help the extension personnel to understand the basic difficulties with the existing technologies and thereby modify technology for farmer's interest. Hence, the question of why farmers adopt production technologies is elementary and apparent; new production technologies are adopted when the techniques are perceived as being in farmers' best interests. Almost everyone, farmers included, would agree with this basic premise. Yet disagreements arise when asking the more interesting and challenging question of why farmers are not adopting new techniques to diversify aquaculture, such as introduction of SIFS in carp polyculture. While disagreements exist, it is the answer to this latter question from which strategies must be built to help farmers make decisions that are economically, agronomically, and environmentally sound. Consequently, answers to the question of why farmers do not adopt must serve as the basis for increasing adoption through modification of the current package. Efforts to increase the rate of adoption of new technologies in fish farming must be based on understanding why farmers reject new production techniques.

Figure 7.1 demonstrates the basic factors involved in the Farmers decision-making process towards adoption of new technology. Usually, fishers do not adopt production technologies for two basic reasons: they are either unable or unwilling. These reasons are not mutually exclusive. Farmers can be able yet unwilling; willing but unable, and, of course, both unwilling and unable. These may sound like minor semantical distinctions, but the difference between a farmer being unwilling or unable is crucial when designing the appropriate remedial (Cramb, 2003). It is generally assumed that farmers make adoption decision based upon their utility consideration (Batz, *et al.*, 1999). While a technology is introduced in a given area, the decision whether to adopt, continue and intensify it or not will depend, among other things, on how a technology meets household objective of food and income security. Hence, socio-economic background of the farmers also highly influences the rate of adoption of modern culture practices.

There is another interesting observation regarding technology adoption by the fish farmers. Fish farming, it has been found, had

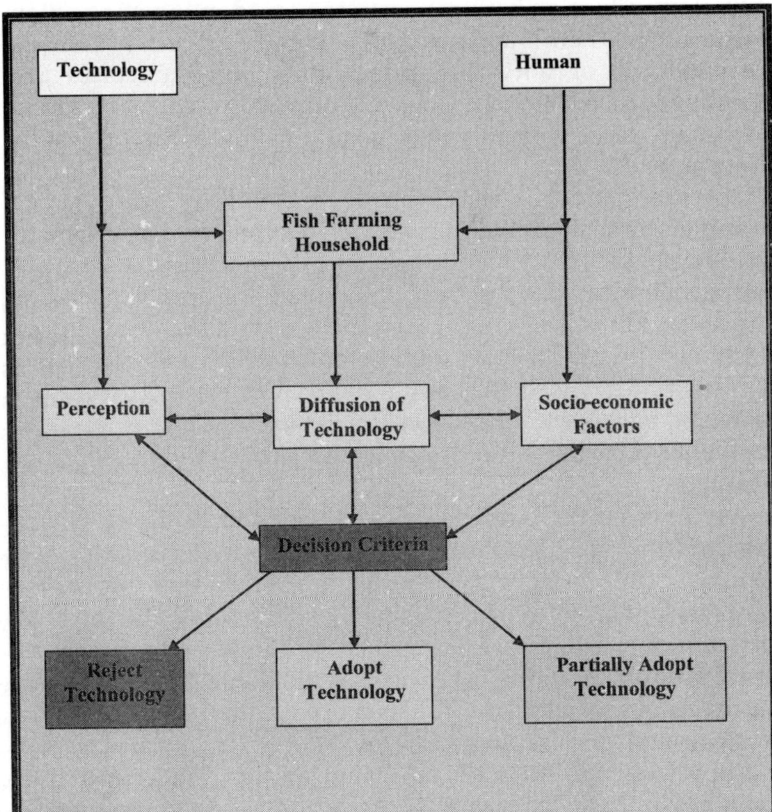

Fig. 7.1: Framework for Farmers' Decision Regarding Adoption of New Technology.

Source: Author's construction from ideas provided by World Fish Centre.

not generated positive effects on the majority farmers' well-being because most of the farmers have been selective; adopting only part of the recommended package of the technology (FAO, 1989). This is contrary to the perception of some researchers who perceive technology adoption as the exact coping or imitation of how the innovation had been used previously in a different setting (Rogers, 1995). In reality, choices available to a potential adopter are not just adoption or rejection; selection or rejection of some components of the innovation or modification and re-invention of the innovation may also be options. Many researchers on technology adoption have concentrated on adoption or rejection of technology. There is apparent lack of knowledge on why farmers are selective or why they adopt only some parts of the recommended technology. Consequently, only some parts of the technology have been adopted leading to discouraging results (Wetengere, 2010).

Farmers' decision-making on technology adoption is prompted by such problems or challenges confronted by them in their business from time-to-time. In this process, the farmers' sources of information fundamentally shape the kinds of decisions they make. Sources of information and acquired knowledge from those sources constitute the foundation on which many decisions of farmers are based (Agbamu, 2006). It is expected that the perceived benefits of adaptation of fish farming technologies can be attained if the farmers did not encounter constraints in decision-making.

Apart from the characteristics of the technology which are already known to affect farmer's decision to adopt, it is suspected that the socio-economic characteristics of the farmer play major roles in adoption of decision-making. Ofuoku, *et al.* (2005) observed that the farmer's decision for or against the adoption of any science-based production technology was described as a mental process, consisting of several stages. The level of education, farm size, farm income, and extension contact all are involved in this process and thereby interrelated with adoption of the fish production technologies. Whether farmers are tradition-bound or progressive depends closely on their socio-economic background.

The objective of this section, therefore, is to determine the level of adoption of diversified aquaculture technologies and identify the variables which determine the adoption of a recommended package of fish farming technology.

7.2 Adoption Level of Aquaculture Diversification Practices

There is no doubt that the fish production has been a traditional enterprise in our study area. In the past it was practiced thoroughly with traditional methods. But during the last few years, precisely after launching of FFDA (Fish Farmers' Development Authority) programmes, certain steps were taken by the fish farmers to adopt modern culture practices. It is of interest now to examine the response of operators to the package of diversified culture practices over time and then to identify the factors that determine the adoption behaviour. In this study, we define adopter-operators as those operators (or fish farmers) who adopt the practices like pre-stocking, stocking, input applications like lime, toxicants, manures, fertilizers, application of supplementary fish feeds, harvesting etc. for their culture of carp with or without SIFS.

Table 7.1: Distribution of Fish Farmers Adopting Modern Culture Practices

Adoption Intensity	*Frequency*		
	Traditional (N=102)	*Progressive (N=780*	*All (N=180)*
Full Adoption	17 (16.7)	29 (37.2)	46 (25.6)
Partial Adoption	56 (54.9)	36 (46.2)	92 (51.1)
No adoption	29 (28.4)	13 (16.6)	42 (23.3)
Adoption Score	**0.37**	**0.53**	**0.44**

Note: Figures in parentheses indicate percentage of respective totals.
Source: Field Survey, 2015-16.

The computation revealed that almost 23.3 per cent of total farmers had not adopted any modern culture techniques to improve farm productivity. More than 25 per cent of total sample went for full adoption, but partial adoption of modern culture practices was quite high (more than 51%) among the farmers. Almost 29 per cent of the traditional farmers had not adopted any scientific culture practice. Adoption of full package of practices is considerably higher in case of progressive farmers (37.2%) as compared to traditional farmers (16.7%). There is high degree of partial implementation of package for both traditional and progressive farmers (54.9% and 46.2%). The adoption rate had increased positively with the diversification practices. The results imply that the adoption level was low generally since a total of 74.4 per cent of the respondents fell under the low adoption category. This is confirmed by the adoption score and index that are likewise low. The adoption levels which formed the dependent variable were determined by computing the number of the stages (like pre-stocking, de-weeding, pond preparation, supplementary feeding etc.) adopted by the fish farmers in the study area. The adoption score was arrived at, by dividing the overall mean adoption score by the number of adoption stages. As such, adoption rate had been found highest among progressive farmers (0.53%), followed by traditional farmers (0.37%). This is attributed to the traditional training and visit system where farmers do not participate in technology development and farmers are not easily reached by Extension Agents. The low adoption of diversification is an index of the poor extension approach to agricultural development. One important observation in this regard is that most of the fish farmers, even though they tend to adopt, did not use the inputs in accordance with proportions and schedules recommended by the technical experts. They normally chose only those combinations of inputs that suited their resource position best.

Adoption level of improved aquaculture practices had been found to depend on two major aspects of institutional effort – training and government assistance in form of subsidized credit, supply of seeds etc. As such, operators have been divided into four different categories, as follows—

Category A : Adopters who received government assistance and trained.

Category B : Adopters who are trained but not received government assistance.

Category C : Adopters who are not trained but received government assistance.

Category D : Adopters who are neither trained nor received assistance.

Table 7.2 provides an overview of the trend with regard to adoption of practices in the districts by size classes of operators, trained and untrained and receiving and not receiving assistance of any kind from different sources. The percentage of operators of the water units of different category who received training and assistance and adopting the package of practices are found to be 10.6 per cent in 2015-16, indicating thereby that the pace of adoption was highly unsatisfactory. As against this, more than 59 per cent of the operators who are untrained and did not receive

Table 7.2: Distribution of Different Types of Operators by Pond Category

Category of Operators	*Distribution of Sample Farmers*			
	Category A	*Category B*	*Category C*	*Category D*
Traditional	09 (08.8)	25 (24.5)	02 (01.9)	66 (64.7)
Progressive	11 (14.1)	26 (33.3)	00 (00.0)	41 (52.6)
Overall	**19 (10.6)**	**51 (28.3)**	**02 (01.1)**	**107 (59.4)**

Note: Figures in parentheses indicate percentage of total number of farms in the respective group.

Source: Field Survey, 2015-16.

any government assistance have so far used package of practices in 2015-16. Again, it is important to note that percentages of trained farmers who have received assistance from government had been found higher among the progressive farmers (14.1%) who were culturing carp with SIFS. Percentage of recipient of only training from extension personnel was considerably higher (28.3%) than that of recipient of only government assistance (just one per cent). This had clearly indicated that without training from institutional sources, it was almost impossible to dig up governmental assistance. Progressive farmers could able to grasp highest share of financial or other assistance compared to traditional farmers, which leads to conclude that diversification of aquaculture is catching the attention of more assistance from institutional sources. Another interesting observation is that almost all the farmers who are both trained and recipient of government assistance had adopted improved fish culture technologies completely. Similarly, all the farmers, who had not adopted culture practices at all, were neither trained nor received any government assistance. Clearly, therefore, the package of practices appealed to those fish farmers who are trained and reasonably backed by financial assistance by way of loan/grant with or without any provision of subsidy. Also, training alone by itself may not necessarily stimulate all the fish farmers, particularly small and medium sized farmers to go in for modern culture practices. Other complementary factors like financial assistance may act as a positive factor. It has also been observed that the fish farmers, particularly the farmers practicing diversified aquaculture, adopt the modern culture practices through receiving the information/ knowledge from the other fish farmers. In our study area, even the traditional farmers are found to become enthusiastic to internalize the externalities of efficient production system taking place elsewhere in other water units.

7.3 Adoption-wise Variation in Technical Efficiency

In order to investigate the effect of adoption intensity upon technical efficiency of fish farms, data envelopment analysis has been followed as earlier. Using meta-frontier methodology, grand and group (according to intensity of adoption) technical efficiency has been calculated and presented in Table 7.3. Taking ratio of the geometric means of group and grand frontier, adoption efficiency has been calculated. From Table 7.3, it has been revealed that, in general, average TE scores are higher among intensive systems for both traditional and progressive farmers. But technical efficiency scores of both group and grand frontiers constructed for progressive farms are considerably higher than that for traditional farms. From the result it can safely be asserted that degree of efficiency of aquaculture practices is directly proportional to intensity of culture if such practices are diversified with introduction of SIFS. In case of diversified practices, farmers' have appeared almost 89 per cent efficient towards optimal allocation of resources. The trend of results has appeared almost similar when TE was measured based on grand frontier. Clearly, technical efficiency increased directly with the increase in adoption intensity, so also the adoption efficiency. There are considerable differences in adoption efficiency among the different category of farmers. Adoption efficiency was highest (0.834) for intensive farmers of progressive category of ponds, whereas the respective figure was as low as 0.564 for semi-intensive farmers under traditional category. Frequency distribution of mean technical efficiency scores for both groups and grand frontier is shown in Figure 6.2. The distribution has been found similar to the TE distributions that were found and reported in previous studies on TE of aquaculture (e.g., Sharma & Leung, 1998, 2000a, 2000b; Sharma, 1999; Dey *et al.*, 2000). Noteworthy is that, taking into consideration the different methods and the set of variables, the TE estimates reported by Sharma & Leung (2000b) for India are in accordance with the estimates reported in this study.

Based on group frontier, the average TE scores of semi-intensive and intensive farms under progressive category are 0.769 and 0.527 respectively, which clearly has an important implications. First, if aquaculture practices are diversified and not intensively practiced by following proper adoption regulations, farmer's efficiency may decrease measurably and second, if it not possible to follow proper adoption rule, it is better to undergo traditional aquaculture practices by not incorporating species other than carp (since, TE score of traditional farms in no-adoption category is higher than progressive farms).

These results have important implications for the development of appropriate and comprehensive extension and research strategies for successful aquaculture diversification. Such strategies would assist operators (especially those who are less educated, younger, and new to farming of diversified aquaculture practices, and are thus technically inefficient) increase human capital by accessing the information needed to increase technical efficiency, to adopt modern diversified aquaculture technologies, and to increase freshwater aquaculture productivity. It is widely stated that the fish farming involves the use of certain "cultural practices" to obtain the maximum yield. No doubt, intensive composite fish culture involves a high degree of skill. But it is observed that fish culture is practised in a very neglected and arbitrary manner; as a result of which, technical efficiency had been found measurably low. Only a small percentage of the adopter-operators in our sample have been found to follow strictly the uses of inputs in accordance with the schedules and doses. In the sample studied, only 11 per cent of the adopter-operators followed preparatory operations like de-weeding, desilting and eradication of predators and weed fishes. Only 7 per cent cultivators used toxicants; 61 per cent of the water had weeds and only 5 per cent of the water units were renovated. The species-mix in seed and the stocking rate – the two major determinants of yield—were not strictly followed. The operators liberated different species of carps without maintaining right proportions. They could not procure quality fish seed. It was also reported that the average survival from spawn to fry stage for SIFS is about 30 per cent which is very low. Netting and soil testing were seldom done. It is also to be noted that use of fertilizers and supplementary feed, which indicates the inability of the users to bear higher cash expenses for cultivation and their ability to bear risk, was not made properly.

Table 7.3: Mean Technical Efficiency of Fish Farms Across Adoption Intensity

Pond Category	*No. of Fish Farms*	*Mean Technical Efficiency*		*Adoption Efficiency*
		Based on Grand Frontier	*Based on Group Frontier*	
Traditional Farms				
Intensive	17 (16.7)	0.731	0.761	0.798
Semi-intensive	56 (54.9)	0.604	0.537	0.564
No Adoption	29 (28.4)	0.572	0.611	0.571
Progressive Farms				
Intensive	29 (37.2)	0.854	0.879	0.834
Semi-intensive	36 (46.2)	0.781	0.769	0.811
No Adoption	13 (16.6)	0.711	0.527	0.632
Overall				
Intensive	46 (25.6)	0.809	0.835	0.806
Semi-intensive	92 (51.1)	0.673	0.628	0.679
No Adoption	42 (23.3)	0.615	0.576	0.623

Source: Data Envelopment Analysis (DEA) results of data received through field survey, 2015-16.

Only 10 per cent of the adopter-operators were found to follow the suggestions made in this regard. Manures for maintaining healthy atmosphere in tank were seldom given. Organic manures were used by about 70 per cent of the operators (the most common being cow dung). Unfortunately, it is also observed that about 95 per cent of the fish farmers in our sample fed their fish irregularly.

The most commonly reported fish feed were rice-bran, leftover cooked rice or fresh cow dung, etc. All these findings lend credence to the fact that the level of technology adoption is inadequate, and the input-mix is sub-optimal.

7.4 Determinants of Adoption Practices

Socio-economic characteristics (like age, experiences or education) of the fish farmers sometimes determine the adoption of improved fish production technologies. Pond size (as proxy of farm size) or extension contacts also affect the level of adoption intensity of fishers. In order to investigate the effects of such variables, multiple regression analytical tool using the ordinary least squares (OLS) method was applied. The linear function was used as the lead equation because its equation indicated goodness-of-fit considering the quality of its coefficient, R-squared adjusted R-squared, and F-ratio. The adoption levels which formed the dependent variable were determined by computing the number of the technologies adopted by the fish farmers in the study area. The adoption index was arrived at, by dividing the overall mean adoption score by the number of adoption stages. The multiple regression model is implicitly specified as follows:

$$Y = f(X_1; X_2; X_3; X_4; X_5; e)$$

Or, $$TE_i = \alpha_0 + \alpha_1 X_1 + \alpha_2 X_2 + \alpha_3 X_3 + \alpha_4 X_4 + \alpha_5 X_5 + \alpha_6 X_6 + e_i$$

where, α_0 is constant and is the e_i error term.

Y = Level of adoption of improved fish farming technologies (number of technologies adopted).

X_1 = Age of farmers (years)

X_2 = Level of education (years spend in school)

X_3 = Experience of fish farmers (years in Carp Culture)

X_4 = Pond size (population of fish)

X_5 = Financial assistance (Rs.)

X_6 = Extension Contact (number of visits by extension agents)

e_i = Error term of *i*th farm

The level of significance used was 0.05.

The parameters of the estimated linear regression model, shown in Table 7.4, has revealed that the age of the fish farmers (X_1) had a negative correlation with adoption at 0.05 levels of significance. This implied that the older farmers are unwilling to accept improved technologies, because they are afraid of risks involved with new technologies. It has implication for the present extension approach of training and visit as the farmers do not make input in the required technology. The change of approach to a client-driven one will erase the fear-psychosis inherent in the older generation. Young entrepreneurs will readily accept any technology they contribute to its development.

In developing countries like India, a general characteristic of farmers is that they are tradition bound. They are understandably afraid of costly risk and will not take them until they are convinced that the new methods are safe, will pay-off and will not violate their values. As mentioned earlier that there was the contention that most farmers are tradition bound because of their low level of education. In situations like this where farmers are tradition bound, a lot has to be done by the extension agent to erase some of these superstitious beliefs. This calls for the application of the Farmer-Group Approach. This will make agricultural extension service more client-driven thus reducing the risk of introducing an innovation that is at variance with the tradition of the farmers. Perhaps this is the reason, coefficient for experience (X_4) in regression coefficient has not been found significant.

The level of formal education (X_2) was, on the other hand, negatively correlated with the adoption of improved fish farming

Table 7.4: Linear Regression Model Estimates of the Determinants of Adoption

Variables	*Index*	*Coefficients*	*Standard Error*	*t-Value*
Age (10^2)	X_1	–1.36	0.0043	–2.28*
Education (10^2)	X_2	4.543	0.0230	2.537*
Experience (10^2)	X_3	0.427	0.0627	1.308
Pond Size (10^6)	X_4	0.247	0.060	0.113
Financial Assistance	X_5	4.254	0.070	4.612*
Extension Contact	X_6	9.126	0.0006	3.52*
Constant	—	0.918	0.413	2.989*

Note: $R^2 = 0.931$; F = 93.169; * significance at 5 per cent level.

Source: Regression results on technical efficiency scores of Data Envelopment Analysis (DEA).

technology at 0.05 levels of significance. The implication is that educated farmers readily adopt improved fish production technologies. This is in consonance with Kumar *et al.* (2004), Dey *et al.* (2005) who noted that technological change is achieved through formal education. Formal education enables farmers to obtain useful information from bulletins, agricultural newsletters, radios and other sources. The formal education usually aid farmers and lead them to accept new farm technologies more readily to enhance their income than those farmers without formal education.

Pond size (X_4) revealed a positive correlation with adoption, but it is not significant at five per cent level. t-value was also not strong (0.113). Result has revealed that fish farmers with large farms more readily adopt improved technologies than farmers with small pond sizes, though not always true. This is where economics of scale in aquacultural production comes in to play.

Financial assistance (X_5) has also revealed a positive correlation with adoption of fish farming technologies. Finance and adoption of innovation go hand in hand. This is the reason why even when new technologies are costly to adopt because it requires large amount of money initially, the poor farmers could not able to adopt them. The fish farmers who adopted most of the improved technologies were the rich farmers and this was observed in the study area also.

Extension contact (X_6) is positively correlated with the adoption of fish farming technologies. This was because the more extension agents visited the fish farmers and educated them on the more recent technologies the better they understand and adopted them. This observation was in agreement with Misra (2011) who reported that the frequency of extension contact influences, the adoption behaviours of farmers. Such frequent contact is nurtured by a change to the farmer field school approach of extension delivery, as the participation of the farmers in the technology development, based on adult learning principles and experimental learning motivates them. This has facilitated farmer demand for knowledge, and offered opportunity for the farmers to choose, test and adapt technologies according to their needs.

Overall, the study revealed that the level of education, farm size, farm income, and extension contact were positively correlated with adoption of the fish production technologies, while age was negatively correlated with regard to fish production technologies.

There is the need to jettison the present training and visit system for farmer-group and farmer field school approach which suits the present day dispensation. As extension has been found significant effect on adoption, more fisheries extension agents should be employed by FFDAs. Efforts should also be made to facilitate interest-free loans (as financial assistance has been found positive correlation with adoption) so that they will be able to expand and by eventually be able to adopt costly innovation. Extension agents should increase the frequency of their visit to fish farmers. Adult education programmes should be organized for the fish farmers who are not literate.

7.5 Constraints Behind Unsatisfactory Adoption

As to why fish farmers are tardy in adopting package of practices becomes clear from the information given in Table 7.5. Perhaps the most important reason for non-adoption is the financial difficulties. A sizeable percentage of traditional operators (more than 76%) have reported this problem. Such problem is more acute for progressive farmers (almost 82% of the farmers have reported problem of financial difficulties). Both types of operators are also facing problems regarding multiple ownerships and percentages of occurrence of such problem were 30.4 and 37.2 respectively for traditional or progressive farming. Risk factor and failure to provide extension services to afford information also account for the non-adoption. About 80 per cent of the operators, on an average, consider risk factor as a deterrent for adoption. The lack of availability of quality fish seed was not that much sensitive for traditional farming; but accessibility of spawn of small indigenous

Table 7.5: Reasons for Non-adoption of Diversified Aquaculture Practices

Questions regarding Nature of Constraints	*Traditional*		*Progressive*	
	Frequency	*%*	*Frequency*	*%*
Facing financial difficulties	78	76.5	64	82.1
Lack of availability of quality seed	47	46.1	72	92.3
Plurality of ownership	31	30.4	29	37.2
Risk factor acting as fear-psychosis	27	26.5	58	74.4
Lack of Proper Extension Services	83	81.4	62	79.5
High Price Spread	22	21.6	31	39.7

Source: Field Survey, 2015-16.

fish species was really a deterrent factor behind non-adoption of aquaculture diversification. More than 92 per cent of the progressive farmers had reported seed problems in the sample area. To sum up, the data reveal that the major causes for non-adoption of diversified aquaculture practices are unavailability of seed, the perception of risk factor and cost factor (or financial difficulties).

Risk involved in adopting intensive practices is greater in the sense that it increases proportionately along with an increase in the cost of cultivation. Again, why some operators perceive higher risk in adopting modern practices entailing high costs may be that, in terms of yield, their performance falls much below expectations for various reasons. Consequently, while costs mount up, benefits remain low; the apprehensions about risk and loss thus become real.

As regards biological and environmental hazards, it is important to note that though initially unwanted predatory fishes or animals can be removed, they may reappear. This poses serious biological hazards. Another serious problem in regard to algal blooms occurring in the ponds is that it creates 'super-saturation' in oxygen levels during day and oxygen 'depletion' during night. This sometimes leads to mass mortality. The 'fear psychosis' of possible occurrence of fish diseases among fish farmers coupled with the lack of fish hospitals is an impediment.

The operational features of the new technology should be examined against the backdrop of prevailing organizational basis of individual water units and pisci-culture as a whole. The new technology is scale-neutral, no doubt; but two problems arise with the farmers in this context – one, as a proposition involving higher cost per acre and second, as a proposition involving more working capital than usual. In this context, there arises the question of financial support necessary to internalize the external economies. The Government of West Bengal through FFDA schemes, Department of Sundarban Affairs and Sundarban Development Board have made arrangements for giving loans and subsidies and other assistances to adopt modern intensive fish culture and diversification practices. But, the success behind such arrangements was not quite satisfactory. There is wide gap between farmers who want to receive assistance and those who actually received it. Table 7.6 gives the distribution of fish farmers

Table 7.6: Distribution of the Fish Farmers who needed and Received Assistance

Types of Assistance	*Number and Percentages of Farmers*			
	Needed		*Received*	
	Number	*%*	*Number*	*%*
Finance	142	78.89	19	10.56
Technical advice/service	145	80.56	67	37.22
Supply of fish feed and other inputs	119	61.11	36	20.00
Others (marketing facilities)	93	51.67	29	16.11

Source: Field Survey, 2015-16.

for whom assistance is needed by type of assistance. It is found that finance is the most important component of assistance needed by the farmers. More than 78 per cent of the sample farmers need financial assistance. Technical advice and services are also important component of assistance, which about 80.5 per cent of the farmers expressed desire to receive. Another important component of assistance, which the fish farmers desired to obtain, is the regular supply of quantity of inputs and arrangements for different infrastructural facilities. 61.1 per cent of the fish farmers under study need those kinds of facilities. Desire to receive marketing facilities has been expressed by 51.7 per cent of the sample farmers.

But unfortunately, it is revealed from Table 7.6 that only a small proportion of the fish farmers received a considerable assistance of any kind. In the case of finance, most of the fish farmers could not able to manage it (10.56%). Technical advice and marketing facilities leave much to be desired. Input supply at cheaper rate has been received by only 20 per cent of the farmers. 37.2 of the farmers, who want to receive technical advice from extension personnel has been deprived. Only 16.11 per cent of the sample farmers have received marketing facilities. Registered and regulated markets are found to be conspicuous by their absence.

As regards the reasons for the unsatisfactory availability of assistances, it is clear from Table 7.7. For example, that quite a significant proportion of the fish farmers interviewed have adequate knowledge regarding financial assistance programmes (only 6% of the farmers did not know about financial assistance).

Table 7.7: Percentage Distribution of the Fish Farmers – Not Receiving Assistance with Reasons thereof

Reasons	*Financial Assistance*	*Extension Services*	*Quality Seed*	*Marketing Facilities*
Did not know	06.24	3.27	06.38	14.74
Know but did not try	14.43	36.72	47.73	67.81
Tried but failed to receive	52.73	07.32	39.19	23.29
Reluctant due to cumbersome procedure	24.96	11.37	24.31	36.18

Source: Field Survey, 2015-16.

But striking was that more than 52 per cent of them failed to receive financial assistance and additional 25 per cent had left the hope to receive it due to cumbersome procedure of loan grant. However, such percentage of not receiving services was significantly low in case of training services provided by extension agents of government. Only 7.32 per cent had tried but failed. However, farmers had appeared reluctant to participate on training programme as evident from sample survey. Almost 37 per cent did not try to receive government training though they have knowledge regarding its positive impact on aquaculture productivity. Marketing facilities through appropriate network have not still developed. Again, cumbersome procedure for applying for receiving assistance also acts as a deterrent factor for the purpose of receiving different assistances from the Government agencies.

7.6 Overall Impression Regarding Adoption

Institutional bodies and research institutions have several recommended fish farming technologies for aquaculture diversification, but the adoption levels were generally low. Some of the reasons for non-adoption of the diversified aquaculture farming were given as dearth of the technologies; complexity of the technologies and lack of extension contacts, prompted by the use of contact farmers to reach out to other farmers and technologies tube adopted by farmers dictated by extension agencies. There are a lot that need to be done in the extension system with regard to empowering the farmers educationally.

It should also be mentioned that there is a prospect of ICAR,

CIFRI and FFDAs in facilitating culture of SIFS along with carp among the fish farmers and obviously, it created a positive impact. Their role in training, demonstrating the attractiveness of aquaculture and arrangements of loans and seed are found to be instrumental in motivating fish farmers for adoption and hence, increasing the production of fish. These institutional activities are based on decentralized planning ideas. The merits of those activities are derived partly from its ability to discover the dormant resources and skills and endeavour to activate them. Its operative part is being carried out at a very fairly decentralized level – districts, blocks or a cluster of villages. It is true that it is essential to know the fish farmers, understand their social, economic and cultural disabilities and understand their local settings and institutions under which low productivity is generated and sustained before solutions can be conceived of and set into action. The programme of aquaculture diversification is required to be area or community specific, taking into account the different development potentials as well as constraints of each area or community. It is difficult to *tend a flock of sheep from the camel's back*. It is equally difficult to eliminate low productivity from the elevation of the central plan, however "thorough and earnest". From these points of view, it is expected that FFDAs would be very much effective. However, it has also been observed that it has left much to be desired. To ensure proper planning, adequate supervision, effective implementation and better monitoring, the institutional effort to incorporate SIFS in carp polyculture need to be re-evaluated.

In the first place, it should be stated that this programme, if it is to succeed completely, calls for the real identification of the beneficiaries. It appears from the survey that there exists a great scope for arbitrariness in the selection of beneficiaries. Secondly, the present operational pattern of linking of subsidy with the loan resulted in some unfortunate situation. This has, in fact, resulted in unscrupulous elements taking advantage of the 'subsidy' rather than the real purpose of improving the productivity. Cases of pocketing of subsidy by the bureaucrats, local political leaders and farmers are not infrequent. This needs rigorous monitoring of the schemes at every stage. Some of the alternative suggestions regarding subsidy may be that an amount may be deposited as fixed deposits in the beneficiaries' account and this could be adjusted after the completion of the repayment by the borrowers. Again, the benefits of subsidy should be linked with the timely repayment. An improvement in the close rapport and co-ordination among the government institutions, the banks and the local panchayat officers involved in the system is essential.

Thirdly, the cumbersome loaning procedure is normally followed. This causes delays and difficulties in the sanction of loan. The transaction costs of loans, which include informal costs like frequent transportations costs for visiting block and bank officials are quite high. It may be suggested that fishery banks should be established in each block to advance loan well in advance at reasonable rate of interest. It is also observed that the money so borrowed for fish farming has been diverted to other purpose. In this context, it should be noted that if the bottlenecks in the production process dominate, the credit absorptive capacity may go down and the subsidized credit may very well get diverted to consumption purpose. The same consequences may follow here also if the credit does not cover the total requirements of consumption, working capital etc.

Fourthly, it was also observed that sometimes the flow of credit disbursement are plagued. This is not only due to steadily rising overdue, but also due to, in many cases, faulty loan proposals, laxity in post-credit-follow-up, lack of monitoring of end-use, lending without an integrated programme etc. In sum, it should be mentioned that (i) credit should be adequate and on reasonable terms; (ii) there is a need for closer supervision and follow-up to ensure proper end-use of credit; (iii) real investment should be backed by adequate infrastructural facilities so that potential income can be translated into actual; and (iv) the assets acquired through credit should generate incremental income (i.e. sufficient to pay back the loan along with interest and still leave reasonable surplus).

Fifthly, government programmes which have yielded good results in many respects are target-oriented. Being target oriented and in the race to reach the target, benefits are sometimes literally passed on to the ineligibles. It was also observed that the staffs of the development administration were all obsessed with the idea of target achievement. Sometimes, banks are found reactive, instead of proactive. So, it is important to add that target should be fixed, keeping in view the availability of infrastructure and other facilities for optimal utilization of resources.

It is important to note that there has been a proliferation of organizations dealing with development activities like FFDAs, CIFRI, ICAR, CIFA etc. at the grassroots level. This sometimes creates the problem of co-ordination, because they emerge as parallel ladders, each operating in its own style and jurisdiction. This also has resulted in certain negative consequences. That is, rural poor are made to go from pillar to post to have access to the benefits that policy offers to them; and agencies sometimes operate at cross-purposes neutralizing the development efforts. Political interferences also seep into every kind of activities here.

On top of all these, the structure of Panchayati Raj or the Government by the local elective bodies began to totter under the heavy weight of political factionalism, scrambles for control over patronage among politicians and bureaucrats etc. A lot of tension was observed in the system due to conflicts and confrontations between politicians and bureaucrats. Again, in the context of rural power structure and weak administrative set up, there is a lot of arbitrariness in the different activities. In an atmosphere of scarcity and unequal distribution of local resources, local officials are found to coalesce with rich cultivators. There are a large number of reported instances of bureaucratic malfeasance. Government officials should also learn how to curry favour with the rural elites. It is not only the rural structure but also the behaviour and attitude of the functionaries that determine the performance and outcome of the different programmes like FFDAs. A certain amount of commitment and enthusiasm is required among the officials engaged in the task.

8
Conclusions and Policy Implications

More conclusion we have, less we experience life.

— *Sadguru*

8.1 General Impression of Study

There is no denying the fact that sustainable development can be achieved only when economic growth benefits the poor and unprivileged section of the population. But, unfortunate enough, India's rural economy, accounting for nearly 60 per cent of the country's household consumption, shows a sign of distress in all respect. Poor nutrition is a key outcome of food insecurity. Food insecurity causes poverty, vulnerability and livelihood insecurity, but, at the same time, is also a result of these conditions. Hunger and undernourishment make it extremely difficult for poor people to improve their own livelihoods and make it impossible for them to contribute towards sustainable and broad-based growth. To address widespread poverty, vulnerability and food insecurity, the Government, since independence, has implemented multiple initiatives. A significant policy lesson has been that macro-level food self-sufficiency has been achieved partly by establishing national system for public grain procurement and distribution, as well as an increasing food production. However, this has proved insufficient to ensure micro-level food and nutritional security for the poor. Also, it has found in many research study that the diet in south and south-east Asia, particularly in India, is mainly cereal-based, the principal source of protein is actually rice, which contributes about 8-10 per cent of an individual's average protein intake (Thilsted, 2012). This, along with other foods like pulses and milk products, is not often adequate to meet the total protein requirement of an individual, causing widespread malnutrition and undernourishment in rural India.

Against this background, fish, as an important source of animal protein and its role for coping livelihood threats among the poor, has already been recognized by the economists. But, by concentrating on fish as a source of protein, one really misses the point that it is also an important source of micronutrients and minerals like calcium and zinc, and vitamins. Though protein is essential, it is not a limiting nutrient. Micronutrient deficiency, sometimes termed as "hidden hunger", since it is difficult to see, is a big problem in countries like India (Roos, *et al.*, 2007). In order to meet such hidden hunger, small indigenous fish species (SIFS) constitute a major component of food basket consumed by rural families, especially by those living closer to freshwater resources. This locally available, highly nutritious component adds diversity to the rice-based diet. It is important to get information about intra-household consumption patterns, particularly on who consumes what within the household, with a particular focus on women and children.

Apart from consumption aspects, role of SIFS in aquaculture cannot be ignored from the production point of view also. Though Indian freshwater aquaculture has grown at a rate of 7 per cent per annum during the last decade, the present production is not enough to meet the increasing demand for food fish in the country. Fish accounts for six per cent of India's food budget as 60 per cent of the country's population eats fish. The projected additional demand for 2030 is about 5.41 million tonnes, of which 90 per cent is expected to be met from freshwater sources (World Bank, 2013). But the "Blue Revolution", occurred during last few decades, which initially triggered production of freshwater fish from aquaculture, has been stagnating for years now. Hence, additional demand must be met by diversifying freshwater aquaculture from the present carp-based production management towards introduction of more small indigenous species into small water bodies spread over 2.41 million hectares area-all over the country.

India, particularly, West Bengal is blessed with adequate diversity of small indigenous fish species (SIFS). It is usually believed that integration of those fish species in the form of commercial culture, along with present carp based production system can increase the overall efficiency of aquaculture production in the country, as well as, can provide food and nutritional security to the poor fish farmers. There is no denying the fact that such diversification of aquaculture has been started to experience in West Bengal within the ambit of commercial management practices. The Government has recently taken steps for intensifying aquaculture diversification and considerable investment has already been committed. Extension services have been geared at the village level. Training programmes for the fish farmers regarding new commercially viable SIFS have been introduced. Despite all these efforts and enormous potentials for intensified aquaculture diversification, the production level and productivity are still not adequate to meet the large gap between potential and actual yields of fish. Sometimes recipients of improved technology have been found to follow only a part of adoption strategy as they are generally circumscribed by different socio-economic factors. It is, therefore, important to locate the efforts of aquaculture diversification and its effect on efficiency of overall aquaculture production on more secure foundation of data and methodology.

The area of research, which has been conducted in this study, is basically an attempt to contribute towards policy development in the management of aquaculture diversification by examining the interaction among socio-economic, social-distributional and technological aspects of fish production. Present proposal is a case study of estuarine delta of Indian Sundarban located in West Bengal. Aquaculture is treated as the backbone of Sundarban economy, which is home of almost 172 different species of fishes. Moreover, Sundarban acts as the nursery ground for nearly 90 per cent of the aquatic species of eastern coast of India. Hence, Sundarban has been chosen as sampling area. The results developed in this study are based on 180 fish farmers interviewed through primary survey during 2015-16.

8.2 Major Findings and Policy Options

Policy Elements *Availability of Quality Seed*

Major Findings ❖ Wide gap between demand and supply of fish seeds have been observed in many parts of the states. Farmers compel to buy adulterated seed from local *Aratdars*.

- Availability of private seed hatcheries is relatively low in sample area.
- Generally, 1.5-3.6 cm size fry was available in government hatchery which have low productivity of fish.
- There is lack of seed quality certification mechanisms in Sundarban.

Policy Options

- Private sector should encourage more in seed production in order to match demand and supply.
- Induced breeding technology has an edge over other systems of seed production. The technique involves collection of (pituitary hormone) glands from matured carps. Attempts should be made to build up such pituitary banks (with quality control) necessary for breeding both Indian and exotic carps.
- The temptation on the part of the seed producers to sell fry with its high mortality rates should be avoided. For this, the rearing space should be enhanced.
- Bigger size fingerlings (size ranges from 8-10 cm) should be stocked in the pond as it grows very fast within 6-7 months period. Government owned hatcheries should make available bigger size fingerlings to the farmers.

Policy Elements *Conservation of Small Indigenous Fish Species*

Major Findings

- Although many SIFS are self-generating species, the present reliance on wild fry limits further expansion of carp-SIFS farming and puts pressure on the local environment.
- The availability of SIFS fry has been declining due to destruction of their natural breeding grounds through human encroachment and environmental degradation in Sundarban.
- Knowledge of indigenous fish species is poor among the communities in Sundarban.

- ❖ Management of small indigenous fish is still a virgin area in local institutional bodies and they are more or less ignorant regarding its enormous importance and therefore, dedicated approach to thrash out problems and issues relating to their promotion and conservation is lacking.

Policy Options

- ❖ It is therefore necessary to explore the possibility of developing SIFS hatcheries to reduce wild fry exploitation and increase wild production.
- ❖ More research and extension work on low cost small indigenous species culture, diversification, upscaling of breeding and its role in nutrition and livelihood at different regional scale to be strengthened including its auto stocking possibility to hatchery production.

Policy Element *Pre-stocking of Pond*

Major Findings

- ❖ It is also observed that seasonal tanks dry up during summer months.
- ❖ Farmers use to avoid pre-stocking activities due to ignorance.

Policy Options

- ❖ The tank bed should be thoroughly ploughed and exposed to the sun. This will help remove the marsh grasses from the inner depth of the bed area and increase the fertility of the bottom soil.
- ❖ Desalting should be done in those tanks which do not dry up completely. *Mohua* oil cake should be used to cautiously so that eradication of predatory factors and weed fishes from the perennial tanks do not hamper the growth of SIFS.

Policy Element *Water Management Policies*

Major Findings

- ❖ It has been found in Chapter 5 that water has been used for irrigation of agriculture land, domestic use as well as aquaculture. Water has been predicted to be most scarce commodity in future. There is no clear cut policy of water management.

- Most of the impounded water units (tanks and ponds) do not retain water throughout the year. In the post-winter, depth of water becomes less than the minimum requirement. Farmers are forced to harvest juvenile uneconomic varieties belonging to different size-groups. As a result, they could not fetch a commercially viable market price.

Policy Options

- Encompassment of holistic water management policy defining roles of each stakeholder is the need of the hour.
- The abstraction of water from water bodies for agricultural purposes, especially during summer season should be rationalized. If the source of water is canal irrigation, water should be released at a very nominal rate. Again, since water is also exhausted due to irrigation or seepage problem, measures may be directed towards rain fed farming on watershed basis or by strengthening the existing canal supplies. The run-off water collected into farm ponds should be used for irrigation. Ponds should be independent of monsoon for assured water supply.
- Pond water is utilized for domestic needs. Judicial/sustainable use of manures should be adopted keeping in view the water quality requirement for the society as well for growing fish.

Policy Element *Feeding Arrangement*

Major Findings

- There is no coordinated programme for developing low cost feed for carp culture due to weak R&D back-up.
- Neither the government machinery nor any standard feed manufacturer in the country made any effort to come up with a standard feed package.

- Farmers in the sample area have a tendency to avoid supplementary feeding.

Policy Options

- The production of on farm cost-effective quality fish diets should be promoted.
- Locally feeding practices by experienced farmers should be incorporated.
- The poultry droppings may be used, as is done in some States like Haryana, Andha Pradesh and Karnataka, to act both as feed and fertilizer.
- Use of farm made feeds, feeding methods and feeding strategies need to be promoted for enhancing production. Use of floating feed that has an advantage for non-deteriorating water quality should be encouraged particularly for seasonal ponds.

Policy Element *Leasing Arrangements*

Major Findings

- Leasing arrangements are oral and bipartite matter mainly on short-term duration. There are wide variations in leasing period, conditions of lease, allotment procedures, conditions of renewal. As a result, eviction of lessees is quite frequent. This is not congenial for good production.
- Many leasing guidelines are not development-oriented, rather regulation oriented. As a result, potential ponds are not available for lease.
- Absence of long term leasing policy is a genuine hindrance. The uncertainty attached with short duration normally dampens the fish farmer's motivation. Since there is no guarantee that he would get the same size of pond and under the same conditions as in previous years, the fish farmers are likely to be wary of undertaking investment unless the water units are leased for a long period.
- The financial institutions like banks are sometimes found to be hesitant to lend finance for fish culture if the lease tenure is of short

duration. Banks are not certain of the fish farmer's repayment capacity.

Policy Options
- The pond lease should continue to be considered as collateral for the loans by the banks.
- There should be legal policies to safeguard the interests of the lessees by framing suitable tenancy legislations. There should be long-term comprehensive lease arrangements for a minimum period of 7 years. Long-term lease arrangements not only increase production but also provide a full-time avocation or employment to the unemployed rural youth.
- There should be single window system for leasing.

Policy Element — *Multiple Ownerships*

Major Findings
- Existence of multiple ownerships is predominant in Sundarban. Village ponds are sometimes owned by Panchayat, sometimes endowments of religious temple were the owners, some were owned by fisheries, forests or irrigation departments.
- Lack of coordination and conflicting interests among the pond owners have been observed.

Policy Options
- The State Government as well as Sundarban Development Authority should enact legislations to the effect that pond improvement work can be carried on with the consent of one of several co-owners.
- Some amount of business element should be introduced in the management of multi-owned ponds. If a tank or pond is found, wholly or partly, unutilized for a certain period, the Government may take it over and give it to a cultivator who intends to cultivate it.
- Multi-owners ponds can be better managed by department of fisheries (DoF) portioning rights to Gram Panchayat or Panchayat Samitis.

Policy Element *Adoption of Improved Culture Techniques*

Major Findings

- ❖ Adoption rates of modern diversified culture practices are measurably low. Findings of this study have shown that farmers allocate resources to those activities, which contribute to household food and income security. For that they sometimes adopt only a part of package of practices and end up with measurable result.
- ❖ Adoption depends on various socio-economic and farm-specific variables.
- ❖ Technical efficiency of fish farmers under study is positively related with intensity of adoption of diversified practices.

Policy Options

- ❖ The gap between research and extension efforts of the FFDAs and fish farmers' commitment should be minimized through frequent visit.
- ❖ The farmers should be motivated through success stories of adoption. Successful farmers can also be included in extension network.
- ❖ Appropriate technology, keeping in view the socio-economic, regional, environmental and ecological differences should be developed.
- ❖ To increase adoption intensity, recommended package of technology should be so developed to contribute household food and income security of the fish farmers.

Policy Element *Aquaculture Extension System*

Major Findings

- ❖ Limited extension services are mainly organized under the Fish Farmers Development Agencies (FFDAs), though some private bodies are also involved. Diffusion of technology in some rural areas is limited or absent.
- ❖ Present extension system in Sundarban as well as in West Bengal is based on a package comprising both technology and subsidy. But it has not been taken care of that lab generated technology is not readily applicable and appropriate under varied local conditions.

- Farmers are provided technology along with subsidy; it does mean that targeted fishers are passive receivers of modern culture practices. Also, effects of various socio-economic and farm-specific variables have been ignored by the extension agents.
- Lack of adequate skilled staff mainly due to absence of regular capacity building programmes for staff. Absence of coordination among DoF and other development agencies like financial institutions, NGOs, PRIs has also been observed.

Policy Options

- Conventional extension system is no longer able to address effectively the changed grassroots level reality. These calls for different extension approaches like participatory extension approaches including success stories of technology adoption, indigenous innovation by farmers, community based management systems.
- Diffusion process must always be followed to adjust technology for the farmers' need. Indigenous knowledge should be linked up with lab generated results.
- Farmer training and extension activities are relatively low cost methods of increasing production efficiency.
- Incentive based private agencies can be involved in the process of extension network.

Policy Element *Aquaculture at par with Agriculture*

Major Findings

- So far, in our study area, it has been found that there is no concessional seed transport facilities or on-field subsidization mechanism which can help farmers to get rid of finance constraints in the middle of production period. Kisan Credit Cards has also not been granted to all fish farmers. Fish culture in many village tanks and ponds are still not considered under NREGA.

- As par Supreme Court order, aquaculture has to be treated as industrial activity. But no tax concession has so far been granted to aquaculturists. Present guidelines for institutional credit and insurance are hard to be satisfied an industrial activity.

Policy Options

- Aquaculture should be treated at par with agriculture in terms of credit, water tariff, land allocation owing to the similar nature of the two sectors, resource use pattern and providing food and livelihood to the rural poor.
- Crop insurance scheme should be extended to the fish farmers to guard their losses from disease outbreak or poaching.
- Aquaculture should be treated as a priority sector for the purpose of credit. Since aquaculture is a season sensitive activity, credit should be provided in time. Micro finance institutions can be used for timely disbursement of credit, through co-operative societies.

Policy Element *Data Regarding Pond Aquaculture*

Major Findings

- In course of reviewing existing literature, lack of data has been found prominent in the study area. Though aquaculture is a state activity in West Bengal, no census has so far been done.
- Small indigenous fishes are usually consumed and sold at local level. Perhaps this is one of the reasons why they remain invisible in national statistics. This invisibility in statistics could account for their poor recognition in fisheries and aquaculture development policies.

Policy Options

- Comprehensive census of inland fishermen and fisherwomen, including those involved in diversified aquaculture practices shall be conducted.
- Fish farmers should be mandated to maintain a stocking record with details in order to

maintain an effective database on fish production. Such information could be useful for seeking institutional finance and insurance claims too.

Policy Element — *Transparency and Accountability*

Major Findings

- Inappropriate and ineffective organizational design of department of fisheries with respect to its expected roles and functions has been prominent in the study. Issue of corruption has also emerged in course of providing subsidy.

Policy Options

- There is a need for change of attitude and motivation of the development bureaucrats. It is, of course, rightly pinpointed that the ability to set into motion a process of change would critically depend on the support the planners at the block levels or grassroots level receive from the political leadership at different levels. To what extent such support would be forthcoming is a moot point. In fact this takes us back to the local socio-political power structure. So, the change in production may be brought about through radical management reform and through changes in the culture of development and bureaucracy.

Policy Element — *Sustainability* Versus *Production Maximization*

Major Findings

- It is also observed that the fish farmers, sometimes in the districts under consideration, for some reason or other, liberate fish fries three or four times in a year and harvest also three or four times from a particular pond.
- Most of the fish farmers are in the business of making a living rather than trying to maximize fish production, regardless of the cost. Again, it is worth noting that being poor, the small fish farmers tend to be risk averse. Their predominant goal is economic survival. They really do trade off lower risk against higher profit or the disutility of increasing risk.

Adequate stability of output and income and the avoidance of major short-term losses take precedence over profit maximization. They tend to maximize utility rather than income where utility is the function of the variance of income as well as its average level.

Policy Options

- An organized way of exploitation, transportation and marketing should be evolved so that fishes are harvested at regular intervals and earn optimal revenue by sale of fish throughout the year. Bulk landing of fish at a time should also be discouraged.
- Some sort of insurance for fish crop might pave the way for stimulating adoption of practices.
- Strengthening of the marketing structures including storage facilities, ice plants, cold chains, roads and transportations in identified aquaculture areas would ensure higher profit margins to the producers.
- The provision of low-interest credit would help to reduce the risks for small and marginal farmers. Farmers require credit at low interest rates from the government and nationalised banks. This is particularly the case for extensive farmers so that they can shift from extensive to semi-intensive farming systems.
- Fisheries can be integrated with National Rural Employment Guarantee Scheme (NREGS).

8.3 Some Emerging Policy Issues

Fisheries sector and its activities in Sundarban region show a path of monetized development in recent years. But monetized development does not mean only pumping money into the economy. Some kind of supporting facilities must have to be provided for its optimal absorption. This involves public participation in the measure which is conductive, not only to their own ultimate benefits, but to the smooth implementations of aquaculture development programmes. For this, following emerging policies may also be prescribed.

Managing Sustainability of SIFS Conservation

Knowledge of indigenous fish species is poor among the communities in Sundarban. Actually, management of small indigenous fish is still a virgin area in local institutional bodies and they are more or less ignorant regarding its enormous importance and therefore, dedicated approach to thrash out problems and issues relating to their promotion and conservation is lacking. The following suggestions and strategies may be adopted to conserve and augment the sustainability of indigenous fishes in Sundarban Biosphere Reserve:

- It is essential to ban indiscriminate and destructive fishing practices to protect the young and juvenile fishes in all river system and other water bodies.
- Existing laws and regulations should be enforced properly to protect fish from destructive fishing.
- Conservation and enhancement of existing gene pools of native fish and SIFS in floodplains, natural depressions, rivers and other related water bodies through establishment and maintenance of fish sanctuaries on fishing areas.
- Public awareness of the necessity of conservation of indigenous fish diversity and wise management of habitats needs to be created through mass media. Through creating freshwater aquatic sanctuaries (FAS) within the protected area, public awareness can be expanded.
- Research and policy framework is essential for diversification of potential cultivable indigenous fishes.
- Avoidance of introduction of exotic species unless completely justified and supported by fool proof environment impact assessment.
- *In situ* and *ex situ* conservation practice is need to be developed in various pockets of Sundarban to protect the native fish gene pool.

Improving Conversion Ratio by Transforming Technical Know-how

To understand the production efficiency of fish production, conversion ratio is an important measure. Use of higher potential species of fish would yield higher quantity of fish. In our study, on an average, the conversion ratio was found to be 61.7, indicating that the use of one kg of fish seeds would produce 61.7 kg of matured fish. It has also been observed that, on an average, carp and exotic fish species have comparatively higher conversion ratio than that of indigenous fish species. Upon enquiry, it was also observed that, low conversion ratio of indigenous species is due to low technical know-how regarding how to minimize the mortality of those SIFS. Hence, improved knowledge of species combination and stocking density is needed as well as simple method of estimation of biomass of small indigenous fishes in a pond must be geared. Efficient and cheap technology for frequent netting and partial harvesting of SIFS is also required. The use of traditional fishing gear (*e.g.* scoop net, cast net and fish trap) or sharing of drag net among neighbouring farmers will help to reduce the cost of netting. Farmers should be trained in "gentle handling" and "gentle netting" of SIFS.

Motivating Rural Youth in Diversified Aquaculture Practices

Increasing unemployment problem of undereducated rural youths in Sundarban region compels them to search alternative occupation for their livelihood. Many of them cannot complete their desired education level due to certain unavoidable circumstances and this is also evident from the results developed in Chapter 5. Under such condition they are unable to get permanent job neither in government nor in private sectors. However, some of them in order to generate family income do experimentation by altering their occupation and in due course of time they get stable job option in rural sectors for livelihood. Several such undereducated rural youths can be transformed by themselves into entrepreneurs through adopting resource-specific need-based alternative remunerative occupations at sustainable level. In search of such occupation, diversified aquaculture practices can be the best option.

Transforming Rural Fish Farming Towards Industrial Business

Quality SIFS seed availability is prerequisite for rapid growth and expansion of rural diversified aquaculture. It holds immense practical relevance for the rural poor in bringing about a positive change in the economic scene. But timely seed supply in rural areas is one of the major constraints. Although attempts have been made by several investigators to produce SIFS seed, but sustainability aspect of it at commercial level in rural area is still lacking. The gap between demand and supply of quality SIFS seeds, by and large, remains a daunting task. This can be mitigated, if rural fish seed producers are graduated to entrepreneurial seed producers to produce quality SIFS seed like *A. mola* at commercial level. This will not only make access to regional rural fish farmers with locally produced and nursed quality seed of SIFS but also stimulate and support them to adopt diversified fish culture within their situation. In view of this, an attempt should be made to develop an entrepreneurial SIFS seed producer from an agriculture farmer through technology demonstrations and constant follow-up technical supports. In this endeavour, transformation of rural farmers into an industrial SIFS seed producer in rural area will assure supply of SIFS seed at district level within easy reach of rural fish farmers while simultaneously creating awareness, generating income and employment for the rural poor. Acquisition of more infrastructures by recycling the hard earned money, increased interest and development of self-confidence, regular participatory training followed by technical guidance and incorporation of new knowledge will make the rural fish farmers to an industrial SIFS seed producer. Within the phase also there will be gradual acceleration both in seed quantity and income generation indicating a gradual evolution of entrepreneurial fish seed producer.

8.4 Final Words

This study takes a view of the diversified aquaculture system of Sundarban region that encompasses an integrated approach to improve productivity and efficiency of aquaculture through introduction of SIFS in carp polyculture system. This investigation follows its journey from research and development to input markets and from farm level production and distribution to final consumer. The development of linkages among these stages is key to achieving an optimal contribution from the diversified aquaculture system to broad based economic growth and transformation through increased value added and employment linkages in downtrodden areas of Sundarban.

Also, there is no denying the fact that interface between the resources and people's livelihood has so far been largely disregarded in the policies of government, especially in case of Sundarban fishery. When fisheries are providing high returns, government should provide more stimuli to spread up those activities, may be at the cost of rice production. Unfortunately, it has not happened. The first thing to be clear about that there is a distinction between *"fisheries policies"* and *"policies for fisheries in development"* as such. The former will always possess an element of self-interest. For example, not all fishers are full time, some are part-timers or occasional. Part-timers have other occupations, often seasonal, but fisheries remain an essential component of their livelihoods. This is the reason to recognize the interdependence of fisheries with agriculture or petty trading, and therefore the need for a well-integrated cross sectional development policy. Aquaculture may not be for the poorest, but ways should be explored by which the poor can gain access to appropriate technologies as part of a livelihood diversification strategy rather than a production led strategy.

Now-a-days, we have been accustomed to use some rhetoric language while prescribing some national policies for formulating or implementing some important issues of national interest in the form of operation or revolution. In case of aquaculture, the wide-spread term silver revolution had been replaced by another new innovative term, "Blue Revolution". Blue revolution deals mainly with two aspects. First, who own these resources, how they are utilized, has the government taken any measures for effective utilization of such resources and also what are the achievement so far. Second, whether the conditions for occurrence of such revolutions are fulfilling. The answer is not much simple. We all are sympathetic to the poor condition of the sector, poor management, poor extension network, poor technical support and also poor livelihood of pond fishing community. But, mere sympathy could not bring the requisite resolution. Here may recall the famous words of Amartya Sen, "While knowledge of torture of someone makes you sick, it is a case of sympathy. While it is not so but you think it is wrong and you are trying to stop it, it's a case of commitment" (Sen, 1982: 28). And today, in present context, what we lack is that commitment. Here lies the answer of the question of whether conditions for occurrence of revolution have been fulfilled or not. The answer is, it is still purely a question of time to test. Before that to be realized, it is better to instill hope in heart rather to beg arms.

Glossary

Aquatic Ecosystem: Any system of interacting aquatic life within its natural and physical environment.

Aquatic Environment: Means the natural and biological resources comprising any aquatic ecosystem.

Aratdar: Commission agent of fish and moneylender.

Baor: Flood plan lake.

Batam cake: Local fish feed.

Bati: Vessel used for measuring quantities of hatcheries.

Beel: Flood plain Lake.

Bheri: Erther pond used for fish production.

Brackish Water: Water having a mineral content intermediate between fresh water and sea water (1000–10,000 mg/*l* dissolved solids).

Capture Fishery: In this kind of fishery, one does not have to sow the fish seeds. Nature is doing the job for sowing. The wild untended stock of organisms is harvested with little human interventions on either habitat variables or the biotic communities.

Co-management: A valuable tool for the sustainable management in fisheries. It can also help in resolution of potential conflicts among user groups. As part of co-management, effective dialogue between local and tourism communities is needed, as it is a commitment on the part of non-resident stakeholders.

Culture Fisheries: In culture fisheries, the whole operation is based on captive stock with a high degree of effective human control over the physio-chemical water quality and other habitat variable. One has to sow the seeds, nurse it and tend it to the proper size before harvesting. Intensive aquaculture of fish and prawn in a pond is a typical example of culture fisheries.

Dalal: Agents and fish availability (or quality) informants used in establishing and securing the transactions of live fish between two parties.

Dayabhaga: One of Hindu laws of Inheritances. The *Dayabhaga* system provides that sons and grandsons had right in the family property even during the lifetime of the father.

Ecosystem: An integrated unit consisting of the community of living organism and the non-living, or physical, environment in a particular area such as a tropical rainforest, coral reef or grassland. The relationship among species in an ecosystem is usually complex and finally balanced, and removal of any one species can often be disastrous.

Enhancements: These are interventions in the life/rearing cycle of the common pool resources. Enhancement technologies involve culture based fisheries/ranching, habitat modification, fertilizations, feeding and eliminations of predators. They use little feed and energy and provide high returns and inputs of labour and capitals. Resource poor sections of the population benefit greatly from the enhancements, which help in generating food, income and other benefits from underutilized, new or presently degraded aquatic resources.

Fashijal: A kind of net, used by the traditional fishermen of Bengal.

Fishery: One or more stocks or species of fish or aquatic life (usually freshwater) that can be treated as a unit for conservation/ management purposes.

Food Chain: A sequence of plants and/or animals generally increasing in complexity and decreasing in numbers with each succeeding species feeding upon its predecessors.

Freshwater: Water having a low mineral content acceptable for portable purposes (< 1000 mg/*l* dissolved solids).

Freshwater Ecosystem: Include Rivers, lakes, freshwater wetlands, geothermal ecosystems and underground aquifers.

Fish Farmers' Development Agencies: The FFDAs are Registered societies, envisaging leasing of tanks and ponds owned by government and local bodies to the fish farmers on long term lease, training of farmers, supply of inputs required, and provision of financial assistance in the form of subsidy for fish pond improvement and inputs. In addition, the extension services were provided to the fish farmers to spread the technology.

Garma: A kind of net, used by the traditional fishermen of Bengal.

Glass Jar Hatchery: It is an example of low cost Chinese type portable hatchery, especially in respect of freshwater variety of fish species, which Government of India has helped to promote in rural and semi-urban areas.

Goldar: Trader who transports large quantities of fish seed by truck (owned or hired).

Habitat: The place or type of site where a biological community naturally occurs.

Hapa: Nylon net cage used for holding fish.

Hindu Law of Inheritance: *Mitakshara* and *Dayabhaga* were two laws in ancient India, the dominance of which continued uninterrupted in the countryside have played an important role in the sub-division and fragmentation of tanks and ponds in India.

Hundi: Small aluminium vessel used for transporting fish (also known as *patil* in Bangladesh).

Jalkar: Rent of water bodies collected by the *zamindaars*/owners.

Majhi: Boatman

Mangrove Swamp: Muddy swamp found on tropical coasts and estuaries, characterized by dense thickels of mangrove trees that are adapted to live in creeks of salt water and send down special breathing roots from their branches to take in oxygen from the air.

Mitaksara: One of Hindu laws of Inheritances. According to the law, father or head of the family was the steward of the property. He could dispose of the property and if he died, property succeeded to his sons who would divide them equally. The eldest son, having no special claim, could get a little consideration amounting to twentieth part of the share.

Nursery pond: This type of pond is used for nursing 2.5 to 7.5 cm fry until the desired size of fish is reached.

Reservoir: A natural or artificial, usually open, impoundment or body of water to be used for recreation, power, flood control or drinking purposes is stored.

Sewage Fed Fishery: A unique example of recycling urban waste for productive use in pisciculture. Sewage Fed Fishery in the eastern fringe of Calcutta is an eye-opener to the world and show how the urban waste can be purified through pisciculture. It not only maintains the eco-system but also continues a major source of fish supply.

Social Fishery: This scheme was introduced in 1987-88 by the Fisheries Department aiming at stocking water bodies owned by the Government, institutions etc. by transferring management to group of persons selected by Panchayats, from among those, living below the poverty line.

Stocking: The protection of natural fish resources is a cost-effective strategy for increasing fish production in inland waters but the effect is sometimes limited by environmental conditions. In those cases, where the composition of natural fish species is not optimal for natural productivity, stocking can effectively increase fish production in inland waters. It involves the release of artificially produced fish seeds into natural water bodies and usually depends on the artificial breeding of the fish species. Two major objectives of stocking are to enhance fish resources, and to establish extensive fish culture production.

Sustainable Yield Cropping: The removal of surplus individuals from a population so that the population maintains a constant size. This usually requires selective removals of animals of all ages and both sexes to ensure a balance population structure. Taking too many individuals can result in a population decline, as in overfishing.

System Approach to Aquaculture: This multidisciplinary approach involves the following steps – stating the problem, identifying the system, classifying and describing the system boundaries and critical factors, analyzing the problem, proposing solution to the problem based on system understanding, testing the solution, and implementing the knowledge on how to solve the problem.

Threatened Species: A species or community that is vulnerable, endangered or presumed extinct.

Wetland: Permanently or intermittently wet areas, shallow water and land water margins that support a natural ecosystem of plants and animals that are adapted to wet conditions.

Zotedar: Landholders.

Zooplankton: Small animals or the larvae of larger animals, which drift in the surface waters of the sea and lakes.

Annexure I

Economics of Aquaculture Diversification in Indian Sundarbans: Nature, extent and impact on efficiency

UGC Sponsored Minor Research Project [PHW – 061/14-15(ERO)]
Dhruba Chand Halder College
PO – Dakshin Barasat, South 24-Parganas,
West Bengal - 743371

SURVEY QUESTIONNAIRE

GENERAL INFORMATION

1. NAME OF FARMER :

2. VILLAGE:	GRAM PANCHAYAT:	BLOCK:
3. AGE: Yrs.	SEX: Male / Female	CASTE: General / SC / ST / OBC / Muslim

4. EDUCATIONAL QUALIFICATION: Illiterate / Literate (Class:)

5. FAMILY MEMBERS: Total: ; (Male: , Female:)

6. INCOME SOURCE: (Tick options)
Agriculture / Animal Husbandry / Fishing / Aquaculture / Service / Business / Others (Specify)

7. FAMILY INCOME: Rs. / year

INFORMATION ON AQUACULTURE

8. TYPE OF AQUACULTURE:
(i) Traditional / Modified Extensive / Semi-intensive
(ii) Monoculture / Polyculture / Integrated
(iv) Carp (Rohu, Catla, Mrigal) / SIFS (Chhoto Maach) / Both

9. TYPE OF PONDS:
(i) Seasonal / Perennial
(ii) Total number of pond: (Grow-out: ; Nursery:)
(iii) Total ponds area: Bigha (Ha.)
(iv) Water Source: Rainwater / Groundwater / Creekwater
(v) Other use of pond water: Household / irrigation / bathing

POND MANAGEMENT AND PRODUCTION

10. POND PREPERATION: (Put Tick Mark)

Dewatering	: Done: ☐	Not done: ☐
Bottom Sediment removal	: Done: ☐	Not done: ☐
De-weeding	: Done: ☐	Not done: ☐
Eradication of predator	: Done: ☐	Not done: ☐
Liming	: Done: ☐	Not done: ☐
Manuring	: Done: ☐	Not done: ☐

11. STOCKING: (i) Seed Source: Hatchery / Natural
(ii) Stocking type: Single / Multiple stocking
(iii) Fish Species stocked:
(iv) Fish stocking rate : / bigha (/ ha)
(v) SIFS Species stocked :
(vi) SIFS stocking rate: / bigha (/ ha)

12. SUPPLEMENTARY FEEDING: (i) Supplementary Feeding done : Yes / No
(ii) Type of feed: Rice bran & oil cake / Farm made / Branded
(iii) Frequency of feeding: Daily / ____ times per week

13. HARVESTING: (i) Mode of harvest : Single / Multiple
(ii) Total Carp production : kg / Bigha / ____________(duration)
(iii) Total SIFS production : kg / Bigha / ____________(duration)

14. INPUTS USED: (i) Pond Preparation : (kg/bigha)
(ii) Fish Seed : (kg/bigha)
(iii) Supplementary Feeding : (kg/bigha)
(iv) Labour : (kg/bigha)
(v) Manure : (kg/bigha)
(vi) Others : (kg/bigha)

ADOPTION OF DIVERSIFICATION PRACTICES

15. KNOWLEDGE IN DIVERSIFIED AQUACULTURE: (Tick options)
Govt. training / NGO training / from other farmers / self taught / from mass media

16. CATEGORY OF ADOPTION:

Category A : Adopters who received government assistance and trained ☐

Category B : Adopters who are trained but not received government assistance ☐

Category C : Adopters who are not trained but received government assistance ☐

Category D : Adopters who are neither trained nor received government assistance ☐

17. REASONS FOR ADOPTION:
(i) Better profit margin
(ii) Family consumption can be supplemented
(iii) To acquire nutritional benefit
(iv) Motivation from experience
(v) Motivation from better extension network

18. TYPE OF ASSISTANCE NEEDED AND/OR RECEIVED:
(i) Finance : Needed ◯ Received ◯
(ii) Technical advice/service : Needed ◯ Received ◯
(iii) Supply of quality seed : Needed ◯ Received ◯
(iv) Marketing Facilities : Needed ◯ Received ◯

19. REASONS FOR NOT RECEIVING ASSISTANCE:
(i) Did not know
(ii) Know but did not tried
(iii) Tried but failed to receive
(iv) Reluctant due to cumbersome procedure

CONSTRAINTS FACED		
20. PROBLEMS ENCOUNTERED IN AQUACULTURE		
Problem	**Answer**	**Rank**
(i) Financial Difficulties	: YES/NO	
(ii) Lack of availability of quality seed	: YES/NO	
(iii) Plurality of ownership	: YES/NO	
(iv) Risk factor acting as fear-psychosis	: YES/NO	
(v) Lack of Proper Extension Services	: YES/NO	
(vi) High Price Spread	: YES/NO	
(vii) Influx of Saline water	: YES/NO	
(viii) Poaching	: YES/NO	
(vii) Any other	: YES/NO	
21. NAME OF FEW THREATENED FISH SPECIES IN THE LOCALITY:		
22. DO YOU CONSIDER THE USE OF WATER AREA FOR ROBI CROP CULTIVATION AT THE COST OF AQUACULTURE? IF YES, WHY:		
23. DO YOU CONSIDER THE PRICE YOU RECEIVED APPROPRIATE?		
24. IS DISTANCE OF LOCATION OF WATER AREA A CONSTRAINT? IF YES, WHY:		
25. IN CASE OF MULTIPLE OWNERSHIP, HOW MANY OWNERSHIP ARE THERE? :		
26. DO YOU THINK ABSENTEE OWNERSHIP A CONSTRAINT? IF YES, WHY:		
27. STATE THE WAYS IN WHICH MULTIPLE OWNERSHIP ACTS AS A DETERRENT FACTOR:		
OTHER INFORMATION		
28. ANY SUGGESTION DO YOU LIKE TO MAKE IN ORDER TO IMPROVE AQUACULTURE DIVERSIFICATION STRATEGIES?		
29. DO YOU FACE ANY PROBLEM REGARDING WATER SHORTAGE?		

30. ARE YOU AWARE OF THE RECOMMENDED SCHEDULE OF STOCKING OF FISH SEED?
31. WHAT IS THE SOURCE OF COLLECTION OF FISH SEED?
32. DO YOU GET ANY ASSISTANCE FROM FFDA SCHEME?
33. WHAT KIND OF SUGGESTION DO YOU WANT TO MAKE TO IMPROVE THE WORKING OF FFDA AND GOVERNMENT PROGRAMME?
34. ANY OTHER INFORMATION DESERVE PARTICULAR ATTENTION
THANK YOU Signature of the Farmer — Signature of Surveyor Date: — Signature of PI Date:

Photo Gallery

Diversified aquaculture if gender just avocation

Female members always participate in aquaculture business

Small indigenous fishes provide nutritional securities

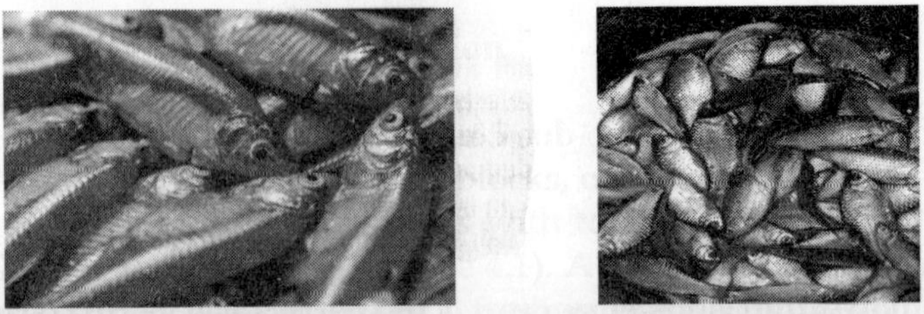

A. *Mola* and *Punti* are always preferred fish species for aquaculture diversification

Lab generated fish seeds are extremely important for productive diversification

Preparation of Nursery and grow-out ponds in the study area

Involvement of both male and female members in aquaculture business

Traditional ways of fish catch in Basanti block of South 24-Parganas

Institutional efforts are increasing to popularize aquaculture diversification

Bibliography

Books

Coelli, T., Rao, D.S.P., Battese, G.E. (1998): *An Introduction to Efficiency and Productivity Analysis*. Kluwer Academic Publishers, Boston.

Dehadri, P.V. (1994): "Export Potential for Fishery Products," Ajit Singh (ed.). *Export of Agricultural Commodities,* Daya Publishing House, New Delhi.

Fare, R., Grosskopf, S., Lovell, C.A.K. (1985): *The Measurement of Efficiency of Production*. Kluwer-Nijhoff Publishing, Boston, MA.

Hayami, Y. and V.W. Ruttan (1971): *Agricultural Development: An International Perspective,* Baltimore: John Hopkins University Press.

Heady, O. Earl and J.L. Dillon (1961): *Agricultural Production Function,* Iowa State University, Princeton.

Jose, Murieker, S.C. (1983): "Inter-linkage of credit and marketing relations in Fish Trade" in U.K. Srivastava and M. Dharma Reddy (ed.) *Fisheries Development in India,* Concept Publishing Company, New Delhi.

Kamal, M. Yusuf (1994): "Aquaculture Technology Development in India", Ajit Singh (ed.), *Export of Agricultural Commodities,* Daya Publishing House, New Delhi.

Kumar, H.D. (2003): *Sustainability and Management of Aquaculture and Fisheries,* Daya Publishing House, New Delhi.

Lawrence, R. Klein (1965): *An Introduction to Econometrics,* Princeton-Hall (Eastern Economy) Press, New Delhi.

Majumdar, T.C. (1985): *Fisheries in India,* Akash Publication, New Delhi.

Marothia, D.K. (2002): "Alternative Governance in Common Pool Resources, in *Institutionalizing Common Property Resources,*" Concept Publishing Company, New Delhi.

Marothia, D.K. (2002): *Institutionalizing Common Property Resources,* Concept Publishing Company, New Delhi.

Misra, S.R. (1987): *Fisheries in India*. Ashish Publishing House, New Delhi.

Pandey, A.C. and J.P. Misra (2000): Economic Feasibility of Fish Culture in the District Faizabad (U.P.) – A Case Study. In *Indian Agricultural Marketing* (eds. J. Prasad and A. Prasad), Mittal Publications, New Delhi, India, pp. 263-269.

Radheyshyam (2002): "Carp seed production for rural aquaculture at Sarakana village in Odisha: A case study". In: *Rural Aquaculture* (P. Edwards, D.C. Little and H. Demaine, eds.), CABI Publishing, New York, USA. CAB International Wallingford, UK, pp. 167-184.

Rahim, K.M.B. and Padhy, M.K. (1994): "Scope and Constraints of Inland Pisciculture in West Bengal: A Case Study in Birbhum district", in the *Role of Fisheries in Rural Development*, Edited by Giriappa S., Daya Publishing House, Delhi.

Ravikesh and R.K. Maurya (2000): "Economics of Inland Fish Production – A Case Study of District MAU, UP." In *Indian Agricultural Marketing* (eds. J. Prasad and A. Prasad) Mittal Publications, New Delhi, India, pp. 271-277.

Rodriquez, V., Puangsumalee, P., and Griffiths, G. (2006): *Indigenous People: Working in Agriculture, Fisheries, and Forestry, ABARE Research Report*, Australian Bureau of Agricultural and Resource Economics, Canberra.

Singh, Ajit (Ed.) (1994): *Export of Agricultural Commodities 2000 A.D. – A perspective.* Wiley Eastern Limited, New Delhi.

Singh, B.B., Singh, R.K.P. and Yadav, R.M. (2000): "Production and Marketing of Inland Fish: A Case Study" in *Indian Agricultural Marketing* (eds. J. Prasad and A. Prasad) Mittal Publications, New Delhi, India, pp. 279-287.

Sinha, M., *et al.* (2002): *Management of Inland Fisheries Resources under Different Property Regimes in Institutionalizing Common Property Resources*, Ed. D.K. Marothia, Concept Publishing Company, New Delhi.

Journals and Working Papers

Agro-Economic Research Centre (1986): *Use of Tanks for Minor Irrigation and Pisciculture in West Bengal*, Visva-Bharati, West Bengal.

Ahmed, N. (2009): "The Sustainable Livelihood Approach to the Development of Fish Farming in Rural Bangladesh", *Journal of International Farm Management*, Vol. 4, No. 4.

Ali, M.H. (1990): "Fishermen's Co-operations in Bangladesh, *Economic Affairs* (Vol. 35, No. 4), pp. 277-282.

Allison, E.H. and Horemans, B. (2006): "Putting the principles of the sustainable livelihoods approach into fisheries development policy and practice", *Marine Policy*, 30: 757-766.

Amilhat, E., Morales, E.J., Yakupitiyage, A., Little, D.C. (2009): "Fisheries production in Southeast Asian farmer managed aquatic systems (FMAS)—Characterisation of systems", *Aquaculture*. 296: 219-226.

Arnason, R. (1988): "Optimal feeding schedules and harvesting time in aquaculture", *Mar. Resour. Econ.,* 7 (1992): 15–35. [2] T. Bjorndal, "Optimal harvesting of farmed fish", *Mar. Resour. Econ.,* pp. 139-159.

Atkinson, S.E., Cornwell, C. (1994): "Estimation of output and input technical efficiency using a flexible functional form and panel data." *Int. Econ. Rev.,* 35: 245–256.

Ayyappan, S., *et al.* (2004): "Fisheries Sector in India: Dimensions of Development", *Indian Journal of Agricultural Economics,* Vol. 59, No. 3, July–September, 2004, pp. 394-410.

Ayyappan, S., Gopalakrishnan, A. (2008): "Resilience in fisheries and sustainability of aquaculture", In: *Souvenir, 8th Indian Fisheries Forum (IFF),* Kolkata, November 22-26, 1-9.

Bagi, F.S. (1982): "Relationship between farm size and technical efficiency in West Tennessee agriculture." *Southern J. Agric. Econ.,* (14): 139-144.

Battese, G.E. (1992): "Frontier production functions and technical efficiency: a survey of empirical applications in agricultural economics." *Agric. Econ.,* 7: 185–208.

Berkes, F. (1986): "Local Level Management and the Common Problems: A Comparative Study of Turkish Coastal Fisheries", *Marine Policy,* Vol. 10, pp. 215-29.

Chakrabarty, S.K. (1968): "Some Problem of Fish Culture in West Bengal — A case study", *Indian Journal of Agricultural Economics,* Vol. 28, Nos. 1-4.

Chakraborty, N.M. and P. Kumaraiah (2003): "Integration of aquaculture with poultry within a watershed tank: A case study." *Fishing Chimes,* 23(9): 10-12.

Chattopadhyay, K.S. (1993): Factors Relating to Underdevelopment of Pisciculture in Birbhum District. Occassional paper.

Coelli, T.J. (1996): A guide to DEAP version 2.1: a data envelopment analysis_computer.program. Centre for Efficiency and Productivity Analysis_CEPA. Working Paper 9608. Department of Econometrics, University of New England, Armidale, Australia.

Copes, Parzival (1986): "A Critical Review of the Individual Quota as a Device in Fisheries Management", *Land Economics,* Vol. 62, No. 3, August 1986, pp. 278-91.

Debnath, B., Krishnan, M., Debnatha, B., Ananthan, P.S., Sharma, A., Sharma, R. (2015): "Gender Perspectives in Adoption of Technological Practices by Fishers and Fish Farmers in Tripura." *Agricultural Economics Research Review,* Vol. 28 (No. 1) January-June, pp. 117-125.

Delgado, C.L., Wada, N., Rosegrant, M.W., and Ahmed, M. (2003): *Fish to 2020 Supply and Demand in Changing Global Markets,* International

Food Policy Research Centre, Washington, DC., and World Fish Centre, Penang, Malaysia, p. 226.

Dhondyal, S.P. and Singh, G.N. (1968): "Benefit Cost Ratios in Fish Culture", *Indian Journal of Agricultural Economics,* Vol. XVIII.

Dubey, S.K., Trivedi, R.K., Chand, B.K. (2015): "Indigenous Freshwater Piscine Resources of Indian Sundarban Biosphere Reserve: Status and Prospects". *World Journal of Fish and Marine Sciences,* 7 (1): 21 28.

Färe, R., Grosskopf, S., Lovell, C.A.K. (1994): *Production Frontiers.* Cambridge University Press, Cambridge.

Farrell, M.J. (1957). "The measurement of productive efficiency". *Journal of the Royal Statistical Society Series,* A 120 _3: 253–281.

Felts, R.A., Rajts, F. and Akhteruzzaman, M. (1996): "Small indigenous fish species culture in Bangladesh, Integrated Food Assisted Development Project (IFADEP), Sub-Project 2", *Development of Inland Fisheries,* Dhaka, Bangladesh.

Gangopadhyay, S. and Giri, A.K. (1990): "Augmentation of Income through Inland Fish Production—A Case Study", *Economic Affairs,* Vol. 35, Issue 3, pp. 163-71.

Garaway, C.J. (2005): "Fish, fishing and the rural poor. A case study of the household importance of small-scale fisheries in the Lao PDR", *Aquatic Resources and Culture Development,* 1: 131-144.

Ghorai, A.K. (1986): Modernization of Small Scale Fish Seed Units, Quality Control and Marketing, Second National Fish Seed Congress, Calcutta.

Gupta, G.S. (1984): "Fresh Water Culture Fisheries: Present Status, Prospects and Policy Issues", *Economic Aspects.* Vol. 28, January–March, No. 1.

Haastrecht, Eline van and Marjanka Schaap (2003): "A Critical Look at the Fisheries Management Practices: The 45-Day Ban on Trawling in Tuticorin District, Tamil Nadu, India", December 2003, University of Amsterdam.

Hardin, G. (1968): "The Tragedy of the Commons", *Science,* Vol. 62, 13 December, pp. 1243-48.

Hatch, U., Tai, C. (1997): "A survey of aquaculture production economics and management". *Aquaculture Economics and Management,* 1: 13-27.

Hayami, Y. (1969): "Sources of Agricultural Productivity Gap among Selected Countries", *American Journal of Agricultural Economics,* 51: 564-575.

Hayami, Y. and V.W. Ruttan (1970): "Agricultural Productivity Differences Among Countries", *American Economic Review,* 60: 895-911.

Indian Journal of Agricultural Economics (1968): All articles in development of fisheries – *Economic Aspects.* Vol. 28, January–March, No. 1.

Jana, R.K. and J.K. Jena (2003): "Freshwater aquaculture in Odisha in national perspective." *Aquaculture International,* December 2003, pp. 12-14.

Jana, R.K. and J.K. Jena (2004): "Overwhelming growth". *The Hindu*, Survey of India, Chennai, pp. 101-103.

Jena, J.K., P.C. Das, B.K. Das, B.C. Mohapatra, N. Sarangi, M.J. Modayil, K.K. Vass, P. Ravichandran and S. Ayyappan (2005): Complied and Edited). *Aquaculture Technologies for Farmers*. Indian Council of Agricultural Research, Krishi Bhawan, New Delhi, India, p. 104.

Katiha, P.K., *et al.* (1997): "Input Resource Management in Reservoir Fisheries", *Indian Journal of Agricultural Economics*, Vol. 52, No. 1, January–March 1997, pp. 125-138.

Katiha, P.K., J.K. Jena, C. Chakraborty and M.M. Dey (2005): "Inland aquaculture in India: Past trend, present status and future prospects." *Aqua. Econ. Manag.*, 9: 237-264.

Kohinoor, A.H.M., Sultana, S. and Hussain, M.G. (2007): "Polyculture of carp with small indigenous fish, bata, Labeo bata (Ham.) at different stocking densities". *Bangladesh Journal of Fisheries Research*, 11(1): 29-36.

Kohinoor, M.A., Hasan, A., Thilsted, S.H. and Wahab, M.A. (2005): "Culture of small indigenous fish species (SIS) with Indian major carps under semi-intensive culture system", *Indian Journal of Fisheries*, 52(1): 23-31, January-March.

Kumar, Anjani *et al.* (2004): "Technical efficiency in Shrimp Farming in India: Estimation and Implication", *Indian Journal of Agricultural Economics*, Vol. 59, No. 3, July-September, 2004, pp. 413-420.

Kumar, P. *et al.* (2004): "A Study of Modelling of Household Demand for Fisheries in India", *Indian Journal of Agricultural Economics*, Vol. 59, No. 3, July-September, 2004.

Kunda, M., Shah, M.N.A. and Mazumder, S.K. (2014): "Production Potential of Nutrient Rich Small Indigenous Species Dhela (*Osteobrama cotio*) in Carp Polyculture System". *World Journal of Fish and Marine Sciences*, 6(5): 453-460.

Kurien, John (2003): "The Blessing of the Commons: Small-Scale Fisheries, Community Property Rights, and Coastal Natural Assets", *PERI Working Paper*, No. 72, August 2003.

Lau, L.J. and P.A. Yotopoulos (1989): "The Meta-Production Function Approach to Technological Change in World Agriculture", *Journal of Development Economics*, 31: 241-269.

Leung, P.S., Shang, Y.C., Chen, G., Ma, S. (1993): "Impacts of the production responsibility system on the development of freshwater pond fish culture in China". *Asian Fisheries Science*, 6: 303-329.

Lobe, Kenton and Fikret Berkes (2004): "The Padu System of Community-Based Fisheries Management: Change and Local Institutional Innovation in South India", *Marine Policy*, Vol. 28, pp. 271-81.

Lorenzen, K., (2008): "Understanding and managing enhancement fisheries systems". *Review of Fisheries Science*, 16: 10-23.

Mathew, Sebastian (1991): "Study of Territorial Use Rights in Small- Scale Fisheries: Traditional Systems of Fisheries Management in Pulicat Lake, Tamil Nadu, India", *FAO Fisheries Circular*, No. 839.

Mazid, M.A. and Kohinoor, A.H.M. (2003): "Research and conservation of small indigenous fish species". In: Wahab, M.A., Thilsted S.H., Hoq M.E., (eds.) *Small Indigenous Species of Fish in Bangladesh*, Bangladesh Agriculture University, Mymensingh, 79-86.

Misra, J. (2010): "Diversifying Carp Culture through Locally Available Fish Species in West Bengal: A Meta Frontier Analysis", *In* Book of Abstracts: Golden Jubilee National Seminar on *Diversification of Aquaculture through Locally Available Fish Species;* Organised by CIFE, Kolkata, p. 107.

Mollah, A.R. *et al.* (1990): "Input-output Relations in Fish Production under various Pond size, Ownership Pattern and Constraints", *Bangladesh Journal of Fisheries Development*, Vol. 3, No. 2.

Mukhopadhyay, P.K. and D.N. Chattopadhyay (2002): "Feed strategies for carp". *Inat. Aqua. Feed*, 5(1): 23-25.

Muralikrishna, M. and Yumi Onishi (2002): "Mussel Muscle", *Samudra*, Issue 33, November 2002, pp. 19-21.

Natarajan, A.V. (1985): "Scope for Scientific and Commercial Fish Farming in West Bengal", *CIFRI Bulletin* No. 25.

Pandey, A.C. (1993): "Fish Farming – Importance and Governmental Assistance", *Unnat Krishi* 32.

Pandey, A.K. and P. Das (2002): "Fish biodiversity conservation: Theory and practice". *Fishing Chimes*, 22(5): 14-24.

Panini, D. (2002): "Addressing Livelihood Issues in Conservation Oriented Projects: A Case Study of Pulicat Lake, Tamil Nadu, India", *Conflict and Cooperation in Natural Resource Management*, Roger J. and Bhasker V. (Eds.) New York: Palgrave, pp. 63-74.

Radheshyam, G. (2001): "Commodity Based Agriculture in India – SWOT, Aquabite", *ICLARM Quarterly*, Vol. 24, November 02, January-June, 2001, pp. 9-15.

Rath, S.C. and S.K. Sarkar (2002): "Utilisation of eco-carp hatchery for mass seed production of common carp (*C. carpio*)." *Fishing Chimes*, 22(8): 36-38.

Ratna Reddy, V., *et al.* (2004): "Ecological and Economic Aspects of Shrimp Farming in Andhra Pradesh", *Indian Journal of Agricultural Economics*, Vol. 59, No. 3, July–September, 2004.

Roos, N., Wahab, M.A., Mostafa, A.R.H., Shakuntala, H.T. (2007): "Linking human nutrition and fisheries: Incorporating micronutrient-dense, small indigenous fish species in carp polyculture production in Bangladesh", *Food and Nutrition Bulletin*. 28 Supplement (2). The United Nations University. S280-S293.

Sarkar, U.K., Lakra, W.S. (2010): "Small indigenous freshwater fish species of India: Significance, conservation and utilization". *Genetics and Biodiversity*. Volume XV, No. 3 July-September, 2010.

Saxena, B.S. (1968): "Inland Fisheries in the National Economy". *Indian Journal of Agricultural Economics*, Vol. 59, No. 3, July-September, 2004.

Shyam, S.S. *et al*. (2004): "Export Performance of Indian Fisheries in the Context of Globalization", *Indian Journal of Agricultural Economics*, Vol. 59, No. 3, July-September, 2004.

Singh, V.D. and Sampath, V. (1983): "Present status, Policy Issues on Inland Fisheries". *Indian Journal of Agricultural Economics*, Vol. 38, No. 3, July-September.

Srivastava, U.K., Dholakia, B.H., Rao, S.S. and S. Vatsala (1990): *Evaluation Study of Fish Farmers' Development Agency Programme for Fresh Water Aquaculture*, Indian Institute of Management, Ahmedabad.

Srivastava, V.S. and S. Vatsala (1983): "Strategy for Development of Inland Fishery Resources in India – by Issues in Production and Marketing". *Indian Journal of Agricultural Economics*, Vol. 38, No. 3, July-September.

Sugunan, V.V. (1995): *Reservoir Fisheries in India*. FAO Fisheries Technical Paper No. 345, Food and Agriculture Organisation, Rome. p. 423.

Sugunan, V.V. (2001): "Status of culture-based fisheries in small reservoirs in India". In S.S. De Silva (Ed.), *Reservoir and culture-based fisheries: Biology and Management*. Canberra: Australian Centre for International Research, 7-15.

Thilsted, S.H. (2012): "Improved management, increased culture and consumption of small Fish species can improve diets of the rural poor, Sustainable Diets and Biodiversity: Directions and Solutions for Policy", *Research and Action*. FAO and Bioversity International, Rome, pp. 176-181.

Thilsted, S.H., and Wahab, M.A. (Eds.) (2014). Production and conservation of nutrient-rich small fish (SIS) inponds and wetlands for nutrition security and livelihoods in South Asia. Proceedings of a World Bank/SAFANSI Funded Regional Workshop on Small Fish and Nutrition. Dhaka, Bangladesh.1st - 2nd March, 2014, p. 47.

Vibol, O., Ngeth, L. and Sopheak, N. (2002): Small-scale fish culture using indigenous fish species in Takeo and Prey Veng provinces of Cambodia. 5th Technical Symposium on Mekong Fisheries, 11th–13th December, 2002.

Wahab, M.A., (2003): "Small indigenous fish species of Bangladesh: potential for culture and conservation", In: Wahab, M.A., Thilsted, S.H., Haq, M.E., (eds.) *Small Indigenous Species of Fish in Bangladesh*, Bangladesh Agr. Univ., Mymensingh, 1-12.

World Bank (2013): Fish to 2030 – Prospects for Fisheries and Aquaculture. Agriculture and Environmental Services Discussion Paper 03. *World Bank Report*, Number 83177-GLB, December, pp. 39-56.

Yamamoto, Tadashi (1995): "Development of Community Based Fishery Management System in Japan", *Marine Resources Economics*, Vol. 10, pp. 21-34.

Reports and Gazetteers

AoA, IFSI, CIFRI and CIFA (2006): Proceedings of National Consultation on Water Management in Fisheries and Aquaculture, New Delhi, 23-24 June, 2006. Association of Aquaculturists, Central Institute of Freshwater Aquaculture, Bhubaneswar and Inland Fisheries Society of India, Central Inland Fisheries Research Institute, Barrackpore.

Ayyappan, S. and J.K. Jena (2003): Indian fisheries and aquaculture: Present status and future prospects. *Souvenir, Fish For All National Launch*, December 18-19, Kolkata, India, pp. 12-24.

Ayyappan, S. and J.K. Jena (2004): Responsible fisheries for sustainable fisheries. Souvenir. *National Seminar on Responsible Fisheries and Aquaculture*, 12-13 February, 2004, College of Fisheries, Odisha, India.

Chand, B.K., Trivedi, R.K., Dubey, S.K. and Beg, M.M. (2012): Aquaculture in Changing Climate of Sundarban: Survey Report on Climate Change Vulnerabilities, Aquaculture Practices and Coping Measures in Sagar and Basanti Blocks of Indian Sundarban, West Bengal University of Animal and Fishery Sciences, Kolkata, India.

Chislam, M. (1962): Field demonstration of composite fish culture in West Bengal, Fish Farmers' Development Agency Officials training in composite fish culture and fish seed production, CIFRI, Barrackpore.

CIFRI (2009): Operational Economics of Different culture system, Background Information on Different Research work and accomplishment of CIFRI, Barrackpore, West Bengal, pp. 16-23.

CSO (2015): National Accounts Statistics, Central Statistical Organisation, Ministry of Statistics and Programme Implementation, New Delhi, p. 232.

DAHD and F. (2015): *Handbook on Fisheries Statistics*, 2014, Department of Animal Husbandry, Dairying and Fisheries, Ministry of Agriculture, Government of India, New Delhi, p. 166.

DAHD and F. (2016a): Performance of Central and Centrally Sponsored Schemes, Department of Animal Husbandry, Dairying and Fisheries, Ministry of Agriculture, Government of India, New Delhi, p. 158.

DAHD and F. (2016b): Material for the Working Group on Fisheries for Twelfth Five Year Plan. Department of Animal Husbandry, Dairying and Fisheries, Ministry of Agriculture, Government of India, New Delhi, p. 158.

Fishery Country Profile (2000): The Republic of India, FID/CP/IND Rev 5; Food and Agricultural Organisation (FAO) 2000.

Fisheries Division, ICAR (2016): Projections in Fisheries, Fisheries Division, ICAR, New Delhi, p. 159.

Government of West Bengal (2014): District Statistical Handbook, South 24-Parganas. Bureau of Applied Economics and Statistics.

Government of West Bengal (2009): District Human Development Report: South 24-Parganas. Development and Planning Department.

Gunaratne, L.H.P. and P.S. Leung (2001): "Asian Black Tiger Shrimp Industry: A Productivity Analysis", Chapter 5 in Economics and Management of Shrimp and Carp Farming in Asia: A Collection of Research Papers Based on the ADB/NACA Farm Performance Survey, Leung, P.S. and K.R. Sharma, eds., Bangkok: Network of Aquaculture Centers in Asia-Pacific (NACA), p. 240.

ICLARM, GoI, GoWB, MSSRF (2003): Fish for all, National Launch, Kolkata, December 18-19, 2003, World Fish Centre (ICLARM), Government of India, Government of West Bengal and M.S. Swaminathan Research Foundation, Chennai, p. 144.

Indian Council of Agricultural Research (ICAR), (2016): *Handbook of Fisheries and Aquaculture*. Directorate of Information and Publications of Agriculture, ICAR, New Delhi, p. 755.

International Food Policy Research Institute (2014): *"Global Food Policy Report, 2013"*, IFPRI Monograph, Washington DC, USA.

Jai-Kisan (2006): Draft National Policy for Farmers, Draft for Comments, Public Debate and Consensus Building. National Commission of Farmers, Ministry of Agriculture, Government of India, New Delhi.

Janaki Ram, K. and A.K. Pandey (2003): Status and prospects of aquaculture development with special reference to Uttar Pradesh. In: *Brain Storming Session on Production Status and Potential of Fisheries in U.P.: Constraints and Opportunities* (January 22, 2003). Uttar Pradesh Council of Agricultural Research, Lucknow. pp. 24-38.

NABARD (2013): Inputs of Twelfth Five Year Plan—National Bank For Agriculture and Rural Development. National Bank For Agriculture and Rural Development, Mumbai.

NABARD (2015): State Focus Paper – 2014-15 (West Bengal), National Bank for Agriculture and Rural Development, January, 2008.

National Centre for Agricultural Economics and Policy Research (NCAP), (2014): Food Demand by 2030. Internal communication, National Centre for Agricultural Economics and Policy Research, New Delhi.

National Council of Applied Economic Review (1992): Export and Prospects of Fish and Fish Products, New Delhi.

National Income Statistics (2002): Central Statistical Organization, Government of India.

NCAP and World Fish Center (WFC) (2004): Strategies and Options for Increasing and Sustaining Fisheries and Aquaculture Production to Benefit Poor Households in India.

Planning Commission (2012): Report of Working Group on Fisheries for Twelfth Five Year Plan (2012-2017). Planning Commission, Government of India, New Delhi, p. 174.

Rahim, K.M.B. and Singh, Katar (1992): Central Fishermen's Co-operative Society, Contai – A case study. A Project Report. Institute of Agriculture, Visva-Bharati and Institute of Rural Management, Anand, Gujarat.

Vass, K.K. (2005): Some Issues on Water. *National Seminar on Management Challenges in Rivers and Associated Ecosystems.* CIFRI, Barrackpore.

Dissertation and ThesisDissertation and Thesis

Misra, J. (2011): An Enquiry into the nature and constraints in the development of Inland Fish Culture in India – Case Study in West Bengal, Thesis submitted in the Department of Economics and Politics, Visva Bharati, West Bengal.

Padhy, M.K. (1993): Constraints in Pisciculture in Bolpur – Sriniketan Block – A case study (an unpublished M.Sc. Thesis).

Web Pages

Allison, E.H. and Mvula, P.M. (2002): Fishing livelihoods and fisheries management in Malawi. LADDER Working Paper No. 22, Norwich, U.K.: Overseas Development Group, University of East Anglia. http://www.uea.ac.uk/dev/odg/ladder/

Bene, C., Minjdimka, K., Belal, E. and Jollet, T. (2001): Evaluating Livelihood Strategy and Role of Inland Fishery in Rural Development and Poverty Alleviation, http://www.oregonstate.edu/dept.

Bene, Cristopher and Neiland, A.E. (2001): Contribution of Inland Fishery in the Context of Rural Livelihood of Africa; http://www.lars2.org/unedited-papers

EU (2003): The Social Dimension of the Common Fisheries Policy. The European Commission (Fisheries), http://europa.eu.int/comm/fisheries/reform/ social_en.html

FAO (2000): Small Scale Fisheries Development: Topic Fact Sheet. http://www.fao.org.

James, M. (2003): Native Participation in Commercial Fisheries – 2003, Ministry of Agriculture, Food and Fisheries, British Columbia, available at http://www.agf.gov.bc.ca/fisheries/reports/NativeParticipationBCFishing03.pdf

Kurien, John (2002): Small-scale Fisheries in the Context of Globalization, CDS Working Papers, Centre for Development Studies, http://www.cds.ac.in.

Payne, Ian (June 2000): The Changing Role of Fisheries in Development Policy, Natural Resource Perspectives (Nov 59), http://www.odi.org.uk.

Srerdrup, Sten (2000): Co-management in Small Scale Fisheries—A Synthesis of Southern and West African Experience, http://www.gt2.dc/fisheries-policies.

Websites Accessed

1. www.aquaculture.tn.nic.in
2. www.bobpigo.org
3. www.dbtindia.nic.in
4. www.icar.org.in/fish.htm
5. www.mpeda.com
6. www.nabard.org
7. www.ncdc.nic.in
8. www.nio.org
9. www.rbi.org
10. www.mospi.nic.in
11. www.fao.org
12. www.thehindubusinessline.com
13. www.indiabudget.nic.in
14. www.dahd.nic.in/stat.htm
15. www.agricoop.nic.in/stats.htm

Index